72 CRA SCROLLSAW PATTERNS

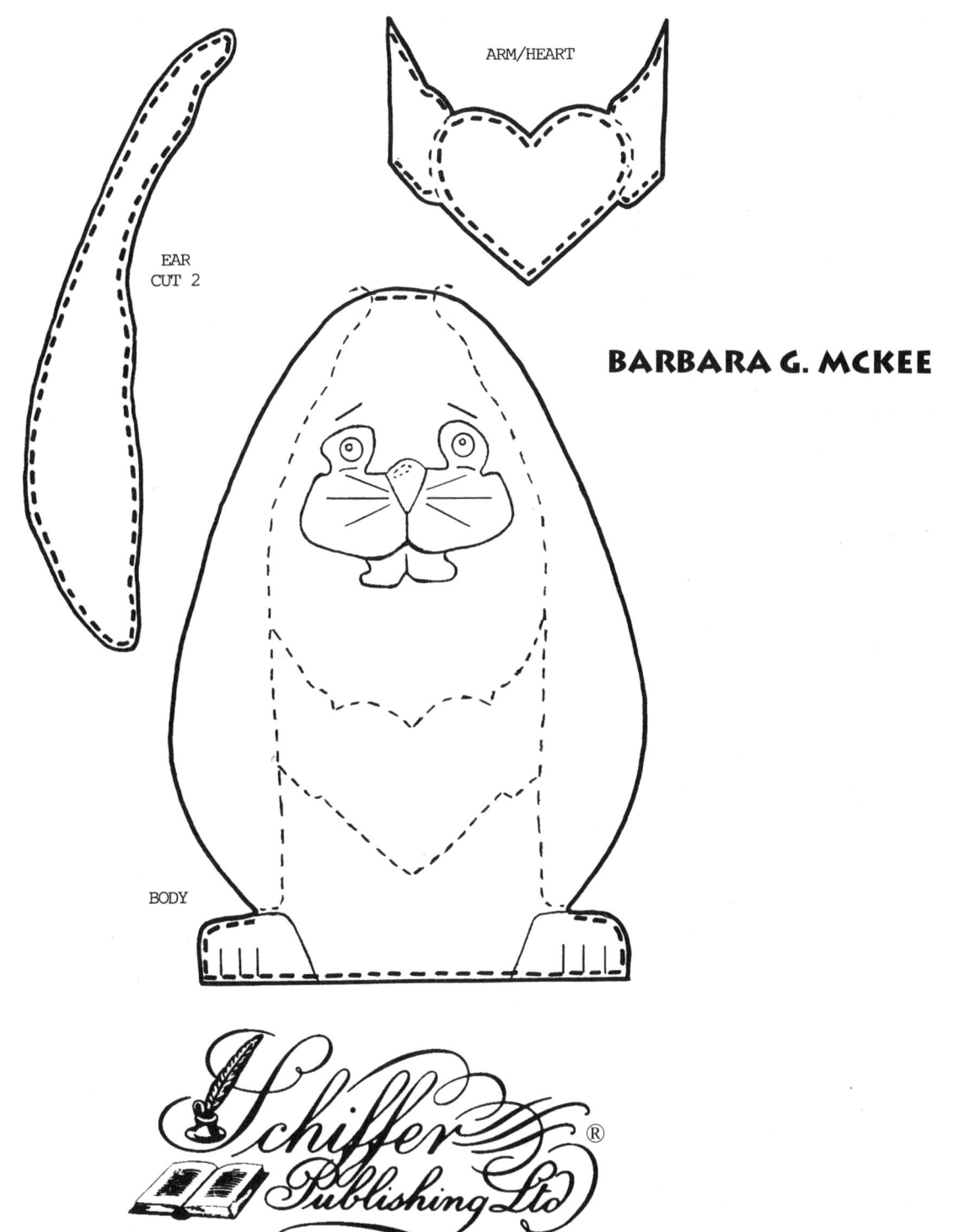

BARBARA G. MCKEE

DEDICATION

To my husband, my children and my grandchildren.
You are my life, my love and my inspiration.
A special thank you to Edward McKee, Joseph McKee, and Jessica and Tom Fish for
their help and support.

Copyright © 1999 by Barbara G. McKee
Library of Congress Catalog Card Number: 99-62072

All rights reserved. No part of this work may be reproduced or used in any form or by any means—graphic, electronic, or mechanical, including photocopying or information storage and retrieval systems—without written permission from the copyright holder.

"Schiffer," "Schiffer Publishing Ltd. & Design," and the "Design of pen and ink well" are registered trademarks of Schiffer Publishing Ltd.

Designed by Bonnie M. Hensley
Type set in Lithograph/Humanist 521 Bd

ISBN: 0-7643-0840-8
Printed in China

Published by Schiffer Publishing Ltd.
4880 Lower Valley Road
Atglen, PA 19310
Phone: (610) 593-1777; Fax: (610) 593-2002
E-mail: Schifferbk@aol.com
Please visit our web site catalog at
www.schifferbooks.com

This book may be purchased from the publisher.
Include $3.95 for shipping. Please try your bookstore first.
We are interested in hearing from authors
with book ideas on related subjects.
You may write for a free printed catalog.

In Europe, Schiffer books are distributed by
Bushwood Books
6 Marksbury Avenue
Kew Gardens
Surrey TW9 4JF England
Phone: 44 (0)181 392-8585; Fax: 44 (0)181 392-9876
E-mail: Bushwd@aol.com

TABLE OF CONTENTS

Introduction 4	Pattern 837: Snowman with Star Vest 38
Scroll Saw Safety 4	Pattern 840: Heart Puzzle 40
Cutting With a Scroll Saw 5	Pattern 841: I-Love-You Heart 40
Puzzle 5	Pattern 844: Spring is in the Air 42
Kerf Line Cutting 5	Pattern 845: Bunny Wreath 43
Round Materials 5	Pattern 846: Six-Egg Basket 44
Stack Sawing Technique 5	Pattern 850A: Toy Bunny 46
Segmenting Technique 5	Pattern 850B: Toy Bunny (fabric ears) 47
Interior Pierce Cutting Technique 5	Pattern 851A: Toy Dog (fabric ears) 48
Blades 6	Pattern 851B: Toy Dog 50
Sizes and Uses 6	Pattern 860: Apple (puzzle) 52
Wood 6	Pattern 861: Pear (puzzle) 53
Standard Sizes of Lumber 7	Pattern 862: Grape (puzzle) 54
Sanding 7	Pattern 867: Cat 55
Copying and Transferring Patterns 8	Pattern 868: Dog 56
Changing a Pattern 8	Pattern 869: Bunny 57
Spray Adhesive 10	Pattern 870: Angel with Flower 58
Glue 11	Pattern 871: Santa with Hat 59
Hot Melt Glue 11	Pattern 872: Snowman with Scarf 60
Paints and Finishes 11	Pattern 873: Reindeer 61
Acrylic Craft Paint 11	Pattern 874: Holiday Tree 62
Spray Enamel 11	Pattern 875: Holiday Turkey 63
Acrylic Latex Enamel 12	Pattern 876: Holiday Eagle 64
Paint Pens 12	Pattern 877: Three Bears 65
Permanent Markers 12	Pattern 878: Goldie 66
Stains 12	Pattern 880: Boy Bunny with Sucker 67
Varnish 12	Pattern 881: Girl Bunny with Balloon 68
One-step Finish 12	Pattern 886: Irish Shamrock Heart 70
Spar Varnish 12	Pattern 887: Irish at Heart Bear 71
Acrylic Medium and Varnish 12	Pattern 888: Sitting Bear 72
Spray Varnish or Spray Wood Sealer 12	Pattern 890: Single Bow 73
Brushes 13	Pattern 891: Double Bow 74
Brush Types and Their Uses 13	Pattern 898: Butterfly Wreath 75
Painting Terms 14	Pattern 899: Butterfly Wall or Lawn Ornament (3-D) 76
Painting Tips 14	Pattern 900: Butterfly Wall or Lawn Ornament (Flat) 78
Decorating with Dots 15	Pattern 901: Inner/Outer Pumpkin 80
Stenciling 16	Pattern 902: Three Pumpkins 82
Sponge Painting 16	Pattern 903: A and B Tall Pumpkins 83
Finishing Touches 17	Pattern 904: Ghosts and Pumpkin 85
Patterns	Pattern 905: Boo-Ghost 86
Pattern 825A: Bunny Puzzle 18	Pattern 906: Speckled Bunny 87
Pattern 825B: Bunny Puzzle (fabric ears) 19	Pattern 907: Flowerpot 88
Pattern 825C: Bunny Holding Heart 20	Pattern 908: Fishbowl 89
Pattern 826A: Dog Puzzle 21	Pattern 909: Welcome Cat 90
Pattern 826B: Dog Puzzle (fabric ears) 22	Pattern 910: Cow 94
Pattern 827: Inchworm Puzzle 24	Pattern 911: Penguin 95
Pattern 828: Tree Puzzle 26	Pattern 912: Lamb 96
Pattern 829: Santa Puzzle 27	Pattern 913: Witch 97
Pattern 830A: Santa Key Chain or Magnet 28	Pattern 914: Turtle 98
Pattern 830B: Santa Tree Ornament 28	Pattern 915: Elephant 100
Pattern 830C: Santa Shelf Decoration 29	Pattern 916: Segmented Pumpkins 103
Pattern 831: Heart Santa 30	Pattern 917: Dinosaur 104
Pattern 832: Santa Heart Face 31	Pattern 918: Scarecrow 106
Pattern 833: Inner/Outer Tree 32	Pattern 919: Bird in Nest Wreath 109
Pattern 834: A and B Standing Tree Puzzles 34	Pattern 920: Angel with Moss Hair 110
Pattern 835: Christmas Angel 36	Gallery 113
Pattern 836: Christmas Wreath 37	

INTRODUCTION

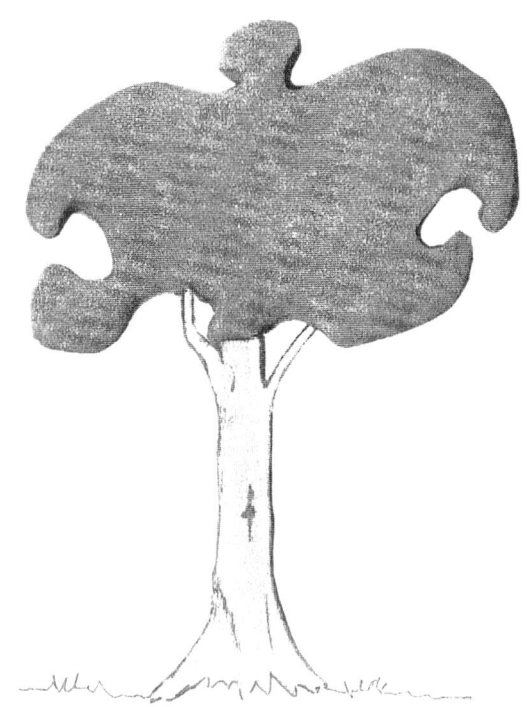

The scroll saw projects in *72 Crafty Scrollsaw Patterns* are all new original patterns and designs, ranging in difficulty from simple to quite challenging. Creating these clever crafts is fun, relatively inexpensive and requires only a few basic tools, making them perfect for craft shows or gift giving. All of the essential information, from selecting the wood right through to the final finishing touches, has been included here to insure your success. Along with a pattern, each project consists of a supply list and detailed cutting and finishing instructions. A color photograph is also included so you can see how the finished project will look. The combined use of these materials provide you with an easy to follow guide, taking you step-by-step through the procedures that are required to complete a professional-looking finished project.

In addition, because your particular wants or requirements may be different from those shown in the pattern, several methods are discussed on ways to individualize a design to fit your specific needs. This detailed information explains how to change, modify or personalize a project design, from changing the pattern's size to adding your own distinct accent touches, in order to help you get the maximum value from each pattern. By imaginatively personalizing a project, you can make it even more special and uniquely your own. Hopefully this book will not only furnish hours of enjoyment but will also inspire you and give you confidence to create your own original designs.

SCROLL SAW SAFETY

- Know how your scroll saw works. READ and FOLLOW the manual instructions. Stay alert and use common sense. Carelessness can cause serious injury.
- Keep children away from the saw.
- Place the saw on a level surface.
- Allow yourself enough working room for handling and supporting the workpieces.
- Make sure the saw is properly grounded to avoid electrical shock.
- If it is necessary to use an extension cord, make sure it's in good condition, the proper size and that it has a 3-prong grounding type plug.
- Bolt the saw to the work table if it tends to walk, slip or slide during cutting.
- Keep the saw clean for safety and to achieve the best cutting results.
- Keep your work area well lit and free from clutter. Cluttered areas invite accidents.
- Never use your saw near flammable liquids, vapors or gases. This can cause a fire hazard.
- Choose the right size and type of blade for the material being cut.
- Be sure that the blade is installed correctly with the teeth pointed down toward the table.
- Adjust the blade tension properly.
- To avoid injury from accidental starting, always turn the saw off and unplug it before removing or changing blades or when you are changing the setup.
- Use the saw only to cut material it was designed to cut. (Wood, wood-like material, plastic and nonferrous metals)
- Keep your face and body to one side of the blade, out of the line of possible thrown pieces if the blade should break.
- Inspect the material to be cut to make sure there are no nails or foreign objects in it.
- Dress for safety. Don't wear loose clothes, gloves or jewelry that can get caught and draw you into moving parts of the saw. Tie back long hair. Wear non-slip shoes.
- Any power saw can throw foreign objects into the eyes causing permanent damage. Always wear safety goggles to protect your eyes.
- Hold the material securely against the cutting table and feed it slowly into the blade.
- Transfer the pattern shapes for very small pieces onto a larger piece of material so that you will have enough waste material to hold on to as you cut. Plan your cuts carefully and use extra caution to keep your hands away from the moving blade.
- Make sure round materials, such as wood dowel, are properly supported. They have a tendency to roll during cutting which can cause the blade to "bite".
- Turn the saw off, wait for the blade to stop and unplug the saw before attempting to free any jammed materials.
- Never leave the saw unattended until it has come to a complete stop.
- Unplug the saw after you are finished using it to prevent injury from accidental start-up.

CUTTING WITH A SCROLL SAW

A scroll saw doesn't cut wood by itself. You allow the saw to cut by guiding the workpiece (the item being cut) into the moving blade. Before starting to cut, be sure that the blade is attached correctly with the teeth pointing down and that the blade tension is properly adjusted. Never force the material into the blade. Feed it into the saw only fast enough to let it cut without binding or twisting the blade. If the saw does jam, turn the saw off and wait for the blade to stop before trying to remove the jammed material. Hold the workpiece firmly against the cutting table so that it will be less likely to lift with the upstroke of the blade. Be prepared for the tendency of the blade to follow the wood grain as you are cutting.

Before cutting thick pieces of wood, check your owner's manual for the thickness-cutting capabilities of your scroll saw. Remember that the thicker the wood, the slower and more controlled your cuts need to be in order to prevent the blade from bending, resulting in slanted cuts. When working with a large piece of material, it's a good idea to rough cut it down to size so that it is easy to handle.

Special care is needed when cutting very small project pieces. Do not hand hold pieces so small that your fingers will go under the blade guard. Transfer very small pattern outlines onto a larger piece of wood than the pattern requires. This will give you more waste material to hold on to. Avoid awkward hand positions where a slip can cause your hand or fingers to move into the blade. Plan your cuts carefully, from start to finish, to avoid injury.

Puzzles must be cut with consistently true, vertical cuts. If the cuts are distorted or slanted the pieces will not interlock properly. The puzzle pieces should fit together and come apart easily. Cut the pieces out slowly and carefully, making certain the blade is not bending or twisting. Use the smallest blade size recommended for the wood thickness so that your cuts will be tight and not look sloppy.

Stand-up puzzles are generally cut from solid wood that is ¾" to 1 ½" thick. The thicker the wood, the more stability the puzzle will have and the better and more substantial looking it will appear. Stand-up puzzles are also easier to move intact when they are make from thicker wood.

Use thicker wood, simpler designs and cut the pieces larger when making puzzles for small children. This will make the pieces easier to handle, while reducing the level of frustration in assembling the puzzle and decreasing the risk of a child choking on the pieces. Avoid cutting sharp corners that can hurt the child or that can break off easily and become a choking hazard. Children's puzzles are apt to receive very tough use; you might want to consider making them out of one of the harder solid woods or using plywood to give them additional strength.

Kerf Line Cutting involves using the scroll saw to cut a defining kerf line (the slot cut by the blade) through the thickness of the wood. The cut-lines provide the project's desired design details and are used to indicate areas of separation. They become part of the overall project design. An example of this technique can be seen in the feathered tail design on "Pattern 875: Holiday Turkey".

Round materials, such as wood dowel, tend to roll during cutting. This can cause the blade to "bite". Use extra caution when cutting these materials. Hold them securely. Using a "V" block can be especially helpful to prevent rolling and give the material proper support.

The Stack Sawing Technique involves layering 2 or more pieces of material on top of each other, securing them together so that they won't slip during cutting and than cutting them out all at once. This time-saving technique will give you identically cut pieces down through the stack. Different materials or types of wood can be layered together; cut and then the pieces can be interchanged to create unusual effects. Be sure that your saw is capable of cutting the combined thickness of the materials. Thicker pieces of material can be held securely by nailing the layers together in their waste areas or by spot gluing the layers together with hot glue. Thinner pieces of material can be held together by wrapping masking tape around them or by placing double-faced tape between the layers.

It is possible to make your own double-face tape by lightly spraying both sides of a piece of paper with temporary spray adhesive. Place the sprayed paper between the layers of material to secure them together.

No matter which method you use, after the securing material is removed, always sand the surface of the workpieces to remove any adhesive residue. An example of this technique can be seen on "Pattern 891: Double bow".

With the **Segmenting Technique**, all of the project pieces (segments) are cut apart along the pattern's main detail lines from a single piece of material. To enhance the design, the front face edges are rounded with sandpaper. For a two-sided project, the front face edges and the back face edges can be sanded. The pieces are finished individually with the desired topcoats and then glued back together in their original positions. DO NOT apply finish to the inside edges where the pieces will join. An example of this technique can be seen in the bird design on "Pattern 844: Spring Is In The Air".

The **Interior Pierce Cutting Technique** is used to cut inside line-work details and to remove waste material from the inside of a project to create an opening in the design. It allows you to make interior cuts without breaking or cutting into the outline or perimeter of the project material.

To make an interior cut, drill a small blade-threading pierce hole through the workpiece at an inconspicuous point on the design, the end of a line-work detail or a corner location of an opening is less noticeable than a hole drilled on a straight or curved pattern line. Remove the blade from the saw. Place the workpiece on the saw table with the drilled pierce hole positioned over the blade access hole. Using the smallest blade recommended for the material thickness being cut, thread the blade through the drilled pierce hole and attach it to the saw. Adjust the blade tension.

To cut inside line-work details, just cut along the desired length of the pattern detail line. Turn off the saw. Remove the blade from the saw and the workpiece. An example of this technique can be seen in the bunny's eye design on "Pattern 906: Speckled Bunny ".

To cut an interior design opening, slowly and carefully cut all the way around, following along the inside pattern line, until the blade is back to the pierce hole. Turn the saw off. Remove the blade from the saw and the workpiece. Separate the pieces. An example of this technique can be seen on "Pattern 841: I-Love-You Heart".

BLADES

To achieve the best results when cutting wood, wood-like products and plastic, it is important that you use the correct blade for the material being cut. A wide variety of 5" plain end or pin end blades can be used in most scroll saws. The various sizes and teeth patterns available are used for cutting different materials and wood thickness. Most blade packages list the materials, wood thickness and cutting radius the blade is intended to cut. As a rule, it is best to use the smallest blade recommended that will effectively do the cutting job required. Always choose a blade that will have at least 2 teeth in the wood at all times.

Some wood fiber "fuzz" or "feathering" on the bottom of the workpiece (the blade exit side) is common. It is not a serious problem as long as there is no splintering. Sanding will remove it. Should splintering occur, try changing to a new blade, a smaller finer tooth blade or supporting the workpiece by placing it on a piece of scrap wood while you are cutting. Using a reverse tooth blade, where the lower teeth are reversed, can also help minimize "fuzz" and splintering on your workpiece.

When cutting thicker wood, you must guide the wood very slowly and carefully into the blade. Make sure that you are not bending or twisting the blade as you cut. This causes excessive blade wear and your cuts will be slanted and not squared.

The teeth on blades wear out in approximately 1/2 hour to 2 hours depending on the material you are cutting. They should be replaced frequently for best cutting results. Overuse will cause your blade to break. Blade breakage can also be caused by poor tension adjustment, twisting or bending the blade, or feeding the wood into the blade too fast. Cutting with slow even pressure, while holding the wood firmly down on the cutting table, will help prolong the life of your blades and result in clean straight cuts.

Thin, Narrow, Fine Tooth Blades are used for:

1. Cutting thinner wood, wood-like products and thin plastics
2. Tight radius cuts and small curves
3. When a smoother cut is required for hard material
4. When cutting at a slower speed

Wide, Thick, Coarse Tooth Blades are used for:

1. For cutting thicker wood, wood-like products and thicker plastics
2. When making straight cuts
3. For large curves
4. When cutting at a faster speed.

BLADE SIZES AND USES

Univ. Number	Width	Thickness	Teeth Per Inch	Description of Uses
2/0	.022"	.010"	28	for extremely intricate sawing, for very thin cuts in material 1/16" to 1/4" thick
2	.029"	.012"	20	for intricate fretwork, for wood and wood veneer, 3/32" to 1/8" thick
4	.035"	.015"	15	for very tight radius cuts in wood 3/32" to 1/2" thick and plastics
5	.038"	.016"	12.5	for very close radius cutting in hard and soft wood 1/8" and thicker and plastics
7	.045"	.017"	11.5	for tight radius cuts in hard and soft wood, and plastics
9	.053"	.018"	11.5	for cutting hard and soft wood and wood-like products 3/16" to 2" thick and plastics
12	.062"	.024"	9.5	heavy duty cutting in 1/2" to 2" thick material faster cuts

---

WOOD

The natural beauty of wood is only one of its many fine qualities. A relatively inexpensive material, wood has great workability, durability and is able to take a finish extremely well. A wide assortment of hardwood and softwood species is available for your craft-making projects. Each is unique, with its own variation of distinct graining and color. Hardwoods such as birch, hard maple and oak have great color and graining along with a harder surface that is more resistant to wear but their higher cost makes them impractical for large volume craft making. Softwoods such as pine, poplar and basswood are less expensive, easier to work with and readily available in a large array of thickness and width.

We have limited our wood selections, using only softwood pine and basswood and in some instances Baltic birch plywood, but most of the projects in this book can by made in the wood type of your choice. While a suitable wood thickness is suggested for each project, this can be varied to meet your own needs. You can also try mixing different types of woods and other materials together to add dramatic visual impact to your project.

Wood is sized as it comes rough-cut from the saw, but the size dwindles as it is fully surfaced or planed on all 4 sides. It is still stocked and referred to by its rough cut size. There can also be slight variations in the wood size, particularly in the width, due to swelling or shrinking. The wood dimensions we give for our projects are the actual sizes of material that you will need for the placement of the pattern pieces.

When buying wood, check it carefully to make sure it isn't warped or twisted and that it doesn't have knots or gouges that will impede your work. Consider buying less expensive softwood that has sound, firm knots when the project is going to be painted with opaque finishes. When you need small pieces of stock for projects, remember that you can get many clear cuttings or pieces between the defects on a piece of common grade board. Take your time and sort though the available stock, this way you can pick the best pieces for the lowest price. When making projects where the wood will show through a transparent finish, you will want to use wood that has a good grain pattern with no defects. DO NOT use pressure-treated wood, it may contain harmful preservatives. Another source of material is to check out building sites where scrap wood is usually free for the asking.

To prepare your wood for finishing, fill any unsightly holes and cracks with wood filler. When the filler has dried, sand the entire piece with 100-grid sandpaper.

Wood is strongest along its length, in the direction of the grain and weaker across the grain. It is harder to break a wood piece across its length and grain pattern. For this reason you will want to try to place the pattern so that the wood grain runs with the longest dimension of the design. Once the pattern pieces have been transferred onto the wood, cut the pieces out with the blade best suited for the wood type and thickness you have selected.

Pine is fairly inexpensive and readily available at any building supply center. It's easy to cut, sands nicely and its natural white to cream color accepts most finishes well. Pine is one of the best and most popular all around domestic softwoods.

Basswood is a soft, fine textured wood with a light, usually uniform cream color. It's a fairly strong wood that cuts smoothly, sands easily and takes finishes well. Basswood is available at most building supply centers and larger craft stores. It's sold in a variety of widths that are 1/16" to 1/4" thick. These features make it a good choice when you need to cut small, thin workpieces.

Plywood is a flat panel that is built up of an odd number of sheets of wood or veneer alternated with various kinds of cores (inner plies). The layers are assembled under pressure, using adhesives, to create a finished piece of sheet material. Because the grain patterns of the wood layers are alternated in direction, at right angles over a center core, it has equal strength in all directions. Although not as attractive, it is stronger, more durable and less expensive than solid wood of the same dimensions. Plywood is available with either hardwood or softwood faces. Avoid using lower grades of plywood, as they tend to splinter and sliver making them unsuitable for craft making. Plywood can be purchased in a variety of thickness at building supply centers. The adhesive used to make plywood is very abrasive and will cause your saw blade to dull and wear out quicker. Change the saw blade often to ensure clean cuts.

Good grade **Baltic Birch Plywood** is a very popular material for craft making. Baltic plywood is comprised of more layers than conventional plywood and is less likely to splinter or sliver. It saws cleanly and smoothly, sands easily and takes most finishes well. Because of its strength, Baltic plywood can be a better choice when making workpieces that have intricate detailed fretted designs or thin, fragile pieces or when making projects that may receive rough treatment, such as children's toys.

Softwood lumber is graded into 3 categories, **select, common** and **structural**. These categories are then sub-divided and priced by the number of defects present in the pieces.

Select lumber is graded by letters into A, B, C and D. Grade A is clear, meaning it has virtually no defects. It is suitable for stains and natural finishes. Grade B contains a few small defects but is also suitable for natural finishes. Grade C contains defects that can be concealed with paint. Grade D has slightly more defects but they can still be concealed with paint.

Common lumber has defects that can prevent you from using a natural finish on your project but it can usually be painted without waste. The quality of common lumber is graded by number. No. 1 is good, with tight knots and few blemishes. It is free of warp, splits, checks or decay. No. 2 is fairly sound, but with defects such as checked ends, loose knots, blemishes and discoloration. No. 3 has defects of all types necessitating some waste removal. No. 4 and No. 5 are not recommended for craft making.

Structural lumber is graded mainly for its strength. Construction grade is the best quality structural material. Standard grade is similar but with a few defects. Utility and economy are not recommended for craft making. Most construction lumber is kiln-dried giving it a good resistance to distortion and checking. It is usually labeled S-P-F species (spruce, pine or fir). Buy the lowest grade if it doesn't have too many knots or defects and the edges are in good condition. The thickness of pine construction lumber is ideal for small projects and stand-up puzzles.

STANDARD SIZES OF LUMBER

Common Boards		Construction Lumber	
Size from saw	Approx. Size after planing	Size from saw	Approx. Size after planing
1 X 4	¾ X 3 ½	2 X 4	1 ½ X 3 ½
1 X 6	¾ X 5 ½	2 X 6	1 ½ X 5 ½
1 X 8	¾ X 7 ¼	2 X 8	1 ½ X 7 ¼
1 X 10	¾ X 9 ¼	2 X 10	1 ½ X 9 ¼
1 X 12	¾ X 11 ¼	2 X 12	1 ½ X 11 ¼

SANDING

Proper sanding is an essential step in making your finished project look professional. In order to have a good surface for finishing; you need to first remove scratches and rough spots from the wood. A smooth even surface is provided by sanding the wood with increasingly finer grades of sandpaper. Start with a medium (100-grid) grade paper. Sand with the grain using long straight strokes. Sand again with fine (150-grid) grade paper for an even smoother finish. Test for rough spots by putting a sock on your hand and running it over the surface of the wood. Re-sand any spots where the sock hits a snag. When the project is completely smooth, wipe the surface with a tack cloth to remove all dust.

Sanding lightly between layers of topcoats or finishes will make your final topcoat smoother. Use a very fine [220-grid] sheet of sandpaper. Do not use steel wool to sand. Strands of steel fiber can get caught in the wood and cause rust spots when coated with any water-based product.

1. To help prevent injuries, sand all the edges and sharp corners of children's toys so they are well-rounded.

2. Children's puzzles are easier to put together if the corners of the pieces are sanded to be slightly rounded.

3. Use a small piece of sandpaper wrapped around a pencil to sand curved areas and for rounding edges and corners.

4. Use a sandpaper block to decrease the time and labor needed when you are sanding large flat areas.

5. Sanding specific areas of a project surface to different depths adds definition and dimension to the design.

6. Sanding can remove small areas of waste wood left when cutting was not close enough to the pattern line.

7. Wet paint can raise the grain on wood. A small piece of brown paper grocery sack makes the finest "sandpaper" available. Let the paint dry, then sand with the brown paper. It will not scratch the paint finish. Any marks it leaves will be covered when the topcoat is applied.

SANDPAPER GRADES AND USES

Very fine	220-grid	Light sanding between topcoats, will not show sanding marks
Fine	150-grid	Fine sanding, cleaning wood surface of grid marks
Medium	100-grid	Moderate removal of surface imperfections
Coarse	60-grid	Heavy removal of wood stock

COPYING AND TRANSFERRING PATTERNS

Pencil can be used to draw a pattern's saw lines directly onto the wood surface. After the sawing is completed, any pencil lines that remain on the surface will be removed during the sanding process. You can lightly sketch the design details with pencil directly onto the project surface, as they are needed. Do not press too hard or you'll indent the wood. Your topcoats of opaque paint should cover the pencil lines but if any lines are still showing, they can be erased after the paint is dry. Make sure that all pencil markings have been removed before you apply any transparent finishes or varnishes or the markings will show through.

Graphite paper is waxless, greaseless and smudge-proof. The graphite lines are erasable and they will not bleed through paint. Graphite paper is available in red, blue, yellow, white, and black at most art supply and craft centers. You can trace patterns directly from the book's pages with a pencil, a piece of graphite paper and a sheet of paper. Place the graphite paper under the pattern (graphite side down). Place a sheet of paper under the graphite. Trace over the pattern lines and design details with a sharp pencil making sure that you don't miss any. You can than use the copied pattern to make the project.

Graphite paper can be used to transfer the pattern onto the wood surface. Place the graphite paper on top of the wood (graphite side down). Place the pattern on top of the graphite paper. Secure in place with a piece of tape. Carefully trace over the pattern saw lines with a sharp pencil. Be sure to go over all the lines. There is no need to transfer the design details yet, as you will be sanding and base-coating over them. The design details can be transferred onto the project surface later, as they are needed, using graphite paper. Do not substitute carbon paper for graphite paper when transferring the design details.

Carbon paper can be used in the same manner as graphite paper but unlike graphite, it is not smudge-proof or erasable. It can leave a greasy residue that will keep paint from adhering properly to the surface of your project and the carbon lines can bleed through your topcoats of paint ruining the design. For these reasons, carbon paper should **not** be used to transfer design details onto the project. Carbon paper can be used to trace patterns from the pages onto a sheet of paper or to transfer the pattern's saw lines onto the wood (when the sawing is completed, sand the wood surface thoroughly to remove any carbon residue).

Copier machines can reproduce patterns quickly, inexpensively and with great accuracy. They eliminate the time consuming task of having to work with layers of graphite or carbon paper and tracing the pattern. Nothing is lost or degraded in the copying process and the cut lines and design details are clear, precise and easy to follow. The copier pattern can be used with graphite or carbon paper to transfer the lines onto the wood or the copy can be temporarily bonded directly onto the wood with a spray adhesive and used as a sawing guide. The instructions for this bonding technique is given in the section headed "Spray Adhesive".

Copiers can also be used to enlarge or reduce a pattern size, from shrinking them down to key chain size to blowing them up to lawn ornament size. Tedious methods of changing the pattern size (like pantographs or the square grid method) are no longer necessary.

CHANGING A PATTERN

By making a few simple modifications, most of the patterns in this book can be used in a variety of different ways. With the aid of a copier machine, changing a pattern design to fit your needs can be accomplished with very little effort.

The changes made to the Santa design in "Pattern 829: Santa Puzzle" are a good illustration of how a single pattern can be altered to make a number of diverse projects. For each of the new projects, the pattern was reduced to the appropriate size and then a few slight changes were made to adapt the pattern for its new purpose. Note that the wood thickness was also changed in each instance to coordinate with the project's new size and purpose.

In "Pattern 830A: Santa Key Chain or Magnet" the pattern was reduced to approximately one-quarter of its original size. The puzzle knobs were eliminated from the design and only the Santa outline was cut out. Depending on the desired use, a magnet is attached to the back or a small hole for a key ring is drilled. The pattern design was painted onto the wood shape.

In "Pattern 830B: Santa Tree Ornament" the pattern was reduced to approximately 40 percent of its original size. The puzzle knobs were eliminated from the design. The Santa outline was cut out and than a small hole was drilled to accommodate the tree hanger. The pattern design was painted onto the wood shape.

In "Pattern 830C: Santa Shelf Decoration", the pattern was reduced to approximately one-third of its original size and the puzzle knobs were eliminated. The Santa shape was cut into segments along the main pattern lines; the pieces were each finished individually and than glued back together. The complete instructions for this technique are given in the section "Segmenting Technique" under the heading "Cutting with a Scroll Saw".

Another good example of the different ways a pattern can be utilized, to get the maximum value from it, is demonstrated in the changes made to "Pattern 825A: Bunny Puzzle". It was altered first to form "Pattern 825B: Bunny Puzzle (fabric ears)". The original pattern was then altered a second time to create "Pattern 825C: Bunny Holding Heart".

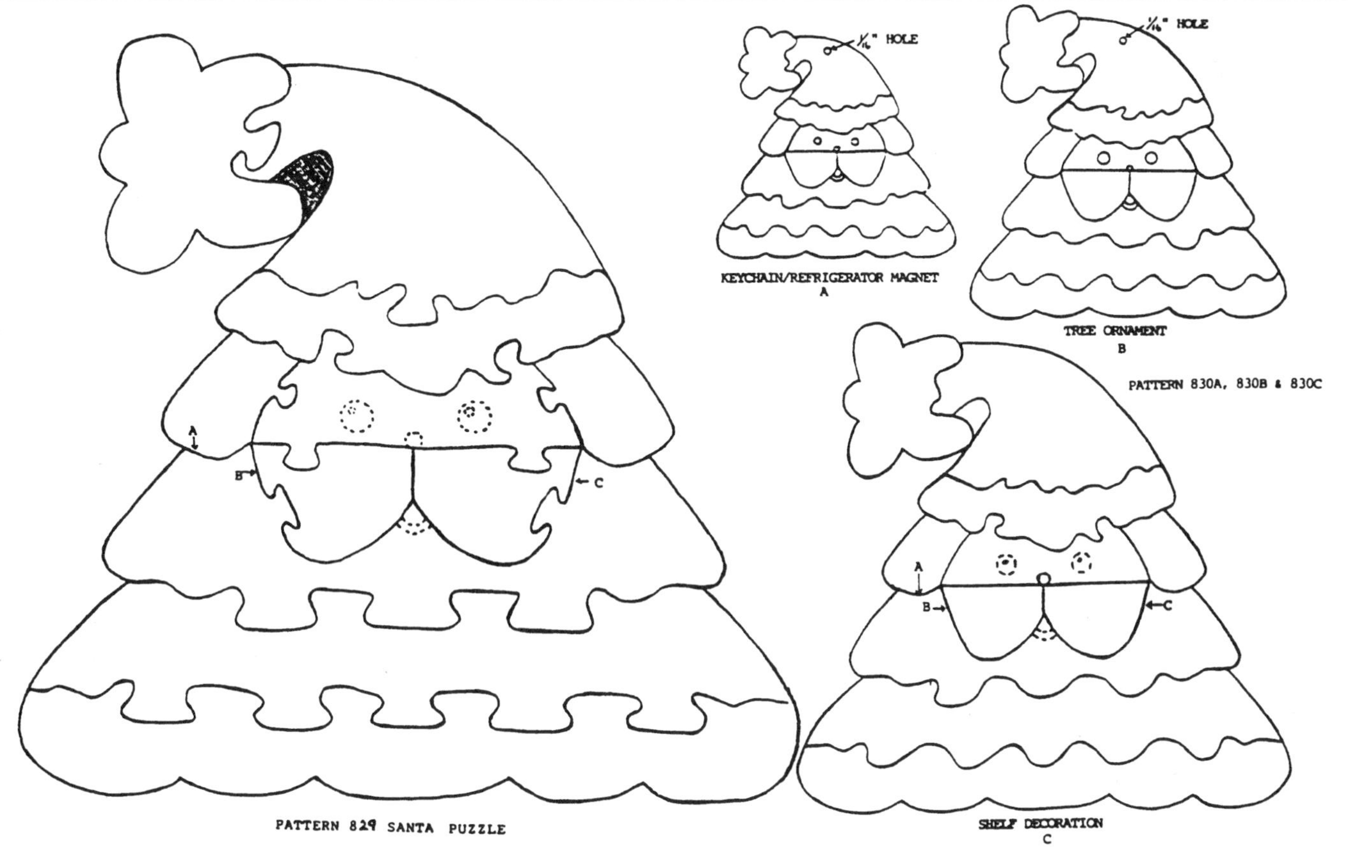

Some of the various ways to change a pattern to fit your particular needs. The original Santa puzzle pattern was changed to form the patterns for the key chain, refrigerator magnet, tree ornament, and the shelf decoration.

To create Pattern 825B, the cut lines for the ear pieces were removed. A hole was drilled into each side of the head where the fabric ears will be attached. Line "A", along with the next 3 horizontal lines, were continued across the body and 2 puzzle knobs were added to each line. An additional horizontal cut line was added to the pattern. The feet pieces, minus the puzzle knobs, were removed to give puzzle a more egg-shaped appearance. The color scheme and the design details of the body were changed. Colorful fabric ears were designed, cut and sewn. They were then tucked and glue into the drilled holes. A ribbon was tied into a bow around the base of the right ear.

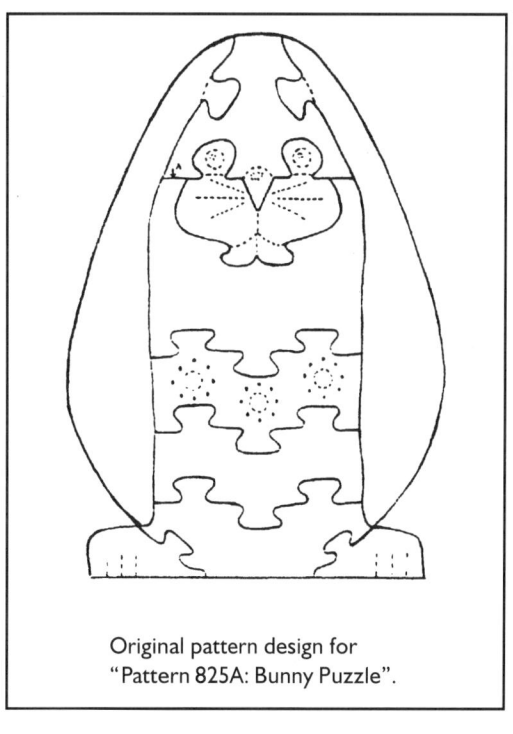

Original pattern design for "Pattern 825A: Bunny Puzzle".

To create "Pattern 825C: Bunny Holding Heart" the original pattern was reduced in size by one-third. Separate ear patterns were made using the ear puzzle piece outlines from the reduced pattern, without the knobs, as a guide. All of the puzzle's cut lines were removed from the project. An arm/heart piece was added to the project design. Only the body outline was cut out. The ear patterns and the arm/heart pattern were transferred onto thin pieces of wood, cut out, finished and than layered onto the body. The color scheme and the design details of the body were changed. A different design of wrapping paper was glued onto the ear pieces and the heart area of the arm/heart piece.

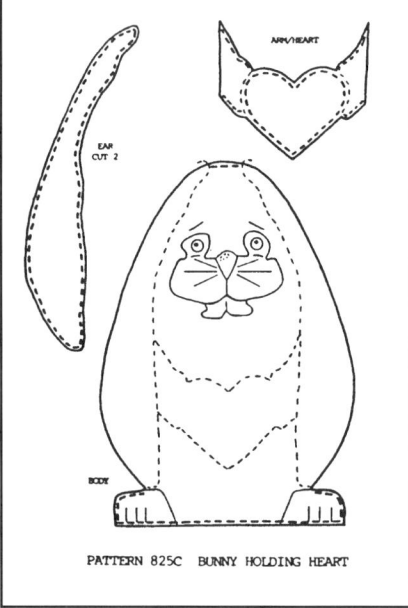

PATTERN 825C BUNNY HOLDING HEART

A second set of changes were made to the original pattern to create "Pattern 825C: Bunny Holding Heart". The size of the pattern was reduced, separate ear pieces were layered onto the body and arms and a heart were added.

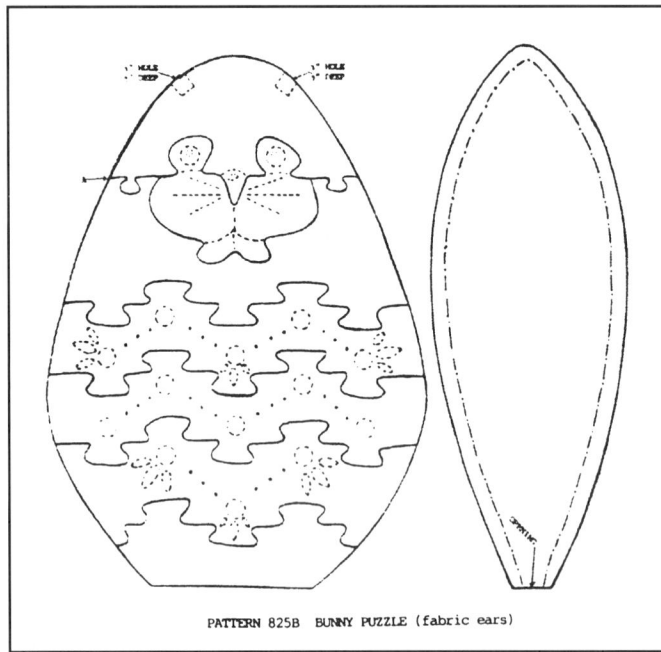

PATTERN 825B BUNNY PUZZLE (fabric ears)

Several changes were made to the original pattern to create "Pattern 825B: Bunny Puzzle". The ear cuts were eliminated, the horizontal cut lines were extended and fabric ears were added.

SPRAY ADHESIVE

Spray adhesive is a clear drying spray that can be used for permanent or temporary bonds. The spray will bond a variety of porous and non-porous materials such as paper, fabric, glass and wood. It dries quickly and resists water. Spray adhesive is available at most craft, hardware and photography stores. Make sure that the product you buy states that it can be used for **both** permanent and temporary bonding.

The surfaces to be bonded should be clean, dry and free of dust. Cover the surrounding area to protect it from the spray mist. Shake the can for one minute before using. Hold the can 8-12 inches from the surface.

Permanent bonds: Spray a medium coat of adhesive onto both of the surfaces to be bonded. Allow the adhesive to dry for about one minute and than press the surfaces together.

Spray adhesive can be used to permanently bond paper designs or fabrics to your project. Spray the back of the paper or fabric and carefully position it onto the wood. Starting from the center and working toward the outer edges firmly press and smooth into place. Make sure it is lying flat with no wrinkles. Let the adhesive dry. Trim off any excess material with a sharp razor blade.

Temporary bonds: Spray a light, uniform coat on only one of the surfaces. Wait a few seconds and then position and press the sprayed surface smoothly in place. To reposition a sprayed item, start at a corner and slowly peel it off. Reposition and press the sprayed surface smoothly in place.

Patterns can be temporarily bonded onto the project's wood pieces with spray adhesive. This great timesaving method eliminates having to trace or transfer the pattern design onto the wood. Rough cut the pattern pieces. Spray a very light mist onto the back of the pieces. Do not spray the wood. Wait 15-30 seconds. Position and press the pattern pieces smoothly onto the wood and you will have a clear and accurate pattern design ready for sawing. Saw along the pattern lines. When the sawing is complete, peel the pattern pieces off the wood. Save the pattern pieces for detail transferring. If there is any sticky residue remaining on the wood, it will be removed during the sanding process.

You can make your own double-faced tape using spray adhesive. Simply spray both sides of strips of paper with a light, uniform coat of adhesive. The sprayed paper will be strong enough to hold thin layers of material together during stack sawing. When the sawing is complete, separate the layers and peel off the paper strips. If there is any sticky residue remaining on the wood, it will be removed during the sanding process. The strips will not damage the wood surface unlike some commercial double-faced tapes which have very aggressive glue that can pull up the woods fibers, cause splinters and can leave a sticky residue that can be difficult to remove.

GLUE

To insure proper bonding the surfaces must be clean, dry, smooth, and free of finishes. Glue will not bond permanently to painted or finished surfaces. To eliminate the need to sand later, leave the areas unfinished where the pieces will join. If you forget, spot sand the finish off to the bare wood where the pieces will join.

Apply a light spread of glue evenly to one of the surfaces when bonding thin material or a heavier spread to both of the surfaces when bonding thicker material. Press the surfaces together. It is important to clamp, rubber band or weight thicker pieces of material together while the glue is still fluid. Insufficient pressure will result in a weak joint because the surfaces will not make proper contact. With a damp cloth wipe off any excess glue from the project surface before the glue sets. Allow the glue to dry thoroughly. Sand the surfaces to remove any remaining traces of glue. Even the slightest trace of glue can effect the way your project will look when it's finished. Glue acts as a sealer preventing stains and finishes from penetrating the wood surface giving your finish a blotchy look. It can also cause topcoats of paint to have a rippled appearance.

White glue will bond most porous and semi-porous materials. It dries clear, is safe and non-toxic. White glue is not waterproof but does resist grease and solvents. Used full strength, it will provide a good bond on wood. White glue can be thinned with a small amount of water and used as an adhesive when decoupaging thin material such as paper.

Wood glue is generally cream colored. It can be used for bonding both hard and soft wood as well as most other porous materials and develops a stronger bond then white glue. Wood glue can actually make a bond that is stronger than the wood itself. It has a strong initial tack and sets fast. It is not waterproof but is highly resistant to heat and solvents.

HOT MELT GLUE

Hot melt glue works well for assembling small pieces of material quickly. Its holding power is good but not as strong as other types of glue. Remember that the glue gun and the glue itself get very hot. Use caution and follow the directions and warning on the glue gun package. Hot melt glue starts to cool and harden as soon as it is applied. It will bond the surfaces together in approximately 60 seconds. No clamping or weighting is required.

Buttons, bows, silk flowers and other decorations can be applied easily to your project with hot melt glue. Hot melt glue can also be used as a temporary means of holding layers of wood together when you are stack cutting material. Simply spot glue in the waste areas of the layers and than press the layers together.

PAINTS AND FINISHES

Paints and finishes add distinction and character to your projects. The designs that we have included in this book were decorated using non-toxic paints and finishes. The color palettes have been kept simple; using colors available at any craft or hardwood store. While we recommend a color palette and paint design for each project, this is where you can really show your own creativity. Have fun! Let your imagination and originality have full rein. Create your own color palette, use your own paint design, and make each project a reflection of your own personality.

We have also kept our painting supplies to a minimum for the sake of both convenience and cost. While not recommending any specific brands, we have included the following list of products that we found work particularly well.

Caution: Some of the following products can be hazardous to your health. Always follow the directions and precautions on the product label. Keep all paint and finishing products away from children. These products can be fatal if swallowed. Some products have vapors that can be harmful to your health. Use them only with adequate ventilation. These products can be highly combustible. Keep them away from heat, sparks and flames. Do not smoke while using them. Dispose of the empty containers properly. Rags that have cleaning solvent, stain or finish on them can ignite spontaneously. Don't leave them lying around. Always dispose of them properly. Most paints, stains and varnishes are non-toxic once they have been applied and allowed to cure.

Acrylic craft paint is one of the most versatile types of water-based paints available for craft making. It's easy to use, non-toxic and dries quickly to a permanent, durable finish. As with any water-based product, it is best to use a synthetic bristle brush to apply acrylic paints. Brushes and paint supplies clean up quickly with soap and water. With the purchase of a few basic colors, you can mix the color just right for your project. Keep in mind that as acrylic paints dry, their color darkens slightly. It is important to shake the bottles of paint before using them. Some colors separate easily because of the amount of pigment used to make the particular color. Shaking them will re-mix the color.

Acrylic paint gives you a low-sheen, opaque (solid) finish. This finish prevents the wood grain from showing through and can hide many minor defects in the wood's appearance. Cracks, small knots, and other flaws can be filled, sanded and covered over with the paint.

Mixing acrylic paint with water will form a transparent wash that allows the wood grain of your project to show through. To add a wash to your project, dilute the paint with water, using approximate 1 part of paint to 3 parts of water. Mix together thoroughly. Load the mixture onto your brush, blot off the excess paint onto a paper towel, and apply to the area where you want the transparent finish. Washes are also a good way to add transparent shadows or highlights over previously painted areas.

Spray Enamel is a quick, convenient and fast drying interior or exterior finish. These spray paints are fade and weather resistant, making them ideal for projects that will be displayed outdoors. Be careful to protect surrounding areas from the spray mist as you paint. To save time, spray all pieces of the same color at the same time.

Shake the can vigorously for 1 minute after the mixing ball starts to rattle to insure uniform color and to prevent clogging. Shake occasionally during use. Point the opening toward the project, holding the can 12 to 16 inches from the surface to be painted. Press the spray button firmly. Use steady, even, overlapping strokes. Several thin coats will product better results than one heavy coat. If clogging occurs, remove the spray button by twisting it off and clean it. Do not stick a pin or any other object into the can. Gently replace the spray button by twisting it back on. Make sure the opening hole is pointed away from you. Clean the spray button immediately after each use by turning the can upside down and pressing the spray button for 5 seconds or until no more paint comes out. Discard the empty can properly.

Acrylic Latex Enamel is a quick, durable interior or exterior finish that provides a bright, smooth, protective coating. This tough, long-lasting finish is fade and weather resistant, making it ideal for projects that will be displayed outdoors. It is fast drying, non-flammable, low odor and washable.

Stir the paint thoroughly in an upward motion to bring the pigment up from the bottom of the can. The paint can be thinned slightly with water if desired. Several thin coats will product better results than one heavy coat. If a second coat is needed let the first coat dry before re-coating. Use a synthetic bristle or form brush to apply the color. Do not over-brush or it could result in brush marks in the coating after the paint dries. Clean brushes and other supplies immediately with soap and water.

Paint pens let you add design details quickly and easily. They are available with a medium, fine or extra-fine tip in a wide variety of opaque colors. These non-toxic, quick drying pens can be used to add details over most painted surfaces.

Paint pens can bleed when applied to raw wood. Applying a thin undercoat of varnish or sealer to the surface, where a natural finish is desired, will help to prevent this. Once the paint pen details have dried, applying a coat of paint or varnish over them should not cause bleeding, but you should always test results on scrap wood before using the paint pens on your project.

Permanent markers are another fast and easy way to add design details, but they can bleed when applied to raw wood or if another topcoat is used over them. Preparing the wood, by painting an undercoat of color or applying a thin coat of varnish or sealer to the surface (where a natural finish is desired), will help to prevent this from happening. Once you have inked over a prepared surface, lightly mist the area with a clear acrylic spray before continuing on with your project. You should always test results on scrap wood before using the pens on your project. Make sure the pen is labeled "permanent ink," "waterproof" and "non-toxic." Permanent markers come in broad and thin tips and a large variety of colors.

Stains are available in a variety of deep, rich colors that can greatly enhance the natural wood grain of your project. A bristle brush, foam brush, or a clean lint-free cloth can be used to apply stain. Always apply a smooth, even coating. Allow the stain to set for 5 to 15 minutes. Stain penetrates into the wood fibers and the longer you let it set, the deeper the color will be. Wipe off the stain with a clean cloth. Wipe across the grain first, then final wipe with the grain. If the color is not deep enough, repeat this process until you get the tone you desire. Allow the stain to dry thoroughly before applying a finish coat of varnish.

We highly recommend the newer water-based stains. While they tend to be a little more expensive, the convenience they offer is well worth the price. They are quick drying, low odor, have no toxic vapors and are non-flammable. Clean up is easy, wash the tools with soap and water and you don't have to worry about the disposal of flammable materials.

Varnish gives your finished project a richer look. It intensifies the colors and adds luster to painted surfaces and raw wood. It helps to protect the wood from moisture, dust and dirt. Varnish can be purchased in satin, semi-gloss or gloss finish. Stir the product gently before using it. Do not shake. Shaking will raise bubbles that can appear later in the finish. Apply a light even coat with a clean brush or a lint-free cloth. Use long even strokes. Allow the varnish to dry. If a second coat is desired, lightly sand the area with very fine (220-grid) sandpaper and wipe off any sanding dust with a tack cloth, before re-coating.

The newer water-based varnishes work extremely well. While a little more expensive than regular varnish, we find the convenience they offer is well worth the additional cost. They provide a tough, crystal clear topcoat over paint or stain. Used as an undercoat, the varnish will seal the wood while allowing the natural grain to show through. Water-based varnish appears milky in the can but dries clear. The product is low-odor, non-flammable, fast drying and non-yellowing. Brushes and other tools can be cleaned with warm soapy water and you don't have to worry about the disposal of flammable materials.

Water-based varnish should be applied with a brush that has synthetic bristles, because natural bristles will absorb the water in the finish. Apply the varnish in very thin coats brushed on in the direction of the wood grain. If a second coat is desired, allow the first coat to dry thoroughly, then sand it smooth with very fine (220-grid) sandpaper. Remove the sanding dust with a tack cloth. Apply the next coat.

One-step finish combines stain and topcoat in one product. With this product, you are able to apply color and protection at the same time. The finish is fast and easy to use, simply brush on a thin smooth coat of the product in the direction of the wood grain. Allow the finish to dry thoroughly. If a second coat is desired, lightly sand the surface with very fine (220-grid) sandpaper. Wipe off the sanding dust with a tack cloth and apply a second thin coat.

Spar varnish should be used when making any outdoor ornaments or signs. It is a product specially designed as an exterior finish. Spar varnish resists weathering, sunlight, moisture and temperature changes. It is also highly resistant to cracks and peeling.

Acrylic Medium and Varnish is a very adaptable craft product that can be purchase in a gloss or matte finish. It can be used to protect and seal raw wood, allowing the natural grain to show through. When applied as an undercoat, it helps to prevent paint pens and permanent markers from bleeding. It provides a fast-drying, gloss finish when applied as a final topcoat on stained or painted projects. Mixed with paint it will add a transparency and gloss to the color. It is an excellent adhesive for applying paper designs to your project. It features soap and water cleanup, is low in odor, and is water-resistant once it dries.

Spray Varnish or Spray Wood Sealer will seal wood and add a clear, thin coat of protection to your projects. They add luster; bringing out the beauty of natural and stained woods and enhance the intensity of paint colors and design details. Sprays dry much quicker than similar brush-on products. They can be purchased in matte, satin or gloss finishes. Although the sprays are too expensive to be used on large areas, they do make finishing small areas quick and convenient. Sprays are particularly useful as an undercoat or topcoat for paint pens and permanent markers (to help prevent bleeding or smudging).

BRUSHES

Your finished project will reflect the materials and tools that you work with, so it pays to invest in a few good, high quality brushes. Choosing a brush size or type is a matter of personal preference. When selecting the best brush for a project, you will want to consider the type of finish being applied, the technique you will be using, the type of surface you are painting and the final effect you wish to create. Always use synthetic bristle brushes when working with acrylic paints or water-based finishes.

Bristle brushes: Take care of your brushes to keep them in top-working condition. Always work the brush hairs in their natural direction when loading, using or cleaning them. Never allow paint to seep into the medal ferrule of the brush. Do not let paint dry on your brushes, clean them promptly and thoroughly with soap and water. Do not leave your brushes sitting in water, especially resting on their bristles. Store brushes lying flat or standing upright (handle down, bristles up) in a container.

Foam sponge brushes are inexpensive applicators for painting larger areas. Water-based paints, stains and varnishes can be applied quickly and smoothly with a foam brush. Purchased at craft or hardware stores, they come in a wide variety of shapes and sizes. A foam stenciling brush can be substituted for a synthetic bristle brush. Do not let paint dry on your brushes, clean them promptly and thoroughly with soap and water.

Old toothbrushes make handy splatter brushes. Splattering gives an aged effect to your project as it softens the finished design. Dip the toothbrush into thinned paint and lightly splatter, flicking tiny dots of paint over the project surface. Practice the technique on scrap wood before trying it on your project.

BRUSH TYPES AND THEIR USES

Brushes come in many sizes, shapes and bristles. Listed below are the most common craft brushes and their uses. We recommend using synthetic bristle brushes for your projects. They are suitable for all finishes and ideal for acrylic paints. Synthetic bristles are durable, inexpensive and work well on wood.

Round: Use on point, thin/thick lines

Wash/Glaze: Washes, basecoats, finishes, highlighting, shading, dry brushing

Liner: Outlining, thin lines, thin lettering, fine details

Detail: Fine details, thin lines, thin lettering

Flat: Blocking in color, highlighting, shading, blending

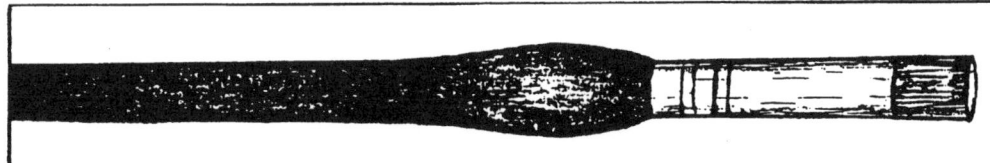

Stencil: Stenciling, dry brushing

PAINTING TERMS

Antique: A finishing technique where the project surface is darkened and made to look old. Can include sanding off areas of paint, especially around the edges, to resemble wear.

Base-coat: Also known as the undercoat. The first coat of paint applied. Filling an area with one continuous color of paint. A neat, smooth base-coat makes re-coating the paint and adding design details easier.

Double loading: Dip each side of a wet, flat brush into a different paint color. Stroke the brush lightly across a paper towel to blend the colors together on the bristle tips before applying on the project. This gives a brush stroke that has a different color on each side with them blended in the middle.

Dry brushing: Painting with a brush almost completely free of paint. A technique used to paint shading and highlights. Make sure the base-coat is completely dry before dry brushing over it. Draw the brush lightly across the area, letting it skip over the base-coat, to allow only partial coverage of paint on the surface.

Floating: Also known as side loading. Load one side of a wet, flat brush with paint. The paint should not travel across the brush bristles. This gives a paint stroke that is dark on one side (where the paint is loaded) fading down to clear on the other side. Use it to create a fading blend for shading or highlighting effects.

Glaze: Clear, translucent finish. Paint thinned with glaze to give it a transparency. It's used to paint or sponge layers over an opaque surface. The more glaze added to a paint color the lighter and more transparent the color will become. Slows down the paint's drying time.

Highlight: Lightening an area to bring it forward so that it looks like it is receiving the most light. Makes an area appear more prominent and adds dimension. Highlighting should be consistent through out the whole project. When applying a highlight, let the base-coat dry, then layer or float a lighter color on in the area to be highlighted. To make a strong highlight, add a light color dot or comma stroke to the area.

Shade: Gives an area depth so that it looks like it's receding. It should be consistent and always on the same side through out the project. When applying shading, let the base-coat dry, then layer or float 1 or more additional darker coats on in the area to be shaded.

Splattering: Also known as flecking or flyspecking. Applying tiny dots of paint onto the project surface using a splatter brush or an old toothbrush. Dip the brush into thinned paint and lightly flick paint dots onto the project surface by running your finger across the brush bristles. When dots are splattered onto a wet paint surface they will somewhat melt into the paint. On a dry background, the dots will remain crisp.

Stippling: Bounce the paint onto the project surface to paint bushes, foliage, fur or fuzzy paint effects. Try to leave some of the background color showing. Hold the brush in a vertical position when loading or applying the paint. Don't overload the brush. Bounce the brush on a paper towel to remove excess paint and to work the paint into the brush bristles.

Wash: Paint thinned with water until it becomes lighter and somewhat transparent. The ratio will vary depending on the paint color being used and the degree of transparency desired. Use it to paint an area for transparent coverage or float it on to add shadows or highlights over base-coat color.

PAINTING TIPS

1. Paint separates as it sits and the paint pigment settles to the bottom. Stir or shake the paint thoroughly before using to re-mix.

2. Paint can be used directly from the container for small areas. For larger areas, pour the paint into a mixing dish and add water until the paint is the consistency of heavy cream. This will give a smoother surface result.

3. Thin the paint with water to an ink consistency when using it to paint design details. This helps you to make long, smooth strokes and gives you better control of the paint. Use a detail or liner brush for painting.

4. If you are custom mixing your own colors, make sure that you mix enough of the paint color for the whole project.

5. Apply the paint smoothly and evenly. Two thin coats of paint will give you better results than one thick coat. Let the paint dry between coat.

6. Allow the base-coat to dry thoroughly before layering paints over it. Paint may feel dry on the surface but could be wet beneath the skin. This can disrupt the base-coat finish or cause bleeding through when you paint the next coats.

7. When painting raw wood, the paint may raise the wood grain, giving it a rough, fuzzy feeling. Sand the wood slightly with very fine (220-grid) sandpaper until it is smooth to the touch. Re-coat with another thin layer of paint, if necessary.

8. Use the largest brush that will fit the design area. This will prevent a lot of tight looking brush strokes.

9. Dip just the tip of the brush bristles into the paint, not so far up as the metal ferrule. This will make cleaning easier and the brush will last longer. Always clean your brush before changing paint colors.

DECORATING WITH DOTS

Applying paint dots is a fun and easy way to create decorative designs on your project. Eyes, flowers, hearts and stars can all be quickly painted with this simple technique. A line of dots can be used to emphasize or accent the line where different areas of paint colors connect. By using different size applicators you are able to make a wide variety of different size dots. Listed below are some of the more commonly use applicators.

APPLICATORS

Stylus: A stylus is a tool with pointed ends that is used to make decorative, multi-sized paint dots or to transfer a pattern onto a surface. They can be purchased at most craft centers.

Paintbrush handle: The handle end of a paintbrush can be used as a paint applicator. By using different size handles you can make bigger or smaller dots.

Round toothpicks: The tip of a round toothpick can be used to apply tiny dots to your design.

Pencil eraser: The unused eraser end of a pencil can be used to apply larger dots. Do not use the eraser for any other purpose. When you are finished painting with the eraser, wipe off the paint and keep it for you're next decorating project.

Stylus: Can be used to make decorative, multi-sized dots

INSTRUCTIONS

Dots: The dots are made in the same manner, no matter what applicator you decide to use. Dip the tip of the applicator into the paint. Touch it straight down on the project surface. Move slowly and lift the applicator straight up to avoid smearing or spattering the paint. Do not let dried paint build up on the end of the applicator or your dots will not be uniform in size. Wipe the paint off of the tip of the applicator frequently. Before applying the design on your project, practice on scrap wood to perfect your technique.

Uniform Dots: Dip and apply one dot at a time to insure uniform size dots.

Descending Dots: To make neatly descending dots, apply 2 or 3 dots before dipping the applicator again.

Hearts: Make 2 uniform dots next to each other. Use a small paintbrush handle or a toothpick to pull some paint from both dots to a central point. This will form the point of the heart. To help you pull the paint in the right direction and to the correct length, make a small pencil mark where you want the point of the heart to end. Pull the paint out to the mark.

Stars: Apply a dot of paint where you want the center of the star. Pull the paint out from the center of the dot with a small paintbrush handle or a toothpick to form the star points. To help you pull the paint in the right direction and to the correct length, make a small pencil mark where you want each point of the star to end. Pull the paint out to these marks.

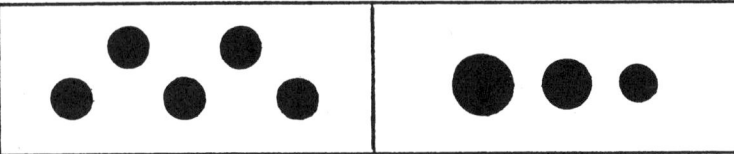

Uniform and Descending Dots

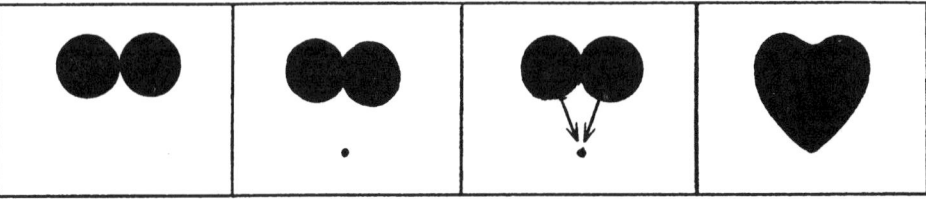

The heart design is painted by placing 2 uniform dots next to each other and than pulling paint down from both of them to form the point.

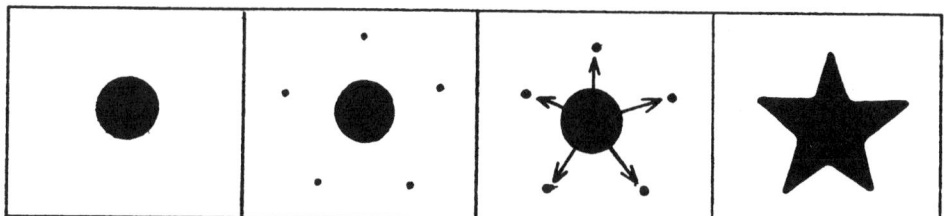

The star design is painted by pulling paint out from a center dot to form the points.

Eyes: An eye can be painted as simply as a single dot or it can be a combination of progressively smaller dots layered on top of each other. A small white highlight dot can add a spark of life to the painted eye.

 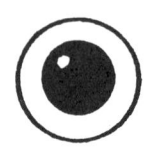  

Various eye designs can be painted using dots.

Flowers: Dot flowers can be painted in a number of ways. A favorite is to apply a large dot in the center and then encircle it with 6 evenly spaced smaller dots. Another design used is to paint 5 uniform dots in a circle, their edges just touching, and then place another dot in the center of them. Painting 3 slightly overlapping uniform dots with a smaller dot placed in the center will give you a smaller flower design.

Dot painting is a fast and easy way to add a flower design to your project.

STENCILING

Stenciling is one of the world's oldest decorating techniques. It's an easy way to add a design to your project. In stenciling, the paint is applied through the openings in the stencil material. Because the stencil defines the stencil design, a repetitive design is simple to paint. Stencils are available in a large variety of pre-cut patterns or you can cut your own designs with a utility knife. Be sure to use a new, sharp blade so your cuts will be clean. A good bristle stenciling brush should be used to ensure crisp, clear design prints. Use the brush dry with very little paint and apply the paint in a circular motion or use a stippling technique.

Acrylics are the most commonly used paints for stenciling. Place the stencil on the project surface and secure with masking tape. Pour the paint color onto a dish. Load your paintbrush by dipping the bristle tips into the paint. Remove excess paint by tapping the tips of the bristles on a paper towel. This will also distribute the paint evenly across the brush tips. If there is too much paint on your brush, it will seep under the stencil, making a messy print. Move the brush around in a circular motion on the opening starting from the edge and working to the center. Complete one color at a time. After all of the colors have been applied, remove the stencil carefully so you do not smudge the paint. Let the paint dry completely. Clean the brush and stencil thoroughly with soap and water.

Dry brush paint looks like a solid cake but has the consistency of lipstick. This non-drip paint won't seep under the stencil. It's an easy to apply product that provides a beautiful, long-lasting color. Place the stencil on the project surface and secure with masking tape. Open the jar and remove the seal from the top of the paint with a paper towel. Swirl the stencil brush in the paint. Blot off any excess paint on a paper towel. Swirl the loaded brush on an uncut area of the stencil to evenly distribute the paint on the brush. Use a circular motion to apply the paint in the cutout areas of the stencil. Re-load the stencil brush with paint as needed. Complete one color at a time. After all of the colors have been applied, remove the stencil carefully so you do not smudge the paint. Let the paint dry completely. Clean the brush and stencil thoroughly with soap and water.

Paint crayons are a neat, easy stenciling medium. The colors are fade-resistant, inter-mixable and blendable. Place the stencil on the project surface and secure with masking tape. Rub the crayon on an uncut area of the stencil. Pick-up the paint with the stencil brush using a brisk, circular stroke. Blot the brush on a paper towel to remove any excess paint as needed. Apply the paint to the cutout areas of the stencil using a circular motion. Work the paint into the surface by repeatedly going over the design. Re-load and repeat the application to darken the color. Complete one color at a time. After all of the colors have been applied, remove the stencil carefully so you do not smudge the paint. Let the paint dry completely. Clean the brush and stencil thoroughly with soap and water.

SPONGE PAINTING

Painting with a **natural sea sponge** is an ideal way to add interesting texture and depth to a project. Sea sponges are available in a variety of sizes with a small, medium or large porous surface texture. The goal in sponge painting is to create a random, uneven pattern and the irregular shape and surface qualities of the sea sponge are perfect for this technique. Always clean the sponge immediately, when you have finished painting, by rinsing it under running water until the water runs clear. If you use the sponge frequently, rinsing it in baking soda once a week will extend its durability and provide better painting results. Let the sponge air dry thoroughly before putting it away.

Sponging looks best when multiple layers of color are applied over the base-coat. Use various shades of one color over the base for a subtle effect. Use 2 or 3 contrasting colors for a more vivid shading effect. The number of paint layers, whether or not you add glaze to the paint and the way they are applied all combine to create very different paint effects. Generally, the darkest color is applied fist, followed by progressively lighter shades layered over it. This helps to create the illusion of depth.

Apply a smooth, even base-coat of acrylic craft paint or semi-gloss, low-luster or gloss latex paint to the area. Allow the paint to dry thoroughly so that it will not bleed through the colors you will be layering over it. The rest of the paint colors can be used as they come from the container or you can mix them with a water-based glaze to give them a lighter, more transparent effect. The more glaze added to the paint, the lighter and more translucent the paint will appear.

Pour the paint or paint mixture into a paint tray. Dampen the sponge in water and squeeze out the excess. Dip the sponge into the paint. Blot off any excess on a paper towel. Lightly press the sponge on the project surface in an overall pattern and texture. Keep your hand moving, over-sponging an area will create a muddled and splotchy surface pattern. Don't try to cover the entire area, the base-coat should be seen through the broken color and space should be allowed for the other colors. Continue this process, rotating the sponge every time you dip it into the paint (to prevent a repetitive pattern) until you have painted the whole area. When you are finished, clean the paint tray and sponge. When applying more than one color refill the paint tray with the next color and repeat the above procedure. Make sure that you leave some of the previous colors showing through.

FINISHING TOUCHES

With a little imagination you can personalize each of your projects by utilizing a wide variety of different materials to add color and interesting effects to its design. The additions of these small decorative touches will not only make your project more attractive, they can also eliminate the necessity of having to tediously hand paint intricate details. Listed below are some of the more common materials that are used in craft making.

1. Ribbon comes in hundreds of patterns, widths and colors. It can be tied on or made into a bow and glued in place.
2. Yarns, twines and strings are available in a multitude of colors, thickness and textures. They can be tied on, attached with glue or threaded through drilled holes in the project pieces to join them together.
3. Wire can be purchased in assorted colors and thickness. It can be threaded through drilled holes in the project pieces to link them together, twisted or curled and then attached to form hangers or glued on as a decorative touch (such as the stem for a flower).
4. Silk or plastic flowers come in every variety, color and size imaginable. They are a great way to add color and dimension to your project. Simply glue them in place.
5. Paper can be cut or torn into pieces and decoupaged onto the project surface. Wrapping paper is an especially wonderful source of colorful patterns and designs.
6. Fabric comes in an almost unlimited array of designs and patterns. It can be tied on to your project or glued in place to create colorful pieces of clothing. When sewing fabric ears for an animal design, your choice of pattern can change the project's whole look.
7. Buttons, beads or bits of lace can be glued on to dress-up a project design.
8. Stickers, decals or rub-on transfers are a quick and easy way to create all sorts of imaginative designs. They are also available in many lettering styles that can be used to personalize a project by adding a name or phase. Apply them according to their package directions.

A piece of wire bent into the shape of eyeglasses, a felt hat trimmed with batting and decorated with artificial holly and a wood button nose dress up this Santa design.

A bit of lace around the neck, a ribbon tied around the ear and a name applied with press-on stickers all combine to add color and interest to the mother bear.

PATTERN 825A:
BUNNY PUZZLE

SUPPLIES

6 ½" x 9" Pine, ¾" to 1 ½" thick
White glue or Acrylic medium & varnish
Black paint pen (fine-tip)
6" x 8 ½" piece of wrapping paper
Varnish (optional)

ACRYLIC PAINTS

White
Black
Light Blue
2 colors chosen to match wrapping paper

Notes: Using the thicker wood will add stability to the puzzle. Cut slowly and carefully, using the smallest blade recommended for the wood thickness you have selected. As you are cutting, make sure the blade is not bending or your cuts will be slanted.

INSTRUCTIONS

Duplicate the pattern on a copier machine or with tracing paper. Transfer the main puzzle lines onto the wood. With a scroll saw, cut along the outline of the bunny. Cut down the pattern lines that form the ears. Cut along pattern line "A" that forms the top of the eyes and the bottom of the nose. Cut out the bunny's face piece. Cut out the rest of the puzzle pieces. Sand all surfaces with 100-grid and then 150-grid sandpaper. Remove the sanding dust with a tack cloth.

Base-coat all surfaces of the puzzle pieces (except for the front areas of the eyes, teeth and nose) with light blue paint. Let the paint dry. Sand lightly to remove the "fuzz" raised by the acrylic paint. Remove the sanding dust with a tack cloth. Apply another coat of the light blue paint. Let the paint dry. Base-coat the eyes and the teeth white. Base-coat the nose black. Let the paint dry.

Transfer the pattern details onto the puzzle. With the eraser end of a pencil apply the large dots that form the flower centers using one of the colors chosen from the wrapping paper. With your second color choice, paint the small flower dots using a paintbrush handle. Dot on the black for the eye pupils using the eraser end of a pencil. Let the paint dry. Dot a white highlight on each eye using a small paintbrush handle. Paint the white highlight on the nose. Use the black paint pen to add the whiskers and the detail lines on the teeth, face and feet.

Transfer both ear outlines onto the wrapping paper. Cut out the wrapping paper ears. Cut the puzzle knobs off the wrapping paper ears. Glue the wrapping paper in place with white glue or the acrylic medium & varnish. Trim off any excess wrapping paper with a sharp razor blade.

Apply a topcoat of varnish to the project for added protection and durability or if a higher gloss finish is desired. Let the varnish dry thoroughly before assembling the puzzle or the pieces will stick together.

These three patterns were reduced at 75%. Enlarge at 130%

Pattern for 825A: Bunny Puzzle

PATTERN 825B:
BUNNY PUZZLE (FABRIC EARS)

SUPPLIES

6 ½" x 9" Pine, ¾" to 1 ½" thick
7" x 9" piece of print fabric
7" x 9" piece of pink fabric
10" piece of ¼" wide ribbon
Black paint pen (fine-tip)
Varnish (semi- gloss finish)
Wood glue

ACRYLIC PAINTS

White
Black
Medium Green
2 colors chosen to match the print fabric

Notes: Using the thicker wood will add stability to the puzzle. Cut slowly and carefully, using the smallest blade recommended for the wood thickness you have selected. As you are cutting, make sure the blade is not bending or your cuts will be slanted.

INSTRUCTIONS

Duplicate the pattern on a copier machine or with tracing paper. Transfer the main puzzle lines onto the wood. With a scroll saw, cut along the outline of the bunny. Cut along pattern line "A" that forms the top of the eyes and the bottom of the nose. Cut out the bunny's face piece. Cut out the rest of the puzzle pieces. Drill the ¼" holes for the ears where shown on the pattern. Sand all surfaces with 100-grid and then 150-grid sandpaper. Remove the sanding dust with a tack cloth.

Varnish all surfaces of the puzzle pieces except the front of the face, eyes, teeth and nose. Let the varnish dry. Base-coat the face, eyes and teeth white. Let the paint dry. Sand lightly to remove "fuzz" raised by the varnish and paint. Remove the sanding dust with a tack cloth. Touch-up paint if necessary. Mix a small amount of black with water to form a wash. Use this mixture to add shading to the face. Let the paint dry.

Transfer the pattern details onto the puzzle. Dot on the black for the eye pupils using the eraser end of a pencil. Base-coat the nose black. Let the paint dry. Dot a white highlight on each eye using a small paintbrush handle. Paint the white highlight on the nose. Use the black paint pen to add the whiskers and the details on the teeth and face. Using one of the colors chosen from the print fabric, paint the large dots on the bunny's body with the eraser end of a pencil. With your second color choice, paint the small design dots using a paintbrush handle. Add the medium green leaves with a detail brush. Let the paint dry.

Apply a topcoat of varnish to the entire project for added protection, durability and a higher gloss finish. Let the varnish dry thoroughly before assembling the puzzle or the pieces will stick together.

Trace 2 ear patterns onto the print fabric and 2 ear patterns onto the pink fabric. Cut out the fabric pieces. Place 1 print and 1 pink ear piece right sides together. Sew a ¼" seam around the edge leaving the opening as shown on the pattern. Turn the ear right side out. Sew and turn the second ear in the same manner. Tuck and glue one ear into each ear hole. Tie a bow around the base of the right ear using the ¼" wide ribbon. Adjust the ears.

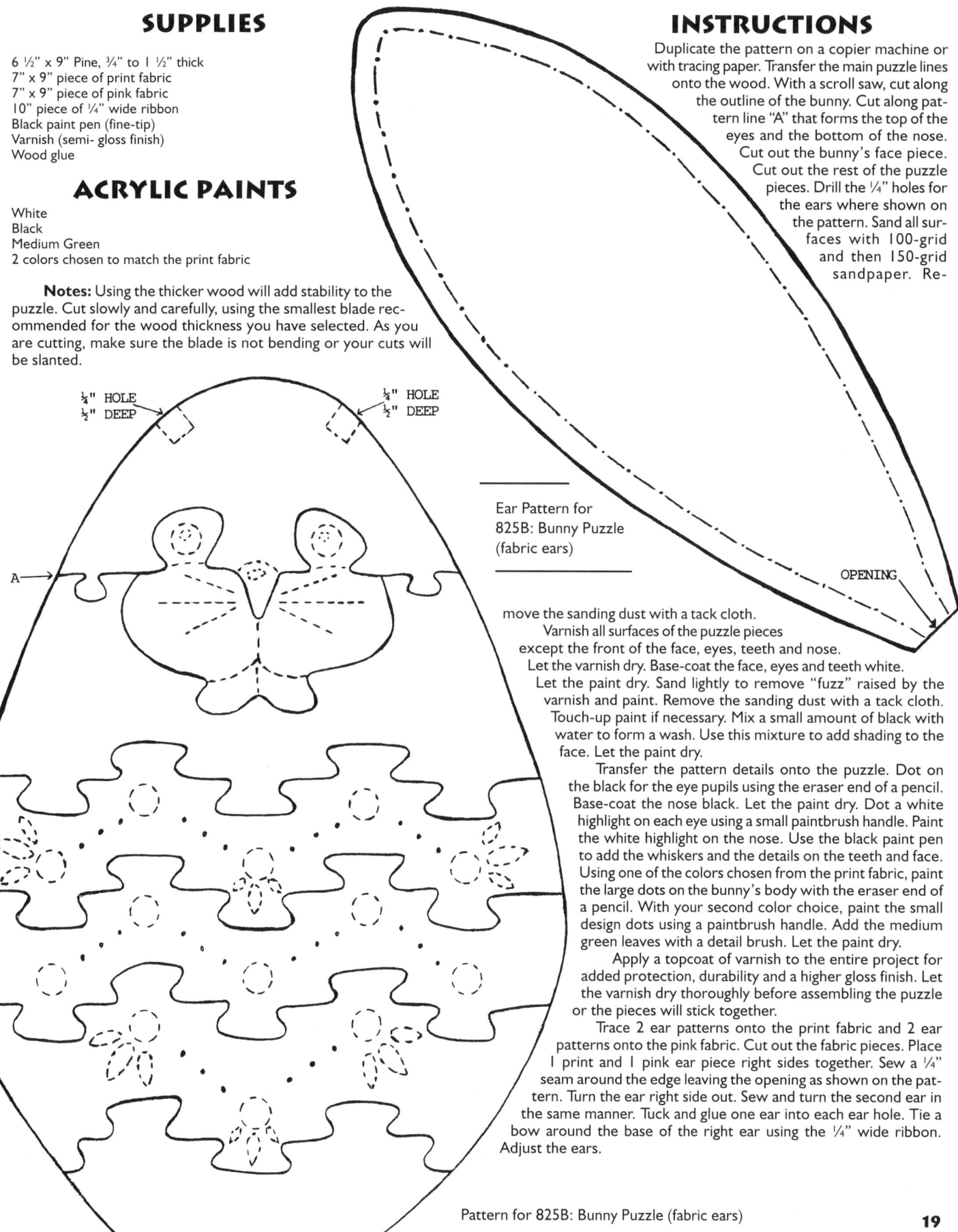

Ear Pattern for 825B: Bunny Puzzle (fabric ears)

Pattern for 825B: Bunny Puzzle (fabric ears)

PATTERN 825C:
BUNNY HOLDING HEART

SUPPLIES

4 ½" x 5 ¾" Pine, ¾" to 1 ½" thick
2" x 5 ¼" Basswood, ¼" thick
2 ½" x 2" Basswood, 1/8" thick
White glue
Wood glue
Black paint pen (fine-tip)
4" x 5 ¼" piece of wrapping paper
Varnish (optional)

ACRYLIC PAINTS

White
Black

INSTRUCTIONS

Duplicate the pattern on a copier machine or with tracing paper. Transfer the body pattern outline onto the 4 ½" x 5 ¾" piece of pine. Transfer 2 ear pattern outlines onto the 2" x 5 ¼" piece of basswood. Transfer the arm/heart pattern onto the 2 ½" x 2" piece of basswood. Cut the shapes out with a scroll saw. Sand all surfaces with 100-grid and then 150-grid sandpaper. Remove the sanding dust with a tack cloth.

Transfer the main pattern lines onto the arm/heart piece. Paint the arm sections of the arm/heart piece white, continuing the color around the edges of the **whole** piece. Paint the edges of both ear pieces white. Paint the back of the ears at the top, where they will stick out from the body, white. Base-coat the body white, continuing the color around the edges and onto the back. Let the paint dry. Sand lightly to remove the "fuzz" raised by the acrylic paint. Remove the sanding dust with a tack cloth. Touch-up the paint if necessary.

Transfer the outlines for the heart and the 2 ears onto the wrapping paper. Cut out the wrapping paper heart and ears. Glue the wrapping paper in place with white glue. Trim off any excess wrapping paper with a sharp razor blade.

Transfer the pattern details of the face and feet onto the body. Paint the detail lines of the face and feet with the black paint pen. Dot on the black for the eye pupils using a large paintbrush handle. Paint the nose black. Let the paint dry. Paint the white highlight on the nose. Dot a white highlight on each eye using the tip of a round toothpick. Use the black paint pen to add the dash lines on the body, ears and arm/heart piece.

If you have painted the glue areas, sand the paint off where the pieces join. Glue the 2 ear pieces and the arm/heart piece in place using the wood glue. Let the glue dry. Apply one or two topcoats of varnish to the project for added protection and durability or if a higher gloss finish is desired. Let the varnish dry.

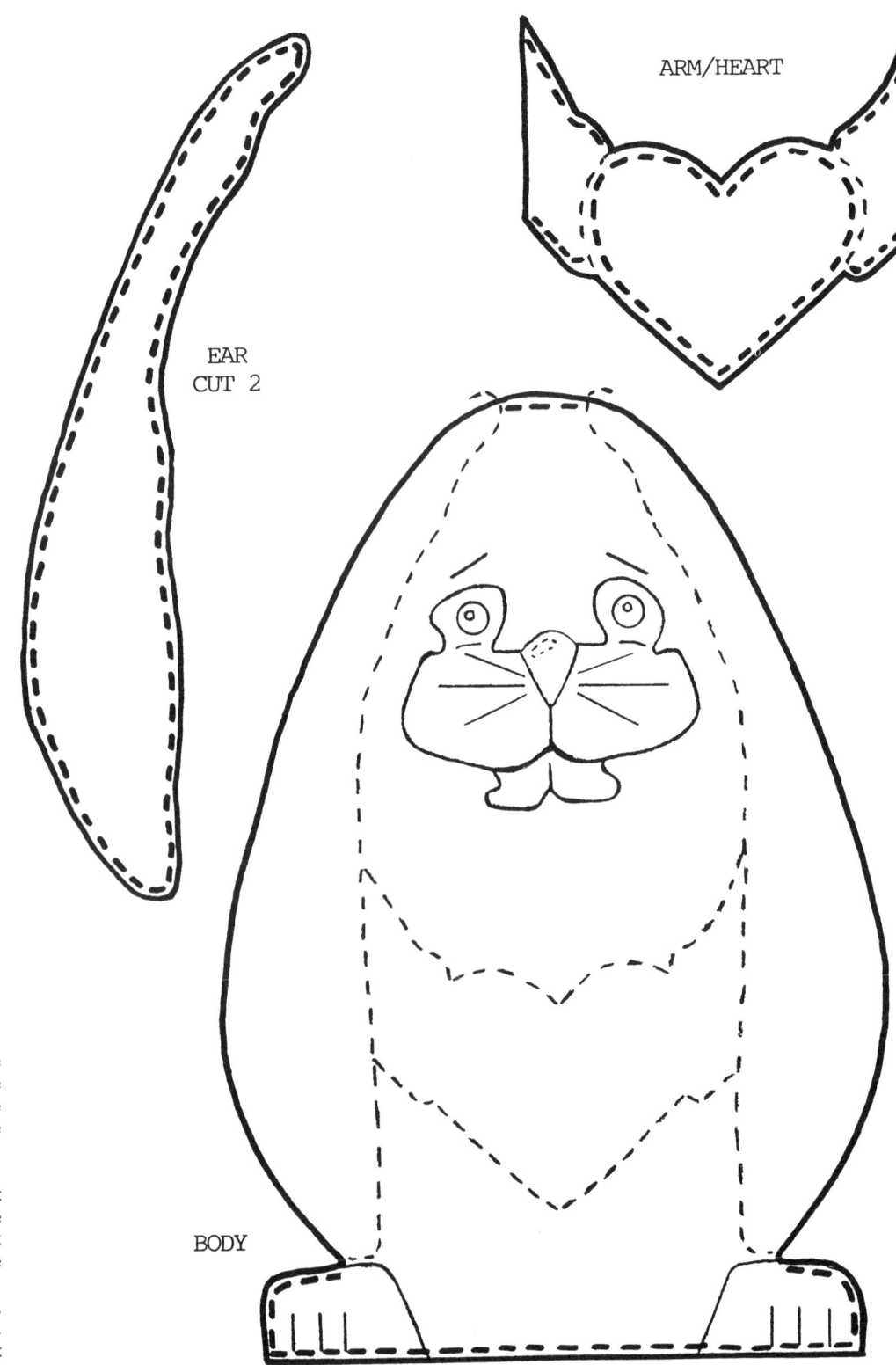

Pattern for 825C: Bunny Holding Heart

20

PATTERN 826A:
DOG PUZZLE

SUPPLIES

6 ½" x 9" Pine, ¾" to 1 ½" thick
Stain (any brown shade)
Varnish (semi-gloss finish)
Black paint pen (fine-tip)

ACRYLIC PAINTS

White
Black
Red

Notes: Using the thicker wood will add stability to the puzzle. Cut slowly and carefully, using the smallest blade recommended for the wood thickness you have selected. As you are cutting, make sure the blade is not bending or your cuts will be slanted.

INSTRUCTIONS

Duplicate the pattern on a copier machine or with tracing paper. Transfer the main puzzle lines onto the wood. With a scroll saw, cut along the dog's outline. Cut down the pattern lines that form the ears. Cut along pattern line "A" that forms the top of the eyes and the bottom of the nose. Cut out the dog's face piece. Cut out the rest of the puzzle pieces. Sand all surfaces with 100-grid and then 150-grid sandpaper. Remove the sanding dust with a tack cloth.

Stain all surfaces of the puzzle pieces except the front areas of the eyes, nose and tongue. Let the stain dry. Stain the ears again to deepen their color. Let the stain dry. Sand lightly to remove "fuzz" raised by the stain. Paint the tongue red. Base-coat the nose black. Base-coat the eyes white. Let the paint dry.

Transfer the pattern details onto the puzzle. Dot on the black eye pupils using the eraser end of a pencil. Let the paint dry. Paint the white highlight on the nose. Dot a white highlight on each eye using a small paintbrush handle. Use the black paint pen to add the whisker dots and the details on the face.

Apply a thin coat of varnish to all surfaces of the puzzle pieces. Let the varnish dry. Sand the surfaces lightly with 220-grid sandpaper. Remove the sanding dust with a tack cloth. Apply a second coat of varnish. Let the pieces dry thoroughly before assembling the puzzle or the pieces will stick together.

This pattern was reduced at 75%. Enlarge at 130%

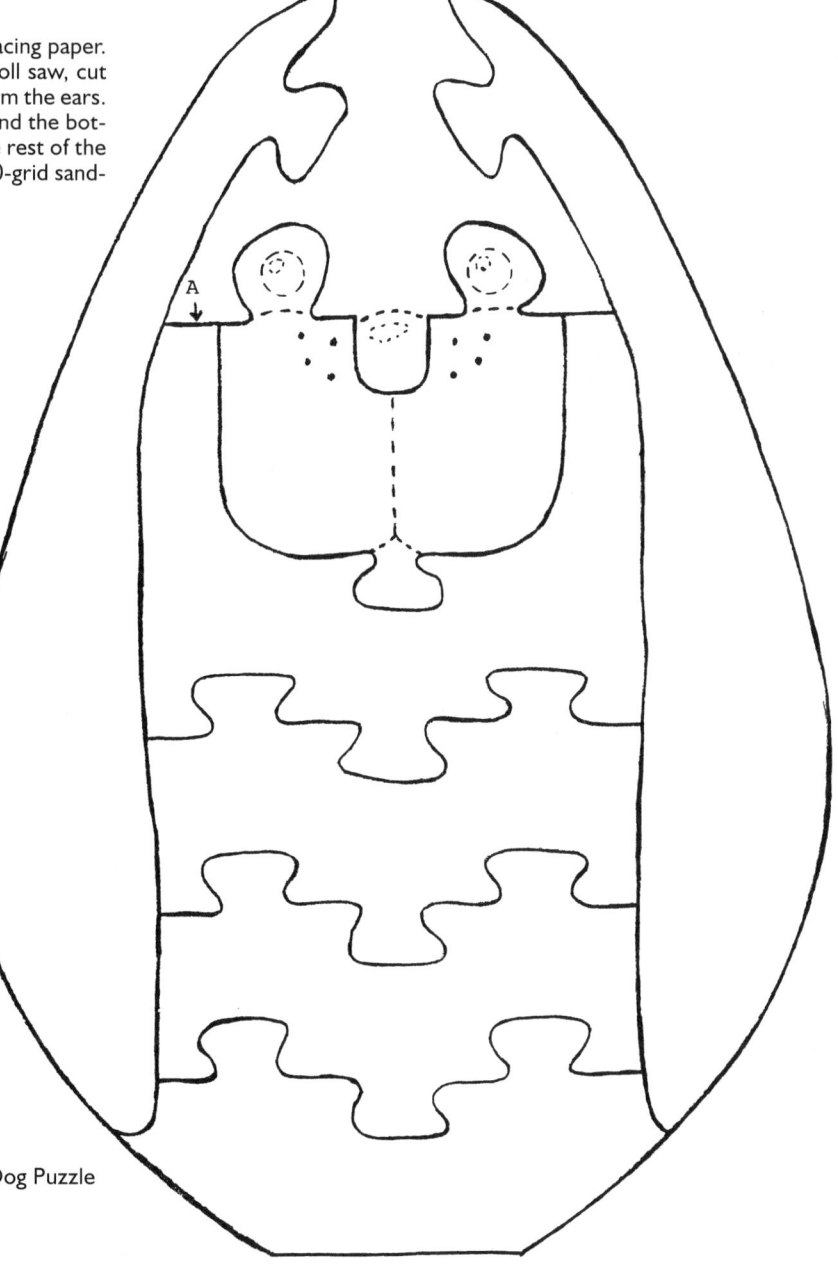

Pattern for 826A: Dog Puzzle

PATTERN 826B: DOG PUZZLE (FABRIC EARS)

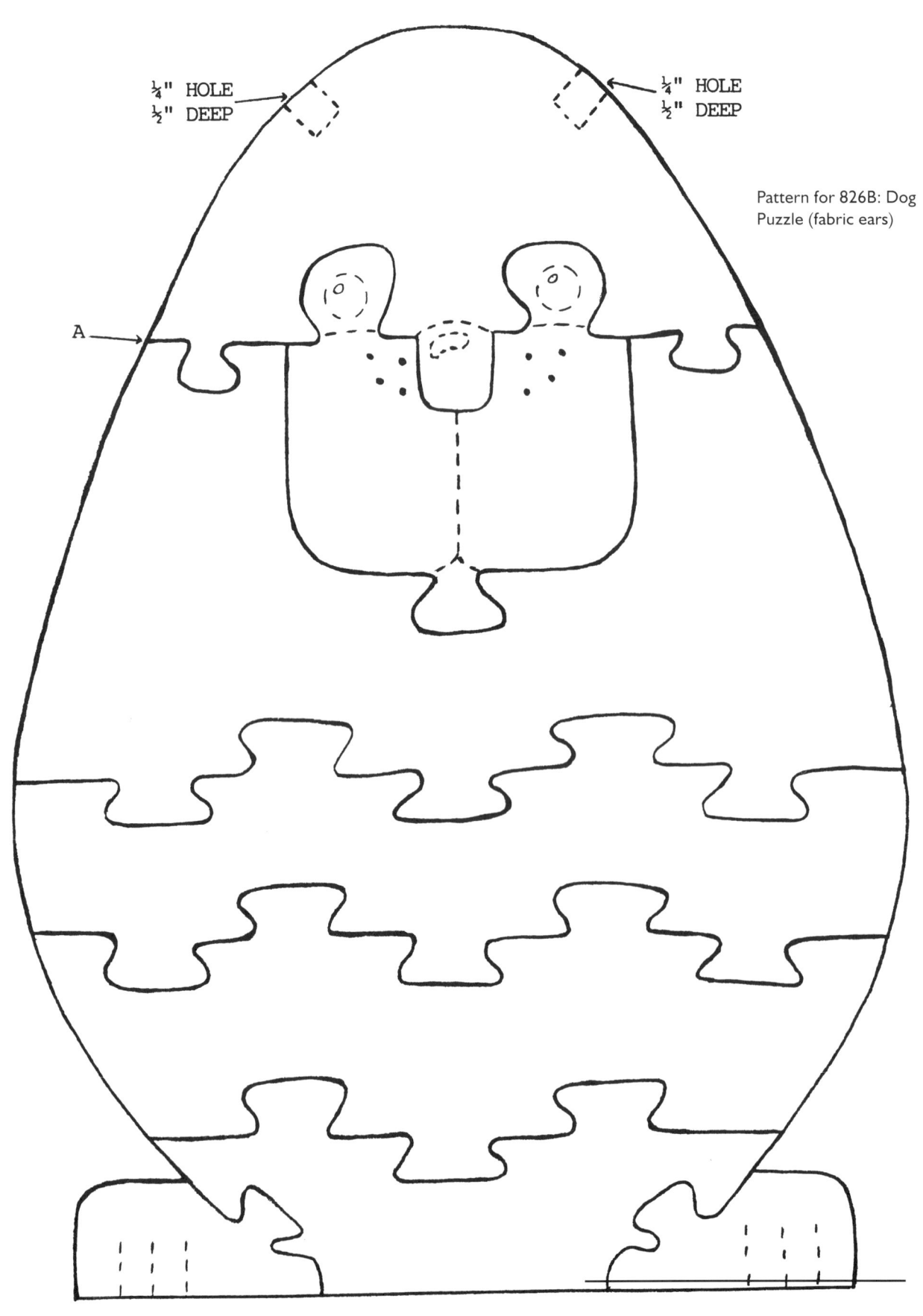

Pattern for 826B: Dog Puzzle (fabric ears)

SUPPLIES

6 ½" x 9" Pine, ¾" to 1 ½" thick
14" x 9" piece of fabric
Black paint pen (fine-tip)
Wood glue

ACRYLIC PAINTS

White
Black
Brown
Red

Notes: Using the thicker wood will add stability to the puzzle. Cut slowly and carefully, using the smallest blade recommended for the wood thickness you have selected. As you are cutting, make sure the blade is not bending or your cuts will be slanted.

INSTRUCTIONS

Duplicate the pattern on a copier machine or with tracing paper. Transfer the main puzzle lines onto the wood. With a scroll saw, cut along the outline of the dog. Cut along pattern line "A" that forms the top of the eyes and the bottom of the nose. Cut out the dog's face piece. Cut out the rest of the puzzle pieces. Drill the ¼" holes for the ears where shown on the pattern. Sand all surfaces with 100-grid and then 150-grid sandpaper. Remove the sanding dust with a tack cloth.

Base-coat all surfaces of the puzzle pieces, except the front areas of the eyes, nose, tongue and face, with a brown wash (approximately 2 parts brown to 1 part water). Let the paint dry. Sand lightly to remove "fuzz" raised by the paint mixture. Remove the sanding dust with a tack cloth. Paint the tongue red. Base-coat the nose black. Base-coat the eyes white. Mix together equal parts of brown and white. Use this mixture to paint the face. Let the paint dry.

Transfer the pattern details onto the puzzle. Dot on the black eye pupils using the eraser end of a pencil. Let the paint dry. Dot a white highlight on each eye using a small paintbrush handle. Paint the white highlight on the nose. Use the black paint pen to add the whisker dots and the detail lines on the face and feet.

Trace 4 ear patterns onto the fabric. Cut out the fabric ear pieces. Place 2 ear pieces right sides together. Sew a ¼" seam around the edge leaving the opening, as shown on the pattern. Turn the ear right side out. Sew and turn the second ear in the same manner. Tuck and glue one ear into each ear hole. Adjust the ears.

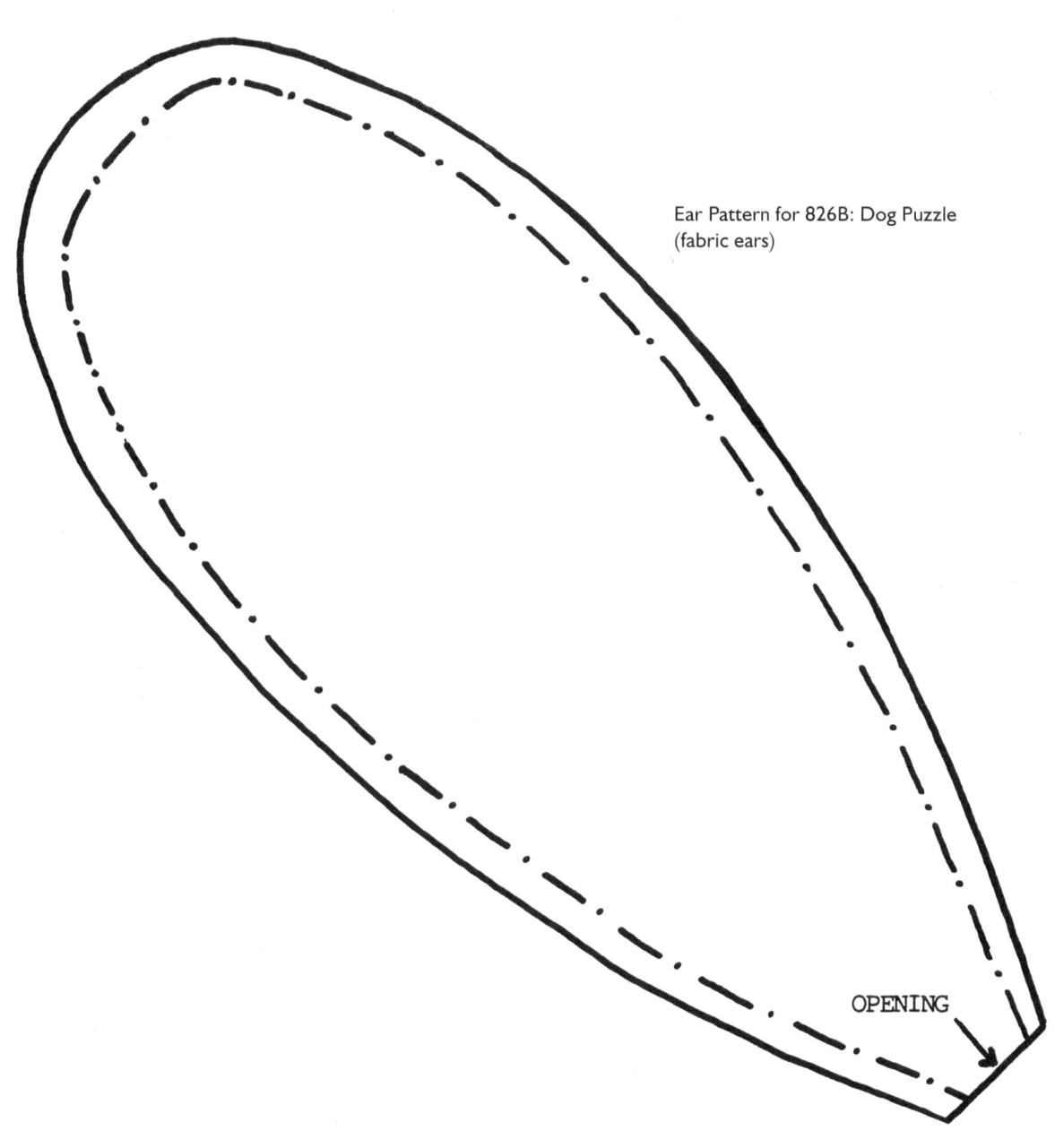

Ear Pattern for 826B: Dog Puzzle
(fabric ears)

OPENING

PATTERN 827:
INCHWORM PUZZLE

SUPPLIES

16" x 7" Pine, 1 ½" thick
Black paint pen (medium-tip)
Varnish (optional)
Splatter or old toothbrush

ACRYLIC PAINTS

Yellow/Green
Yellow
Green
Black

Notes: It's important to use wood that is 1 ½" thick for this project. It gives the puzzle the stability it requires. Cut the wood slowly and carefully, using the smallest blade recommended for the wood thickness. As you are cutting, make sure the blade is not bending or your cuts will be slanted.

INSTRUCTIONS

Duplicate the pattern pages for the front and back sections of the inchworm on a copier machine or with tracing paper. Line up and tape together the 2 pattern sheets to form 1 full pattern. Trim off excess paper. Place the pattern on the wood workpiece so that the bottom edges of pieces 1, 2, 8 and 9 run along the bottom edge of the wood. Transfer the pattern cut lines onto the wood. With a scroll saw, slowly cut along the outline of the inchworm. Slowly cut out the puzzle pieces. Sand all surfaces with 100-grid and than 150-grid sandpaper. Remove the sanding dust with a tack cloth.

Base-coat the puzzle pieces with yellow/green, continuing the color around the edges and onto the backs. Let the paint dry. Sand lightly to remove the "fuzz" raised by the acrylic paint. Remove the sanding dust with a tack cloth. Touch-up the paint if necessary.

Float green shading onto the pieces. Highlight the pieces with yellow. Let the paint dry. Dilute black with water to ink consistency. Dip a splatter brush or an old toothbrush into the thinned paint and splatter the pieces. Let the paint dry. Dilute yellow with water to ink consistency. Dip a splatter brush or an old toothbrush into the thinned paint and splatter the pieces. Let the paint dry.

Transfer the pattern details onto the puzzle pieces. With a small detail brush, paint the eye and the numbers black. Use the black paint pen to add the dot/dash details around the inchworm's outline. Let the paint dry.

Apply one or two topcoats of varnish to the project pieces for added protections and durability or if a higher gloss finish is desired. Let the varnish dry thoroughly before assembling the puzzle or the pieces will stick together.

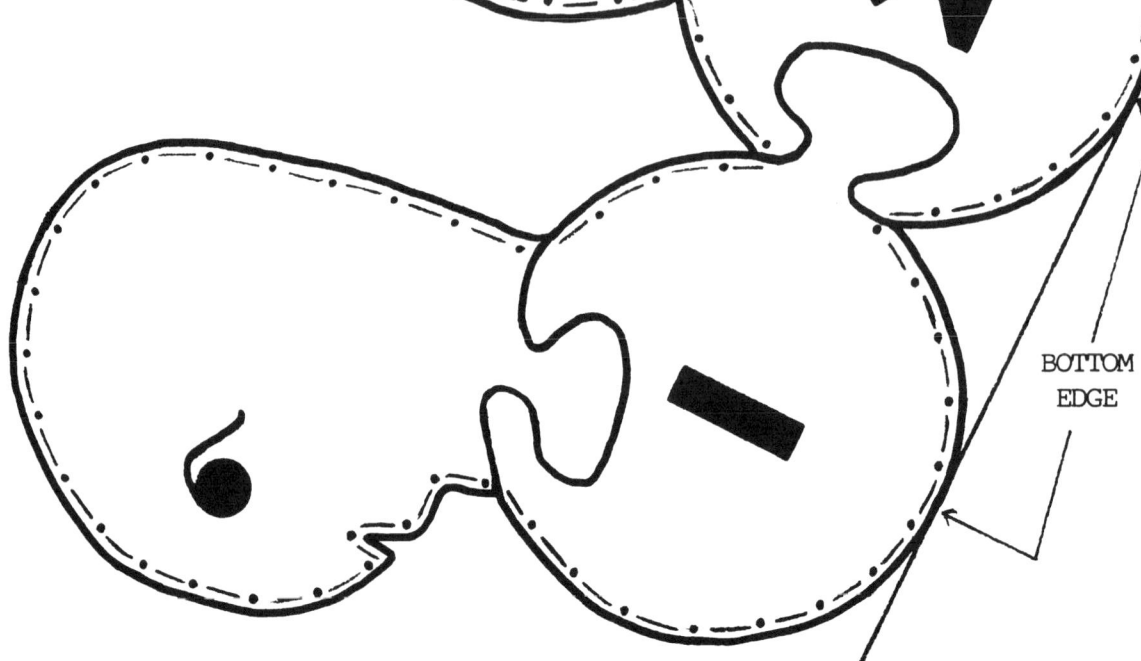

Pattern for 827: Inchworm Puzzle (front half)

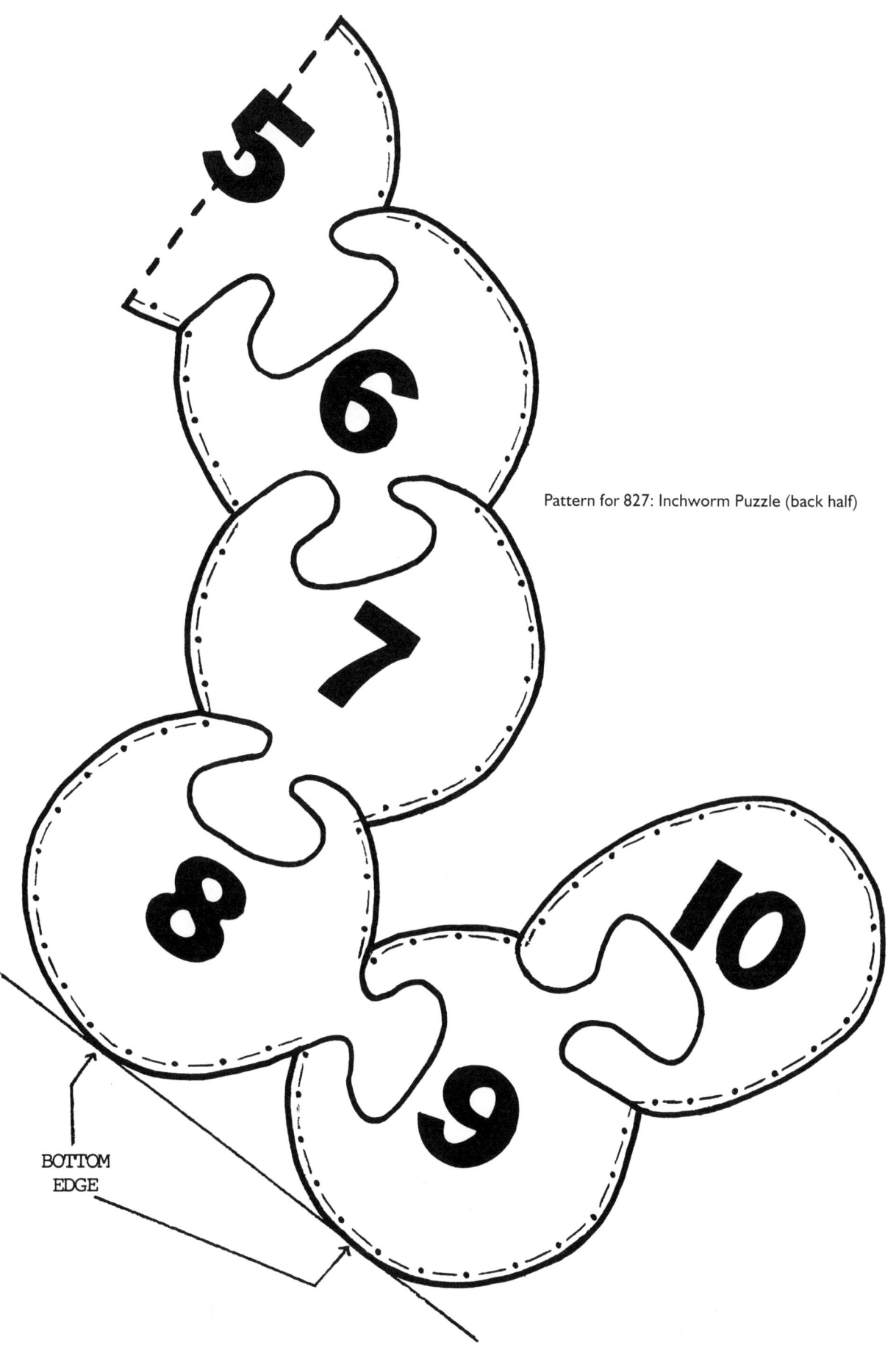

Pattern for 827: Inchworm Puzzle (back half)

BOTTOM EDGE

25

PATTERN 828:
TREE PUZZLE

SUPPLIES

8" by 8 ½" Pine, ¾" thick
Black paint pen (fine-tip)
Sea Sponge

ACRYLIC PAINTS

Red
Green
White
Black

INSTRUCTIONS

Duplicate the pattern on a copier machine or with tracing paper. Transfer the pattern lines onto the wood. There is no need to transfer the bow details yet. With a scroll saw, cut along the outline of the tree. Cut out the puzzle pieces. Sand all surfaces with 100-grid and then 150-grid sandpaper. Remove the sanding dust with a tack cloth.

To increase the difficulty level in assembling the puzzle, paint the front and back of the pieces the same. Base-coat the bow with red, continuing the color around the edges and onto the back. Mix three parts of green paint with one part white. Use this mixture to base-coat all surfaces of the tree pieces. Don't forget to paint the green tree area on the bow piece. Let the paint dry. Sand lightly to remove the "fuzz" raised by the acrylic paint. Remove the sanding dust with a tack cloth. Touch-up the paint if necessary.

Mix three parts of red and one part of green with a small amount of water. Use this mixture to add shading to the front and back of the bow. Sponge paint green over all surfaces of the tree pieces (be sure to leave some of the base-coat showing through). Let the paint dry.

Mix three parts green and one part black with a small amount of water. Apply this mixture, using the sea sponge, to add a shading effect to the front and back of the tree pieces. Let the paint dry.

Transfer the bow details to both sides of the bow piece. Using a black paint pen, paint the details on the bow. Let the paint dry thoroughly. Assemble the puzzle. Sponge White onto the tree and bow to create a snow effect.

DETAILS FOR BOW

This pattern was reduced at 75%. Enlarge at 130%

Pattern for 828: Tree Puzzle

PATTERN 829:
SANTA PUZZLE

SUPPLIES

8" x 8 ½" Pine, ¾" thick
Varnish (semi-gloss finish)

ACRYLIC PAINTS

Red
White
Black

INSTRUCTIONS

Duplicate the pattern on a copier machine or with tracing paper. Transfer the main pattern lines onto the wood. With a scroll saw, using the smallest blade recommended for the wood thickness, cut along Santa's outline. Slowly cut along pattern line "A" that forms the bottom of the hair and the top of the mustache. Cut along pattern line "B" that forms the bottom of the left side of the mustache. Cut along pattern line "C" that forms the bottom of the right side of the mustache. Cut out the rest of the puzzle pieces. Sand all surfaces with 100-grid and than 150-grid sandpaper. Remove the sanding dust with a tack cloth.

Varnish the front of the face piece. Let the varnish dry. Paint the hat piece red, continuing the color around the edges and onto the back. Paint all remaining surfaces with white. Let the paint dry. Sand lightly to remove the "fuzz" raised by the paints. Remove the sanding dust with a tack cloth. Touch-up paints if necessary.

Transfer the pattern details onto the puzzle. Dot on black for the eyes using the eraser end of a pencil. Dot on a red nose using the handle of a paintbrush. Paint the red for the mouth. Let the paint dry. Paint the details on the mouth with black. Dot a white highlight on each eye using a small paintbrush handle. Let the puzzle pieces dry thoroughly before assembling or the pieces will stick together.

Pattern for 829: Santa Puzzle

This pattern was reduced at 75%. Enlarge at 130%

PATTERN 830A:
SANTA KEY CHAIN OR MAGNET
&
PATTERN 830B:
SANTA TREE ORNAMENT

SUPPLIES FOR 830A

Red acrylic paint
White acrylic paint
Black acrylic paint
2 ½" x 2 ¾" Pine, 1/8" thick
Varnish (semi-gloss finish)
Black paint pen (extra-fine tip)
Key chain or Magnet
Wood glue

SUPPLIES FOR 830B

Red acrylic paint
White acrylic paint
Black acrylic paint
3 ¼" x 3 ½" Pine, ¼" thick
Varnish (semi-gloss finish)
Black paint pen (extra-fine tip)

INSTRUCTIONS

Duplicate the pattern on a copier machine or with tracing paper. Transfer Santa's outline onto the wood. With a scroll saw, cut along Santa's outline. If you are making the key chain or the tree ornament, drill the hole where shown on the pattern. Sand all surfaces with 100-grid and than 150-grid sandpaper. Remove the sanding dust with a tack cloth.

Transfer the main pattern lines onto the wood. Paint the hat red, continuing the color around the edges. Varnish the face area. Let the paint and varnish dry. Paint all remaining surfaces white. Let the paint dry. Sand lightly to remove the "fuzz" raised by the paints. Remove the sanding dust with a tack cloth. Touch-up the paint if necessary.

Transfer the pattern details onto the wood. Dot on black for the eyes using the handle of a paintbrush. Dot on a red nose using a very small paintbrush handle. Paint the mouth red. Let the paint dry. Dot a white highlight on each eye using the tip of a round toothpick. Paint the detail lines on with the black paint pen. Let the paint dry.

For a Key chain... attach the key chain to the project
Refrigerator magnet... glue the magnet on to the back of the project

Pattern for 830B: Santa Tree Ornament

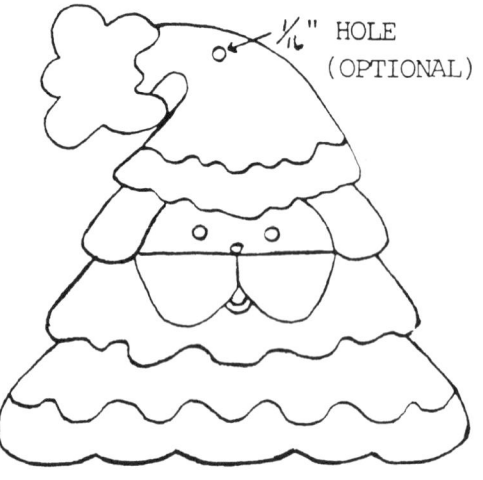

Pattern for 830A: Santa Key Chain or Magnet

PATTERN 830C:
SANTA SHELF DECORATION

SUPPLIES

5 ¼" x 5 ½" Pine, ¾" thick
Varnish (semi-gloss finish)
Black paint pen (extra-fine tip)
Wood glue

ACRYLIC PAINTS

Red
White
Black

Note: For this project, the wood is cut along the pattern lines into separate pieces. Each piece is finished individually and then the pieces are glued back together. Cut slowly and carefully, using the smallest blade recommended for the wood thickness being used.

INSTRUCTIONS

Duplicate the pattern on a copier machine or with tracing paper. Transfer the main pattern lines onto the wood. With a scroll saw, cut along Santa's outline. Slowly cut along pattern line "A" that forms the bottom of the hair and the top of the mustache. Cut along pattern line "B" that forms the bottom of the left side of the mustache. Cut along pattern line "C" that forms the bottom of the right side of the mustache. Slowly cut out the rest of the pieces. Sand the front edges of each piece with 100-grid sandpaper until they are well-rounded. Sand all surfaces with 100-grid and than 150-grid sandpaper. Remove the sanding dust with a tack cloth.

Do not paint the edges where the pieces will be joined together. Paint the hat piece red, continuing the color around the edges and onto the back. Varnish the front of the face piece. Let the paint and varnish dry. Paint all remaining surfaces white. Let the paint dry. Sand lightly to remove the "fuzz" raised by the paints. Remove the sanding dust with a tack cloth. Touch-up the paint if necessary.

Transfer the pattern details onto the pieces. Dot on black for the eyes using the handle of a paintbrush. Dot on a red nose using the handle of a paintbrush. Paint the Red for the mouth. Let the paint dry. Paint the details on the mouth with Black. Dot a white highlight on each eye using the tip of a round toothpick. Let the paint dry.

If you have painted the glue areas, sand the paint off where the pieces join. Glue the pieces back together.

Pattern for 830C: Santa Shelf Decoration

Pattern 831:
HEART SANTA

SUPPLIES

3 ¼" x 3 ½" Pine, ¾" thick
1 ½" x 2 ½" Basswood, ¼" thick
1-1" White pom-pom
Wood glue
White glue
Varnish (semi-gloss finish)

ACRYLIC PAINTS

Red
White
Black

INSTRUCTIONS

Duplicate the pattern on a copier machine or with tracing paper. Transfer the heart outline onto the ¾" thick wood. Transfer the outline of the feet onto the ¼" thick wood. Cut the shapes out. Sand all surfaces with 100-grid and then 150-grid sandpaper. Remove the sanding dust with a tack cloth.

Transfer the main pattern lines onto the heart. Continue pattern lines 1, 2, 3 and 4 around the edges and onto the back of the heart.

Varnish the face area. Paint Santa's suit and hat red, continuing the color around the edges and onto the back. Let the paint dry. Paint the belt black, continuing the color around the edges and onto the back. Paint the feet black, continuing the color around the edges and onto the bottom. Let the paint dry. Paint the hat trim white, continuing the color around the edges and onto the back. Paint the beard and mustache white. Let the paint dry. Sand lightly to remove the "fuzz" raised by the paints. Remove the sanding dust with a tack cloth. Touch-up the paint as necessary.

Transfer the pattern details onto the heart. Paint the eyes white with the eraser end of a pencil. Let the paint dry. Paint the black eye pupils with a paintbrush handle. Paint the mouth black. Paint the red nose with a paintbrush handle. Let the paint dry. Mix black with water until it is the consistency of ink. Use this mixture to paint the details for the hat trim (continuing the detailing around the edges and onto the back), the beard and the mustache. Paint a white highlight on each eye with the tip of a round toothpick. Let the paint dry.

If you have painted the glue areas, sand the glue off where the pieces join. Glue the heart in place on the feet piece using the wood glue. Glue the pom-pom onto the hat point using the white glue.

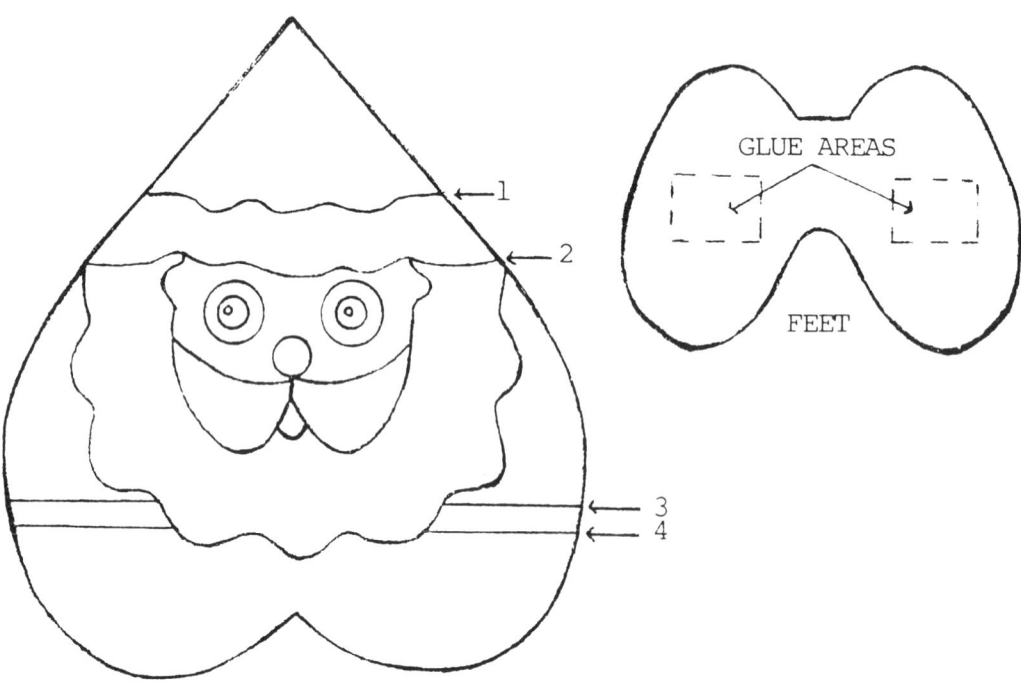

Pattern for 831: Heart Santa

PATTERN 832:
SANTA HEART FACE

SUPPLIES

3 ¼" x 3 ½" Pine, ¾" to 1 ½" thick
1-1" White pom-pom
½" x 8" strip of polyester batting
White glue
Varnish (semi-gloss finish)

ACRYLIC PAINTS

Red
Black
White

INSTRUCTIONS

Duplicate the pattern on a copier machine or with tracing paper. Transfer the heart outline onto the wood. Cut out the shape. Sand all surfaces with 100-grid and then 150-grid sandpaper. Remove the sanding dust with a tack cloth.

Transfer the main pattern lines onto the heart. Continue pattern lines 1 and 2 around the edges and onto the back of the heart. Varnish the face area, continuing the varnish around the edges and onto the back. Let the varnish dry. Paint Santa's hat red, continuing the color around the edges and onto the back. Let the paint dry. Paint the beard and mustache white, continuing the color around the edges and onto the back. Let the paint dry. Sand lightly to remove the "fuzz" raised by the paints. Remove the sanding dust with a tack cloth. Touch-up the paint as necessary.

Transfer the pattern details onto the heart. Paint the eyes white with the eraser end of a pencil. Let the paint dry. Paint the black eye pupils with a paintbrush handle. Paint the black area of the mouth. Let the paint dry. Paint the red area of the mouth. Paint the red nose with a paintbrush handle. Let the paint dry. Mix black with water until it is the consistency of ink. Use this mixture to paint the details for the mouth, beard and mustache (continue the detail for the beard around the edges and onto the back). Paint a white highlight on each eye with the tip of a round toothpick. Let the paint dry.

Glue the pom-pom onto the hat point. Glue the strip of batting around the bottom of the hat, starting and ending in the middle of the back. Clip off any excess batting.

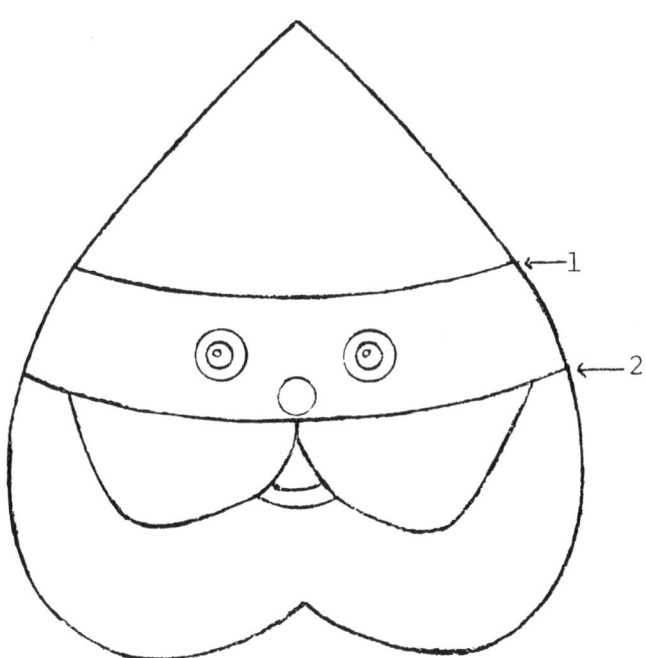

Pattern for 832: Santa Heart Face

PATTERN 833:
INNER/OUTER TREE

SUPPLIES

7 ½" x 9" Pine, ¾" thick
1 ½" x 1 ½" Pine, ¼" thick
Brown paint pen (fine-tip)
8" Brown twine
40" of 20-gauge wire
Wood glue
Sea sponge

ACRYLIC PAINTS

Black
Green
Yellow
Light Orange
White

INSTRUCTIONS FOR INNER/OUTER TREES

Duplicate the pattern on a copier machine or with tracing paper. Trace the main pattern lines of the tree onto the ¾" thick wood. Transfer the star pattern for the outer tree onto the same piece of wood. Transfer the star pattern for the inner tree onto the ¼" thick wood. Cut out both stars with a scroll saw. Cut along the outer tree's outline. Cut in at line "A" to the inner tree pattern line. Continue cutting all the way around the inner tree's outline and exit back out of line "A". Separate the trees. Cut the rest of inner tree pieces. Glue cut line "A" back together. Let the glue dry. Drill all holes where shown on the pattern. Sand all surfaces with 100-grid and then 150-grid sandpaper. Remove the sanding dust with a tack cloth.

Paint both stars yellow, continuing the color around the edges and onto the backs. Let the paint dry. Sand lightly to remove the "fuzz" raised by the paints. Remove the sanding dust with a tack cloth. Touch-up the paint if necessary. Shade the front and back of each star with light orange. Let the paint dry. Use the brown paint pen to add the dash lines to the front and back of both stars. Paint a thin light orange line all the way around the edge, on the front and back of each star.

FOR OUTER TREE

Base-coat the tree with green, continuing the color around the edges and onto the back. Let the paint dry. Sand lightly to remove the "fuzz" raised by the paints. Remove the sanding dust with a tack cloth. Apply a second coat of green to all surfaces of the tree. Let the paint dry.

Knot one end of the brown twine. Thread the other end down through one of the holes at the top of the tree. Thread the twine through the hole in the outer star and then back up through the other hole in the tree. Knot the twine on this side. Adjust the star to hang in the middle of the tree.

FOR INNER TREE

Base-coat all surfaces of the tree pieces yellow. Let the paint dry. Sand lightly to remove the "fuzz" raised by the paints. Remove the sanding dust with a tack cloth. Touch-up the paint if necessary.

Sponge paint all surfaces of the tree with green. Be sure to leave some of the base-coat showing through. Let the paint dry. Mix green paint with a small amount of black. Use this mixture to sponge shading onto all surfaces of the tree pieces. Let the paint dry.

Transfer the ornament placement from the pattern onto the front and back of the tree pieces. Dot on the yellow ornament design using the eraser end of a pencil. Shade the bottom of each ornament with light orange. Dot a small white highlight on each ornament with a small paintbrush handle. Let the paint dry.

Cut 6 – 3 ½" long pieces of wire. Bend each piece of wire into a "U" shape. Insert the wires into the drilled holes (from back to front) to connect the tree sections. Curl the wire ends with needle nose pliers.

Cut a ½-inch piece of wire. Dip one end of the wire into glue and push it into the hole in the inner star. Dip the other end of the wire into the glue and push it into the hole at the top of the tree. Make sure the star is straight. Let the glue dry.

To form the hanger, wrap the remaining piece of wire loosely around a large paintbrush handle six or seven times. Insert one of the wire ends through each of the hanger holes (from back to front). Curl the wire ends with needle nose pliers. Bend the wire into a pleasing shape.

Pattern for 833: Inner/Outer Tree

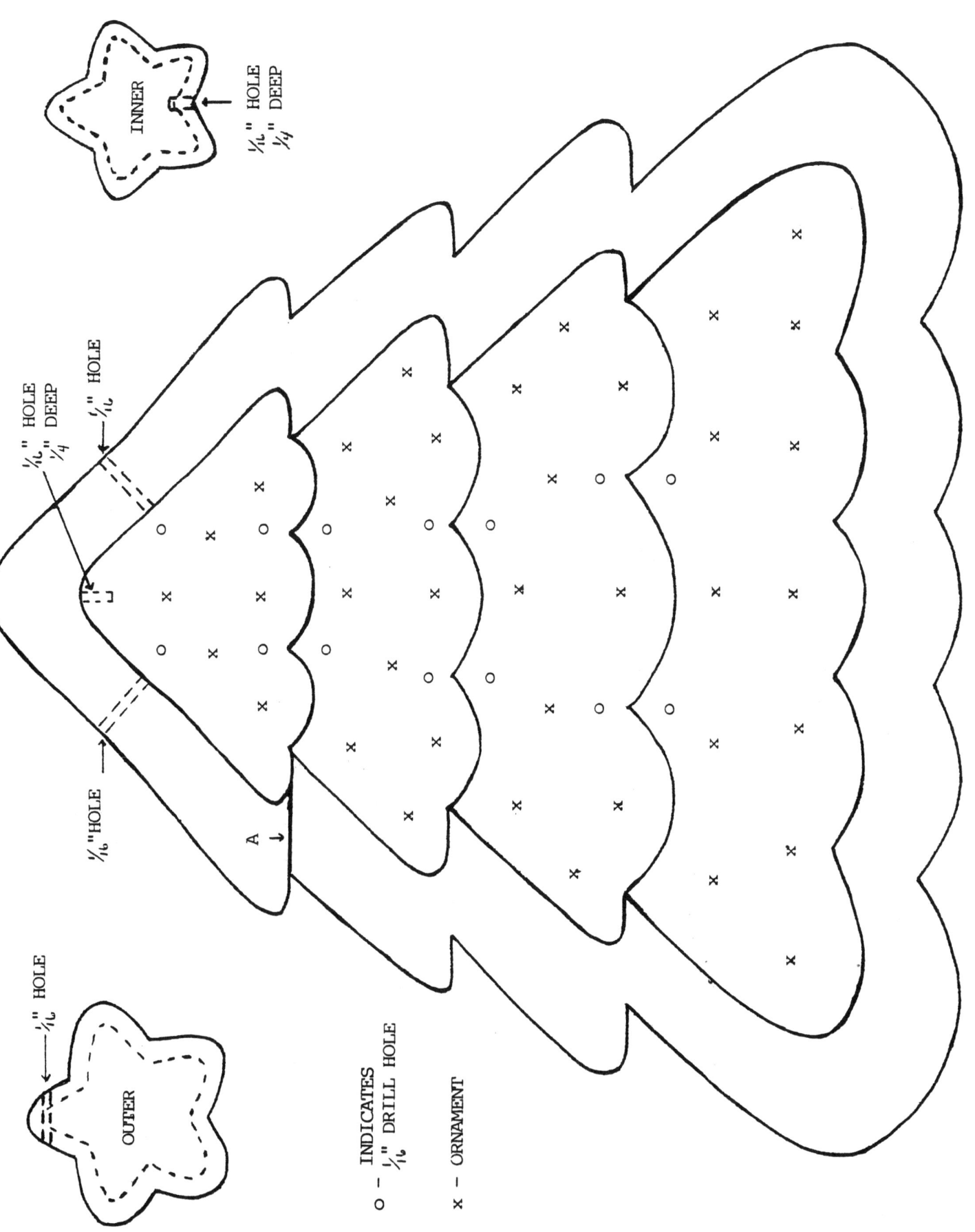

PATTERN 834 A AND B:
STANDING TREES

SUPPLIES

6 ½" x 7 ½" Pine, ¾" thick
1 ½" x 1 ½" Basswood, ¼" thick
2 ½" of ¼" Wood dowel
18" of Raffia
Wood glue

ACRYLIC PAINTS

Green
Yellow
Red
White
Brown

INSTRUCTIONS

Decide which tree you want to make. Duplicate the pattern on a copier machine or with tracing paper. Transfer the main pattern lines of the tree onto the ¾" thick wood. Transfer the outline of the base onto the same piece of wood. Transfer the star outline onto the ¼" thick wood. Cut out the tree shape with a scroll saw. Cut out the puzzle pieces of the tree. Cut out the base piece. Cut out the star shape. Drill all holes where shown on the patterns. Sand all surfaces with 100-grid and then 150-grid sandpaper. Remove the sanding dust with a tack cloth.

Paint the base brown, continuing the color around the edges and onto the bottom. Paint the wood dowel brown. Paint the star yellow, continuing the color around the edges and onto the back. Base-coat all surfaces of the tree puzzle pieces green. Let the paint dry. Sand lightly to remove the "fuzz" raised by the paints. Remove the sanding dust with a tack cloth. Touch-up the paint if necessary.

Mix 3 parts of green and 1 part of brown with a small amount of water. Use this mixture to add shading to the tree pieces. Let the paint dry thoroughly or the pieces will stick together. Assemble the four tree pieces.

Transfer the ornament placement from the pattern onto the tree. Use the eraser end of a pencil to apply the red ornament dots. Let the paint dry. Mix 3 parts red with 1 part of green and use to shade the bottom of each ornament. Dot a small white highlight on each ornament using a paintbrush handle.

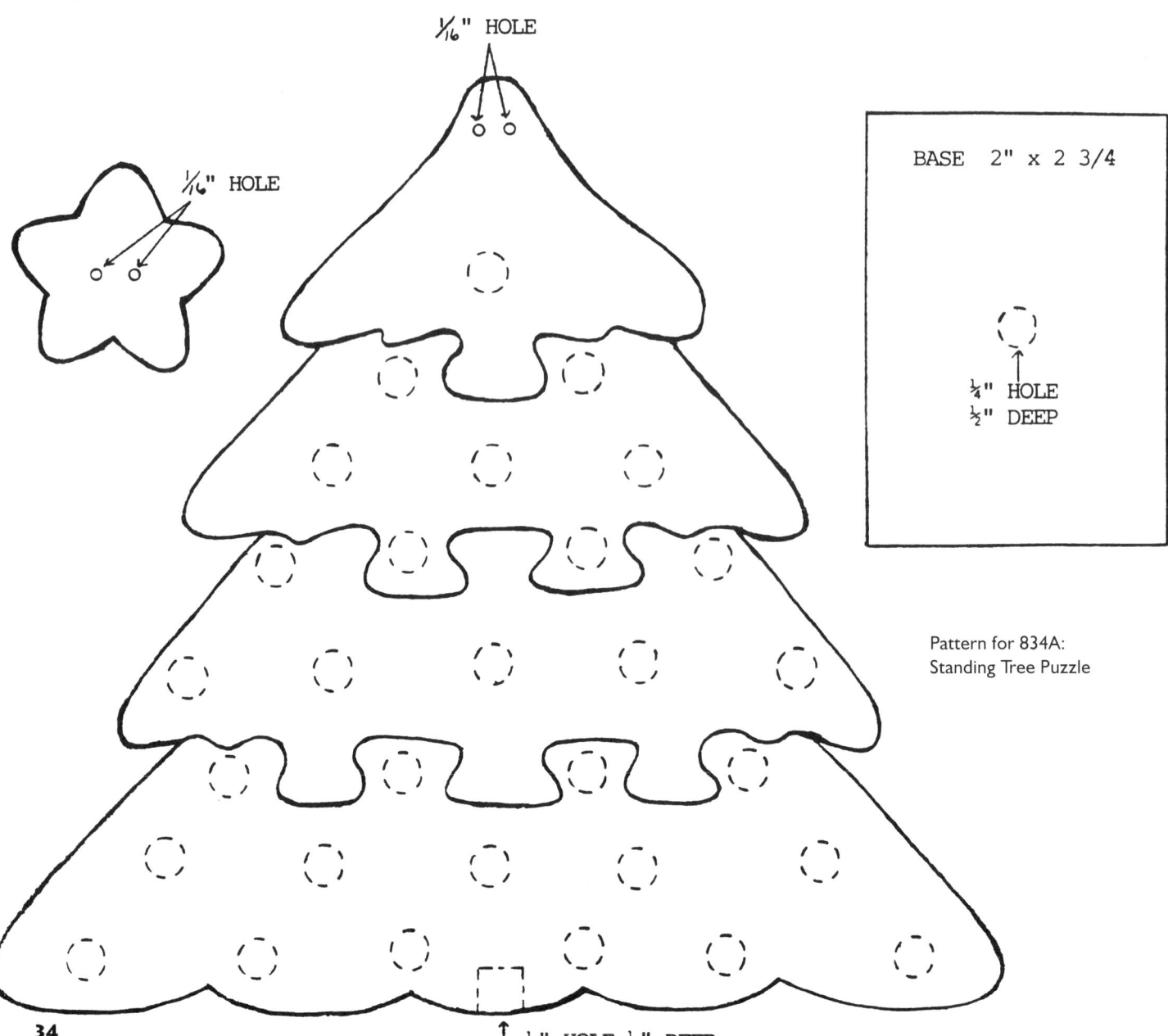

Pattern for 834A:
Standing Tree Puzzle

Dip one end of the wood dowel into the wood glue and push it in the hole on the bottom of the tree. Dip the other end of the dowel into the wood glue and push it in the hole in the base. Make sure the tree is standing straight. Let the glue dry.

Thread the raffia through one of the holes in the star, then through one of the holes on the front of the tree. Thread the raffia back through the second tree hole and the second star hole. Pull the ends of the raffia even and tie into a bow.

Pattern for 834B: Standing Tree Puzzle

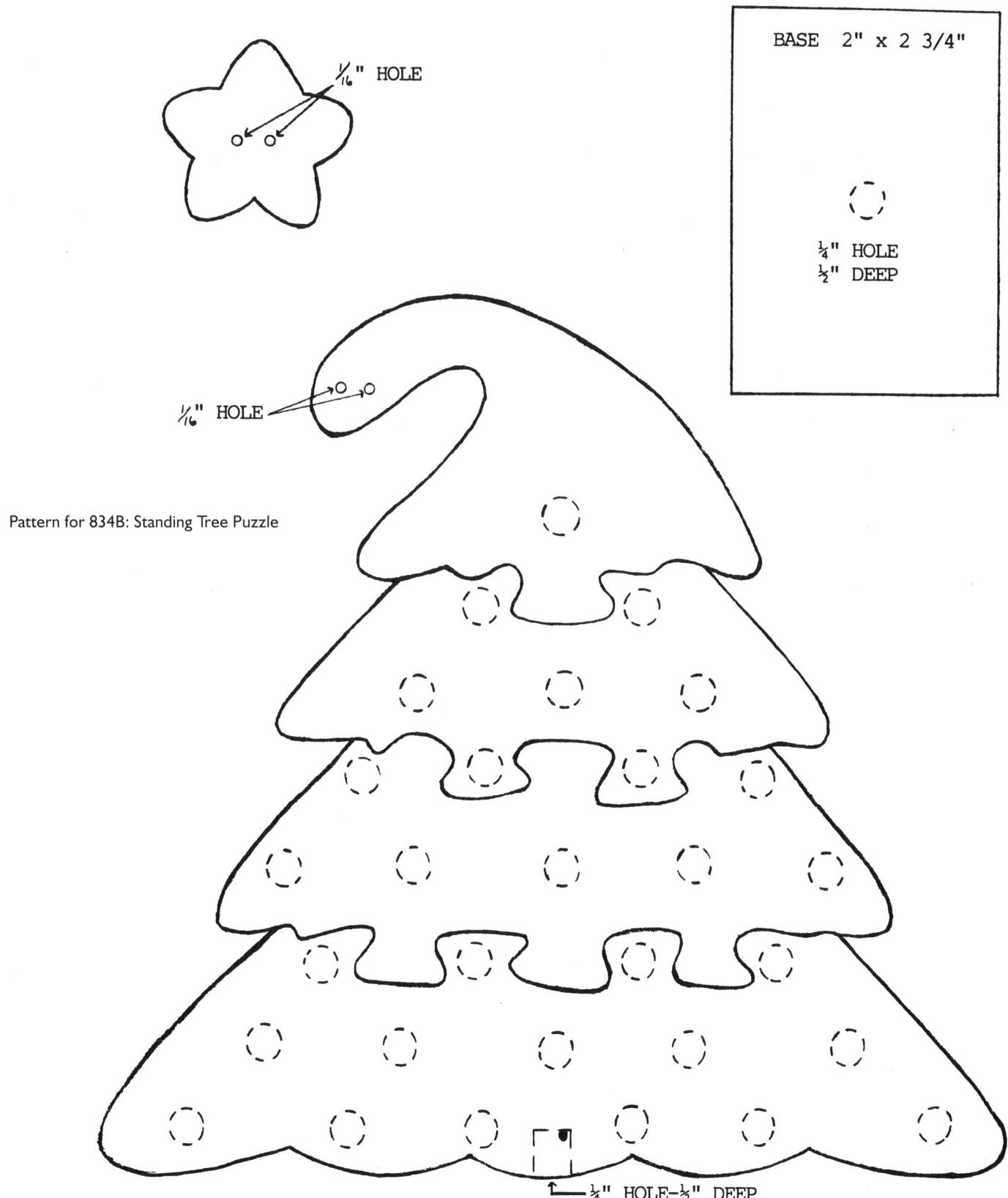

PATTERN 835:
CHRISTMAS ANGEL

SUPPLIES

7 ¼" x 7 ¼" Pine, ¾" thick
2 ¼" x 2 ¼" Pine, ⅛" thick
1 ¼" of ⅜" Wood dowel
Wood glue
½" piece of string for candle wick

ACRYLIC PAINTS

White
Gold

INSTRUCTIONS

Duplicate the pattern on a copier machine or with tracing paper. Transfer the outline of the angel pattern onto the ¾" thick wood. Transfer the arm outlines onto the ⅛" thick wood. Using the smallest blade recommended for the wood thickness, cut around the wing outline and across the bottom hem of the dress. Cut in along the pattern line of the angel's body. Separate the 2 pieces. Cut out the arm pieces. Drill the hole for the candlewick in the wood dowel, where shown on the pattern. Sand all surfaces with 100-grid and then 150-grid sandpaper. Remove the sanding dust with a tack cloth.

Lay the wing piece down on a flat surface. Place a ½" thick piece of scrap wood in the center of the wings. This is used to support the angel's body in place as you are gluing. Run a line of glue around the outside edge of the **body**, approximately ¼" in from the back. Set the body in place on top of the supporting piece of scrap wood. Make sure it's level. Run a line of glue around the cut edge of the body where it joins the wing piece. Wipe off any excess glue. Let the glue dry thoroughly. Turn the angel over and run a line of glue along the line where the pieces join on this side. Wipe off any excess glue. Let the glue dry thoroughly. Lightly sand all of the glue areas with 150-grid sandpaper to remove any excess glue. Remove the sanding dust with a tack cloth.

Base-coat the angel and wings white, continuing the color around the edges and onto the back. Base-coat the arm pieces white, continuing the color around the edges. Let the paint dry. Sand lightly to remove the "fuzz" raised by the paints. Remove the sanding dust with a tack cloth. Touch-up the paint if necessary.

Transfer the pattern details onto the pieces, as they are needed. With a small detail or liner paintbrush, slowly paint the detail lines on the angel's body, wings and arm pieces with gold.

To paint the stars on the halo: With a paintbrush handle, put a dot of gold paint in the spot where you want the center of the star. Pull the paint out from the center of the dot, with the tip of a round toothpick, to form the points. Try a few practice stars on scrap wood before doing your good ones on the halo. Paint the wood dowel candle gold. Let the paint dry.

If you have painted the glue areas, sand the paint off where the pieces join. Dip one end of the string into glue and push it into the hole in the wood dowel candle, leaving a ¼" wick sticking out. Glue the arms in place on the front of the body. Glue the candle on between the hands.

Pattern for 835: Christmas Angel

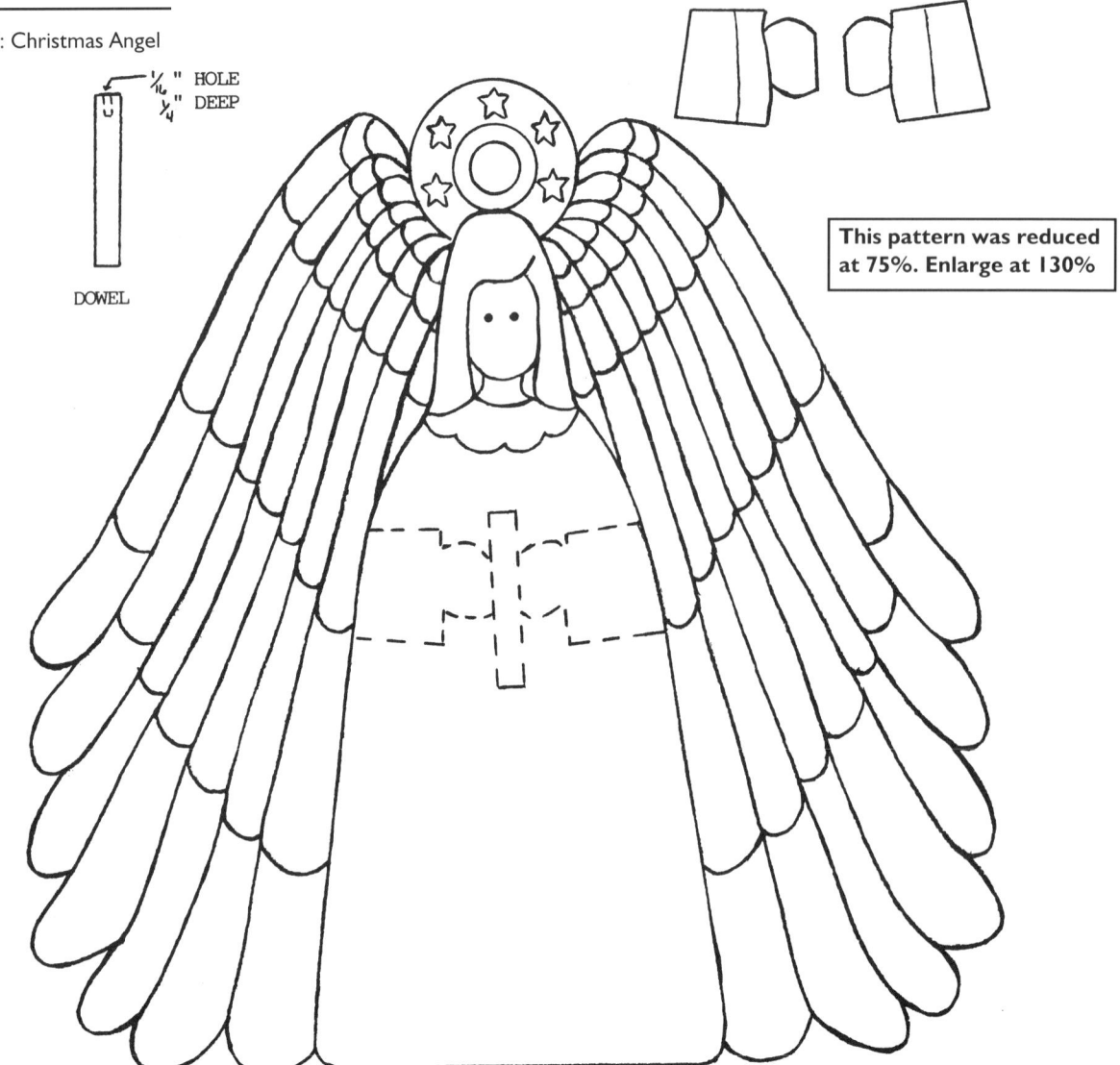

This pattern was reduced at 75%. Enlarge at 130%

PATTERN 836:
CHRISTMAS WREATH

SUPPLIES

5 ½" x 5 ½" Pine, ¾" thick
2" x 7" Pine, 1/16" thick
15" of 1 ½" wide red ribbon
Black paint pen (fine-point)
1 picture frame hanger
Hot glue gun
Wood glue

ACRYLIC PAINTS

Green
White

INSTRUCTIONS

Duplicate the pattern on a copier machine or with tracing paper. Transfer the wreath pattern onto the ¾" thick wood. Transfer 2 small leaf patterns and 6 large leaf patterns onto the 1/16" thick wood. Cut around the outline of the wreath. Cut in at line "A". Continue cutting all the way around, following the inner circle pattern line, and exiting back out of line "A". Cut the leaves out. Glue line "A" back together. Sand all surfaces with 100-grid and then 150-grid sandpaper. Remove the sanding dust with a tack cloth.

Paint the inside and the outside edges of the wreath green. Paint the back of the wreath green. Paint the leaves green, continuing the color around the edges. Paint the back of the leaves green only where they will stick out from the wreath. Let the paint dry. Paint the front of the wreath white. Let the paint dry. Sand lightly to remove the "fuzz" raised by the paints. Remove the sanding dust with a tack cloth. Touch-up the paint if necessary.

Transfer the grid pattern lines onto the front of the wreath. Paint the green checks. Let the paint dry. With the black paint pen, paint the grid lines on the front of the wreath. Let the paint dry.

If you have painted the glue areas, sand the paint off where the pieces join. Glue the leaves in place using the wood glue. Make a bow with the red ribbon. Attach it to the wreath with the hot glue gun. Attach the picture frame hanger on the back of the wreath.

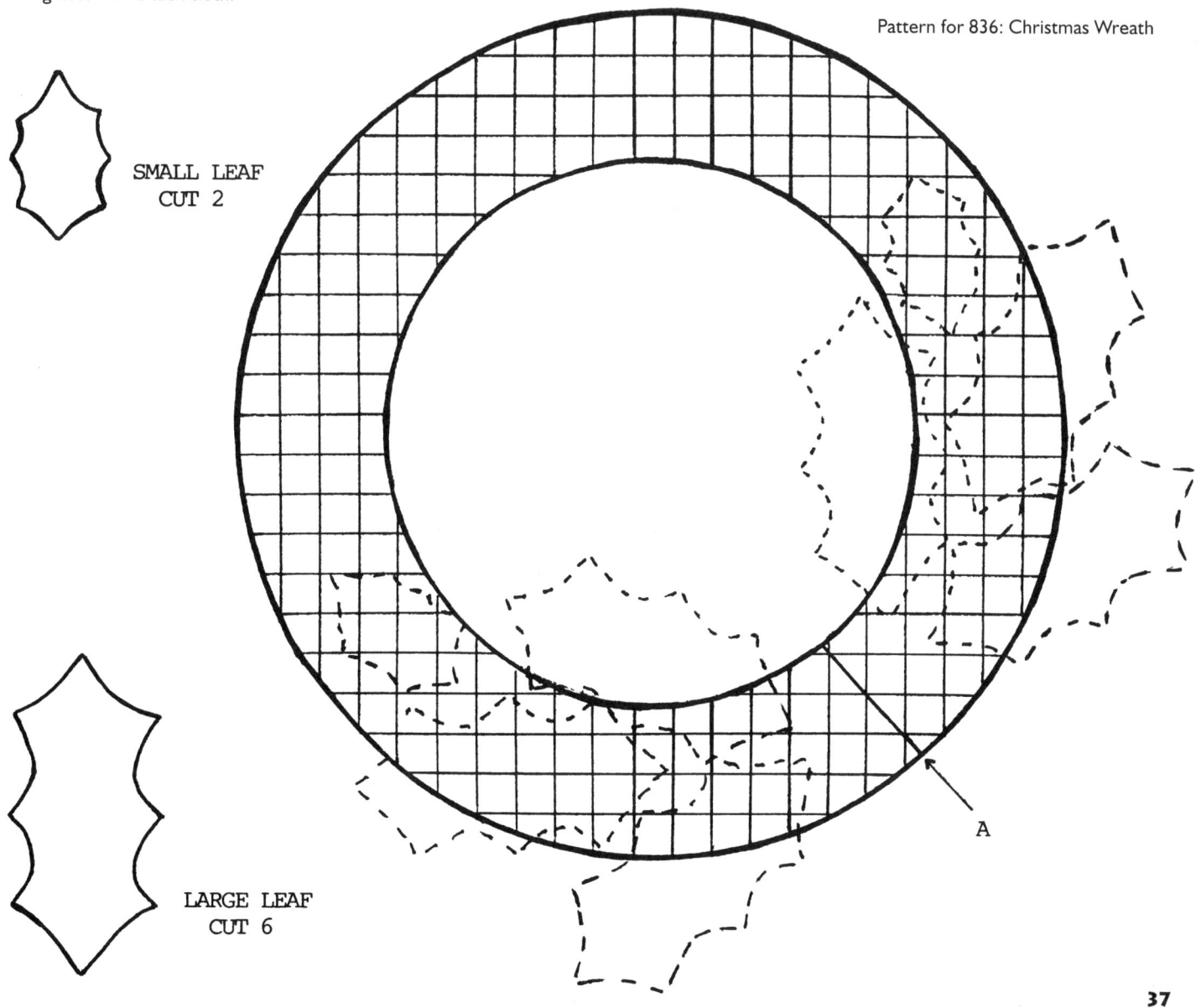

Pattern for 836: Christmas Wreath

SMALL LEAF
CUT 2

LARGE LEAF
CUT 6

A

37

PATTERN 837:
SNOWMAN WITH STAR VEST

SUPPLIES
6 ½" x 16" Pine, 1 ½" thick
Black paint pen (fine-tip)

ACRYLIC PAINTS
White
Beige
Blue
Orange
Brown
Red
Yellow
Black

INSTRUCTIONS
Duplicate the pattern sheets on a copier machine or with tracing paper. Line up and tape together the 2 halves of the snowman, trimming off the excess paper. Transfer the pattern outline onto the wood. Cut the shape out with a scroll saw. Sand all surfaces with 100-grid and then 150-grid sandpaper. Remove the sanding dust with a tack cloth.

Transfer the main pattern lines onto the wood. Base-coat the snowman and the hat pom-pom white, continue the color around the edges of the entire piece and onto the back. Let the paint dry. Base-coat the hat and scarf beige. Let the paint dry. Base-coat the vest blue. Let the paint dry. Sand lightly to remove the "fuzz" raised by the paints. Remove the sanding dust with a tack cloth. Touch-up the paint if necessary.

Shade the snowman's face, arms and body with blue. Shade the hat pom-pom with black. Let the paint dry.

Transfer the pattern details onto the workpiece, as they are needed. Paint the stripes on the hat and scarf red. Paint the scarf fringe red. Base-coat the carrot nose orange. Paint the stars on the vest yellow. Dot on the yellow vest buttons with the eraser end of a pencil. Dot on the blue eye irises with the eraser end of a pencil. Let the paint dry.

Dot on the black eye pupils with a paintbrush handle. Shade the hat and scarf with brown. Add brown shading to the bottom of each button. Mix orange with a small amount of brown and use to shade the carrot nose. Mix blue with a small amount of black and use to shade the vest. Let the paint dry.

Draw on the remaining eye details, the mouth and the lacing for the vest with the black paint pen. Add detailing to the carrot nose with the black paint pen. Dot a white highlight on each eye with the tip of a round toothpick. Highlight the top of each vest button with white.

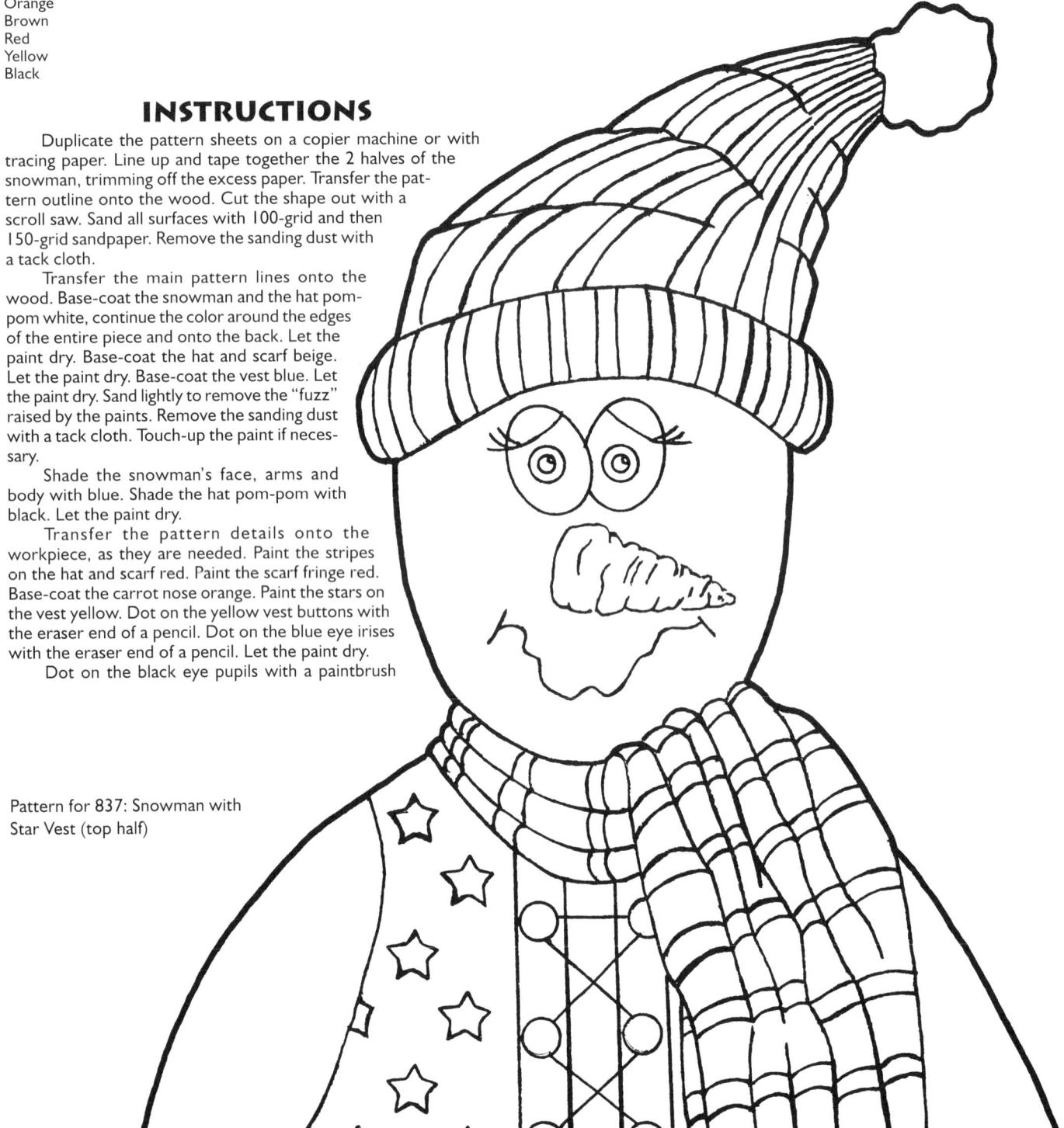

Pattern for 837: Snowman with Star Vest (top half)

Pattern for 837: Snowman with Star Vest (bottom half)

PATTERN 840:
HEART PUZZLE

SUPPLIES

7" x 6 ½" Pine, 1 ½" thick
1 ½" x 3 ½" Pine, ¾" thick
12" of ¼" Wood dowel
Varnish (semi-gloss finish)
Wood glue

ACRYLIC PAINTS

Red
Black
White
Brown

INSTRUCTIONS

Duplicate the pattern on a copier machine or with tracing paper. Transfer the heart pattern lines onto the 1 ½" thick wood. Transfer the arrowhead and the feather outlines onto the ¾" thick wood. Cut out the arrowhead and the feather pieces. With the smallest blade recommended for the wood thickness, cut out the heart shape. DO NOT CUT THE PUZZLE PIECES OUT.

Lay the heart on its right side. Position the tip of the ¼" drill bit at point "A". KEEP THE DRILL STRAIGHT. Drill down as deep as the drill bit will go. Pull the drill bit straight out. Carefully cut off piece number "1". Place the heart back on its right side. Insert the drill bit into the starter hole in piece number "2". Drill straight down as deep as the drill bit will go. Pull the drill bit straight out. Carefully cut off piece number "2". Place the heart back on its right side and continue this drilling and cutting process until all 7 puzzle pieces have been cut. Drill the holes in the arrowhead and the feather pieces where shown on the pattern. Sand all surfaces with 100-grid and then 150-grid sandpaper. Remove the sanding dust with a tack cloth.

Paint all surfaces of the heart puzzle pieces red. Paint all surfaces of the arrowhead black. Paint the brown area on the front of the feather piece, continuing the color around the edges and onto the back. Let the paint dry. Sand lightly to remove the "fuzz" raised by the paints. Remove the sanding dust with a tack cloth. Touch-up the paint if necessary. Varnish the wood dowel. Varnish the middle stripe on the feather piece. Let the varnish dry. Paint the thin black stripes on the feather piece. Paint the white feather design using the dry brush technique. Let the paint dry thoroughly before assembling the puzzle or the pieces will stick together.

Put the heart puzzle together. Dip one end of the wood dowel into glue and push it into the feather piece. Push the other end of the wood dowel through the heart puzzle until it comes out approximately 2 ¼" on the arrowhead side. Insert, but DO NOT GLUE the wood dowel into the arrowhead. Adjust the arrow until the puzzle can stand on the heart point.

PATTERN 841:
I-LOVE-YOU HEART

SUPPLIES

7" x 7" Pine, ¾" thick
3" x 1 ¼" Pine, ½" thick
7" x 1 ⅛" Pine, 1/8" thick
5" of 3/8" Wood dowel
Wood glue
Black paint pen (extra-fine tip)
Varnish (semi-gloss finish)

ACRYLIC PAINTS

Pink
Yellow
Hot Pink
Red
Light Blue
Black
Light Green
Green
Brown

INSTRUCTIONS

Duplicate the pattern on a copier machine or with tracing paper. Transfer the heart outline, including the pattern cut lines for the "I", small inside heart and the "U" onto the ¾" thick wood. Transfer the feather and arrowhead outlines onto the ½" thick wood. Cut out the feather and arrowhead shapes. Cut the 1/8" thick wood for the base to size. Cut the wood dowel into 2 – 2 ½" pieces. With the smallest blade recommended for the wood thickness, cut along the outside pattern line of the heart shape.

The piercing technique is used to cut out the 2 open areas of the heart. Drill the 2 blade-threading (pierce) holes, for the inside piercing cuts, where shown on the pattern. Thread the blade through the hole next to the "U" and re-attach it to the scroll saw. Cut all the way around the inside pattern line of the large heart and the top and sides of the "I", the small inside heart and the "U", until the blade is back to the pierce hole. This is one continuous cut. Remove the blade from the saw and separate the pieces.

Thread the blade through the second pierce hole and re-attach it to the saw. Cut all the way around the sides and bottom of the "I", the small inside heart, the "U" and the inside pattern line of the large heart, until the blade is back to the pierce hole. This is also one continuous cut. Remove the blade from the saw and separate the pieces. Drill the 3/8" holes in the heart, arrowhead and feather pieces where shown on the pattern. Sand all surfaces with 100-grid and then 150-grid sandpaper. Remove the sanding dust with a tack cloth.

Paint the edges of the large heart, the "I", the small inside heart and the "U" pink, continuing the color onto the back. Let the paint dry. Paint the front of the large heart Pink. paint all surfaces of the arrowhead black, except the bottom glue area. Paint the edges and the back of the feather piece brown. Base-coat the front of the feather piece brown, leaving a 3/8" strip down the middle unpainted. Paint the wood for the base hot pink, continuing the color around the edges and onto the bottom. Let the paint dry. Sand lightly to remove the "fuzz" raised by the paints. Remove the sanding dust with a tack cloth. Touch-up the paint if necessary. Varnish both pieces of wood dowel and set them aside to dry.

Transfer the main pattern lines onto the pieces. Paint the thin black stripes on the feather piece. Paint the white feather design using the dry-brush technique. Paint the hot pink, yellow, light green and light blue areas on the inside heart. Paint the 3 white stripes (in the pink and white stripe area) on the inside heart. Paint the hot pink areas of the "I" and the "U". Let the paint dry.

Transfer the remaining pattern details onto the inside heart. Paint the red dots on the hot pink area with the tip of a round toothpick. Paint the white dots on the yellow area with a small brush handle. Paint the white dots on the light blue area with a large brush handle. Mix green paint with water until it is the consistency of ink. Use this mixture to paint the plaid design on the light green area and to add the leaves to the light blue area. Paint the pink stripes. Let the paint dry.

Layer a hot pink dot on the center of each white dot in the light blue area, with the tip of a round toothpick. Paint the white border on the "I", the small inside heart and the "U". Let the paint dry. Add the design details to the "I", the small inside heart and the "U" with the black paint pen. Let the paint dry. Varnish all surfaces of the entire heart and the feather piece. Varnish all surfaces of the arrowhead piece, except the bottom glue area. Let the varnish dry. Apply a second coat of varnish. Let the varnish dry thoroughly.

If you have applied finish to the glue areas, sand the finish off where the pieces join. Dip one end of a 2 ½" piece of wood dowel into glue and push it into the arrowhead. Dip the other end of the dowel into glue and push it into the bottom drill hole in the heart. Dip one end of the second piece of wood dowel into glue and push it into the feather piece. Dip the other end of the dowel into glue and push it into the top drill hole in the heart. Glue the heart point and the bottom of the arrowhead to the wood base. Make sure that the heart is standing straight. Let the glue dry.

¼" HOLE

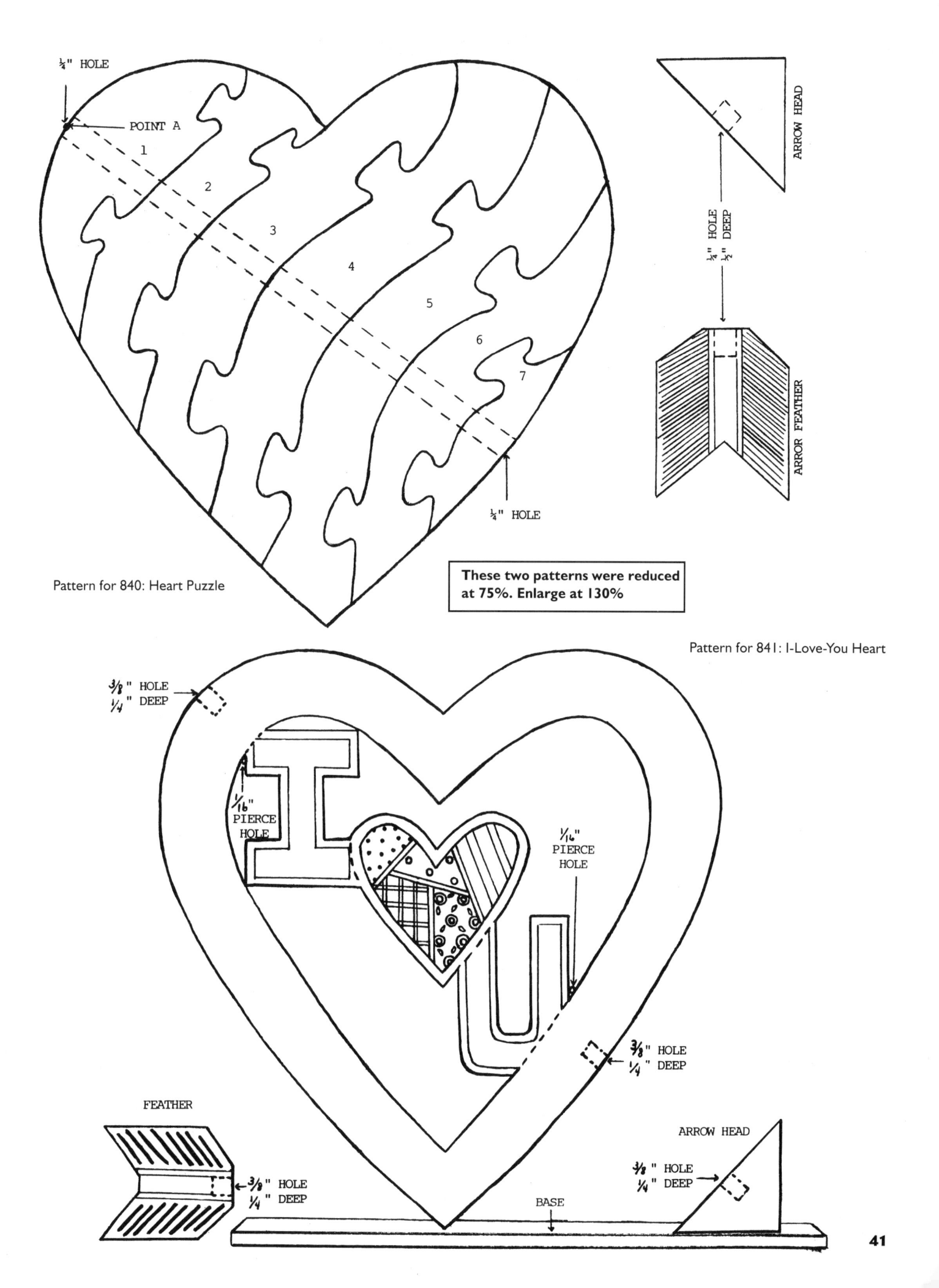

POINT A

1
2
3
4
5
6
7

¼" HOLE

Pattern for 840: Heart Puzzle

ARROW HEAD

¼" HOLE
½" DEEP

ARROW FEATHER

These two patterns were reduced at 75%. Enlarge at 130%

Pattern for 841: I-Love-You Heart

⅜" HOLE
¼" DEEP

1/16" PIERCE HOLE

1/16" PIERCE HOLE

⅜" HOLE
¼" DEEP

FEATHER

⅜" HOLE
¼" DEEP

BASE

ARROW HEAD

⅜" HOLE
¼" DEEP

PATTERN 844:
SPRING IS IN THE AIR

SUPPLIES

8" x 4 ½" Basswood, ¼" thick
6" of 20-gauge wire
Varnish (semi-gloss finish)
Black paint pen (medium tip)
¼" Checkerboard stencil
Picture frame hanger
Stain (red-tone)
Stain (brown-tone)
Wood sealer
Wood glue

ACRYLIC PAINTS

Brown
Black

INSTRUCTIONS

Duplicate the pattern on a copier machine or with tracing paper. Transfer the main pattern lines onto the wood. Cut out the bird and banner outlines. Drill the holes where shown on the pattern. Cut the bird into 9 pieces following the pattern lines. Sand the front face edges of the bird pieces until they are well-rounded. Sand all surfaces of the bird pieces and the banner with 100-grid and than 150-grid sandpaper. Remove the sanding dust with a tack cloth.

DO NOT apply finish to the edges of the bird pieces where the pieces join. Apply wood sealer to the banner and to pieces 2, 5 and 8 of the bird, continuing the sealer around the edges and onto the backs. Apply the red-tone stain to pieces 1, 3, 6, and 9 of the bird, continuing the stain around the edges and onto the backs. Apply the brown-tone stain to pieces 4 and 7 of the bird, continuing the stain around the edges and onto the backs. Let the sealer and stains dry. With the red-tone stain, stencil the checkerboard pattern on the banner. Let the stain dry.

Transfer the pattern details onto the banner. Using the black paint pen, apply the lettering lines to the banner. Paint the black end dots on the letters with a small paintbrush handle. Paint the brown dash lines around the banners outline. Paint the brown dot around the banner outline with a small paintbrush handle. Let the paint dry.

If you have applied finish to the glue areas of the bird pieces, sand the finish off where the pieces will join. Glue the bird pieces back together. Let the glue dry.

Apply a thin topcoat of varnish to the bird and banner. Let the varnish dry. Apply a second thin topcoat of varnish to the pieces and let it dry.

Cut the 6" piece of wire into 2 pieces, one 2 ½" long and one 3 ½" long. Wrap each piece around a small paintbrush handle to coil them. Dip one end of the 2 ½" coiled wire in glue and push it into the hole in the bird's head. Dip one end of the 3 ½" coiled wire into glue and push it in the hole in the birds tail. Dip the other end of both wires into glue and push them into the appropriate holes in the banner. Let the glue dry. Adjust the wires so that the bird is centered beneath the banner. Attach the hanger on the top center of the banner's back.

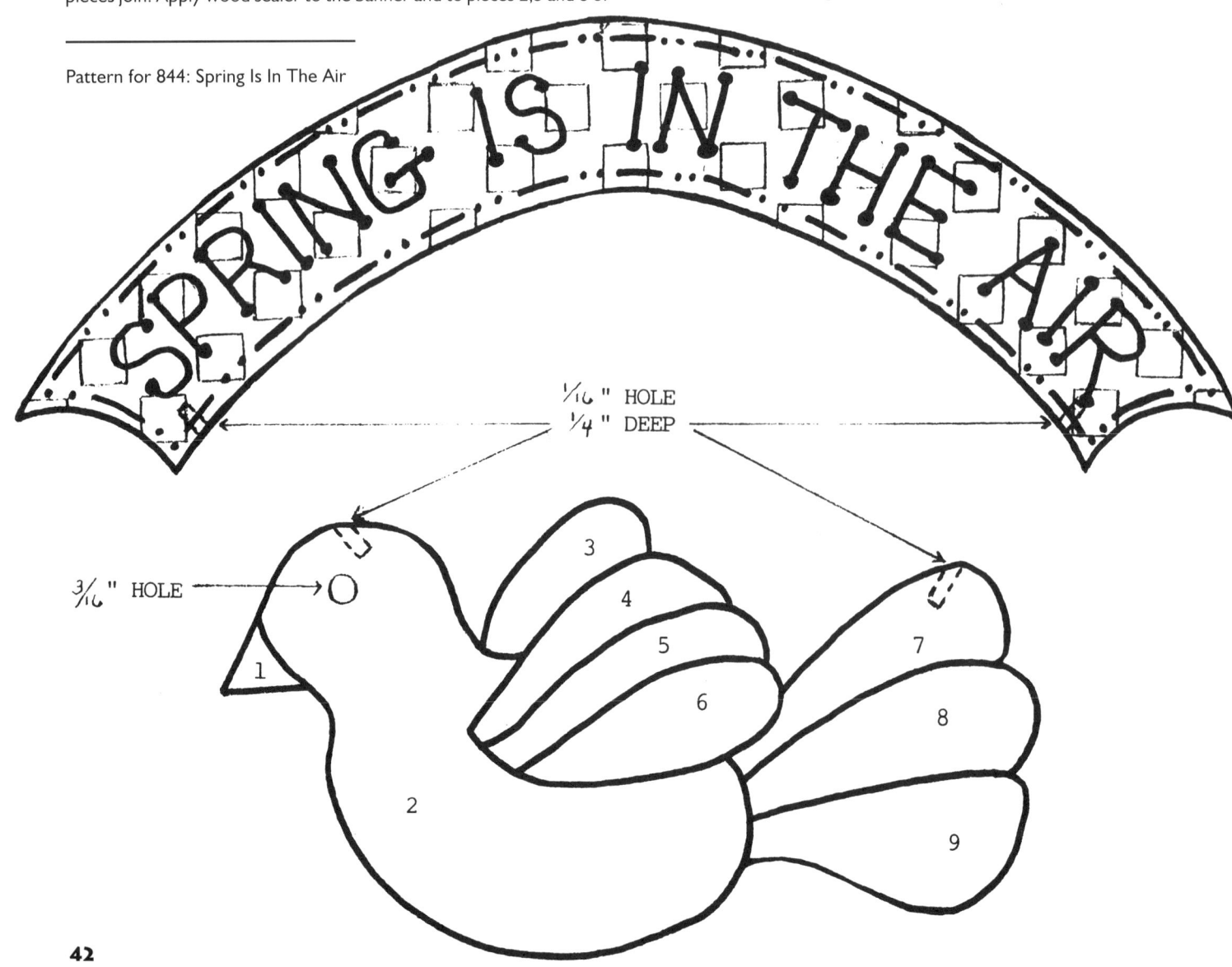

Pattern for 844: Spring Is In The Air

Pattern 845:
BUNNY WREATH

SUPPLIES

5 ½" x 7" Pine, ¾" thick
6" x 9" Pine, ¼" thick
9" x 5 ½" piece of fabric
Picture frame hanger
Black paint pen (extra-fine tip)
Wood glue

ACRYLIC PAINTS

Lavender
Gray
Black
White
Hot Pink
Light Blue

INSTRUCTIONS

Duplicate the patterns on a copier machine or with tracing paper. Transfer the head/wreath outline onto the ¾" thick wood. With a scroll saw, cut along the outline. Cut in at cut line "A" to the inner circle. Cut around the inner circle pattern line and exit back out of the line "A" cut. Glue line "A" back together. Transfer the outlines of the other pieces, except the ears, onto ¼" thick wood. Cut the shapes out (use the detail instructions that follow). Drill the two ear holes as shown on the pattern. Sand all surfaces with 100-grid and then 150-grid sandpaper. Remove the sanding dust with a tack cloth.

Base-coat the front wreath area with lavender, continuing the color around the edges. Paint the edges and backs of the lettering pieces with light blue. Let the paint dry. Base-coat the bunny's head area gray, continuing the color around the edges. Paint the back of the head/wreath gray. Paint the front and back paws gray, continuing the color around the edges and onto the backs. Paint the muzzle white, continuing the color around the edges. Paint the front of the lettering pieces hot pink. Let the paint dry. Lightly sand all pieces to remove the "fuzz" raised by the acrylic paints. Touch-up the paint if necessary.

Transfer the head/wreath pattern details onto the bunny. Paint the eyes and teeth white. Paint the mouth gray. Paint the white dots on the wreath using a paintbrush handle.

Transfer the remaining details on, as they are needed. Mix 1 part of hot pink with 1 part of white. Use this mixture to paint the nose and the light pink areas on the back paws. Let the paint dry. Dot on the light blue for the eyes using the eraser end of a pencil. Paint the hot pink on the back paws. Mix the hot pink paint with a small amount of water and use to shade the nose. Dot on the black eye pupils using a large brush handle. Let the paint dry. Add the details to the muzzle, paws, mouth and eyes with the black paint pen. Dot a white highlight on each eye using a paintbrush handle.

If you have painted the glue areas, sand the paint off where the pieces join. Glue the muzzle, paws and lettering pieces in place.

Trace 4 ear patterns onto the fabric and cut them out. Place 2 ear pieces right sides together. Sew a 1/8" seam around the edge leaving the opening, as shown on the pattern. Turn the ear right side out. Sew and turn the second ear in the same manner. Tuck and glue one ear into each ear hole. Adjust the ears.

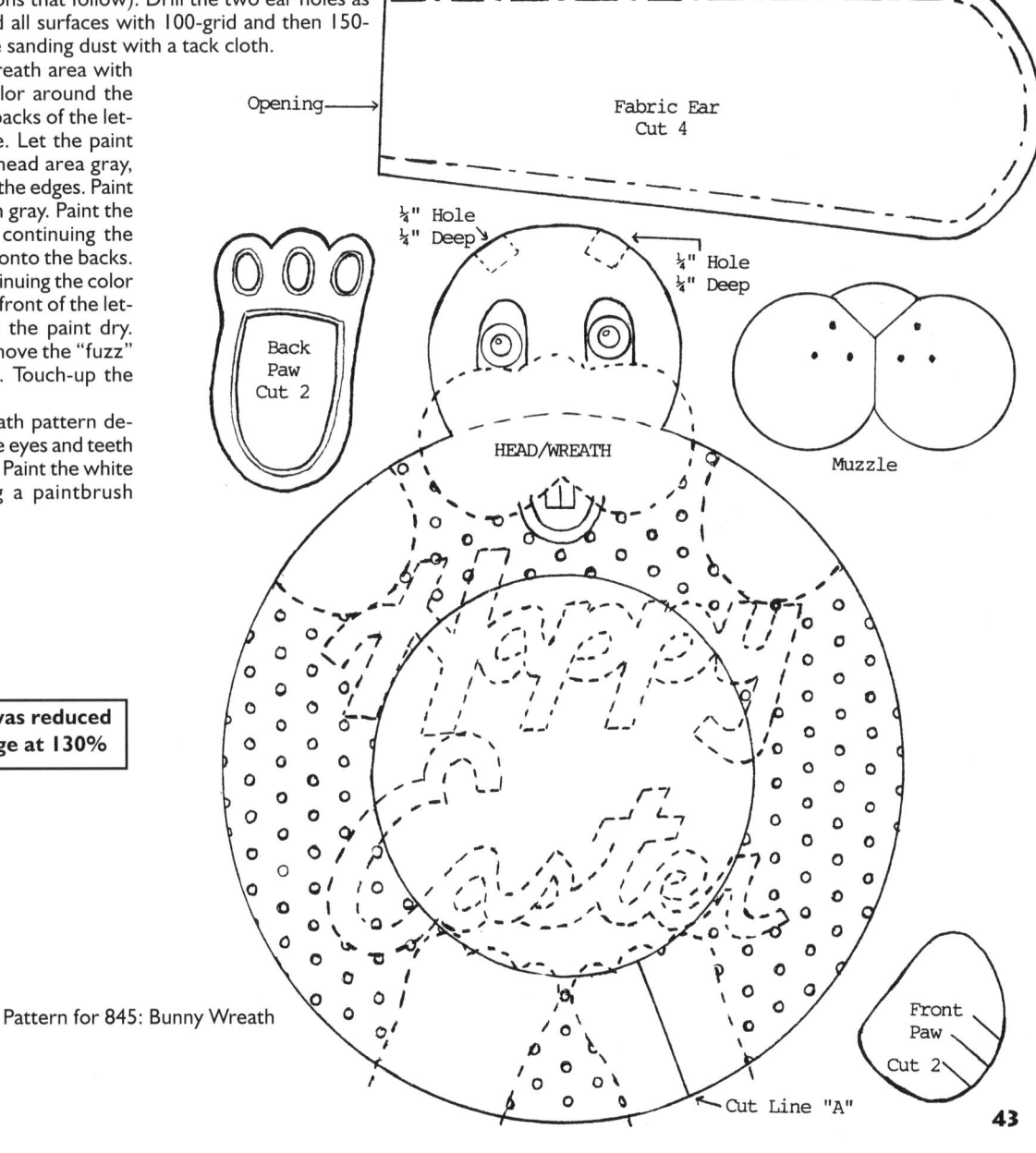

This pattern was reduced at 75%. Enlarge at 130%

Pattern for 845: Bunny Wreath

Fabric Ear Cut 4
Opening
¼" Hole ¼" Deep
Back Paw Cut 2
HEAD/WREATH
Muzzle
Front Paw Cut 2
Cut Line "A"

INSTRUCTIONS FOR CUTTING THE LETTERING PIECES

Duplicate the lettering patterns on a copier machine or with tracing paper. Transfer each lettering pattern onto a separate piece of 1/4" thick wood. Keep the pattern handy so you can refer to it as you are cutting. Use a #5 or smaller blade in your scroll saw.

Happy: Cut a line in to the start point on the lettering piece. Slowly cut along the pattern line that forms the tops of the letters until you reach the end point. Continue sawing straight off the wood. Position the piece so the blade is back at the start point.

Slowly cut along the pattern line that forms the bottom and inside areas of the letters until you reach the end point again.

Carefully sand all surfaces with 100-grid and then 150-grid sandpaper. Remove the sanding dust with a tack cloth.

Easter: Cut a line in to the start point on the lettering piece. Slowly cut along the pattern line that forms the top of the letters and the inside of the "e" until you reach the end point. Continue sawing straight off the wood. Position the piece so the blade is back at the start point. Slowly cut along the pattern line that forms the bottom and inside areas of the letters until you reach the end point again.

Carefully sand all surfaces with 100-grid and then 150-grid sandpaper. Remove the sanding dust with a tack cloth.

Lettering Patterns for 845: Bunny Wreath

This pattern was reduced at 75%. Enlarge at 130%

PATTERN 846: SIX-EGG BASKET

SUPPLIES

5" x 5 1/2" Pine, 3/4" thick
3 5/8" x 18" Basswood, 1/4" thick
1" x 15" Basswood, 1/16" thick (for handle)
6 – 12" pieces of raffia
Wood glue
2 Rubber bands

ACRYLIC PAINTS

Light Blue
Purple
Red
Orange
Green
White

INSTRUCTIONS

Duplicate the pattern on a copier machine or with tracing paper. Transfer the base pattern onto the 3/4" thick wood. Transfer 6 egg pattern outlines onto the 1/4" thick wood. Cut the shapes out with a scroll saw. Cut the wood for the handle piece to size. Drill the 2 holes into each egg where shown on the pattern. Sand all surfaces with 100-grid and than 150-grid sandpaper. Remove the sanding dust with a tack cloth.

Place the handle piece in hot water, weight it down so that it will stay submerged and allow it to soak for 1 hour. **Slowly** bend the handle piece into a "U" shape, as shown in the illustration. You must bend it slowly and carefully or it will break. If it doesn't bend easily, soak it a little longer in hot water and than try again. Once the handle is shaped, place a rubber band around it to hold the shape and let it dry thoroughly.

Glue the 6 egg shapes around the base. Make sure that the eggs are standing straight with their sides just touching at their widest point.

Fasten a rubber band around the egg bottoms, at the base, to hold them securely in place and let the glue dry thoroughly.

Remove the rubber band from the handle piece. Glue the handle piece in place, with the ends going all the way down to the base piece. Use a clamp on each side to hold it securely until the glue is completely dry.

Base-coat the entire basket with light blue. Let the paint dry. Sand lightly to remove the "fuzz" raised by the paint. Remove the sanding dust with a tack cloth. Touch-up the paint if necessary.

Transfer the pattern details onto the 6 eggs. Mix equals parts of purple and white together and use the mixture to paint the 3 small flowers on each egg. Mix equals parts of orange and white together and use the mixture to paint the center stamen of the large flower on each egg. Mix equal parts of red and white together and use the mixture to paint the 5 petals of the large flower on each egg. Mix equal parts of green and white together and use the mixture to paint the stem and leaves of the large flower on each egg. Let the paint dry.

Shade the 3 small flowers on each egg with purple. Shade the center stamen of the large flower on each egg with orange. Shade the 5 petals of the large flower on each egg with red. Shade the stem and leaves of the large flower on each egg with green. Use a small detail paintbrush to paint the stem and center stamens of the 3 small flowers on each egg green. Let the paint dry. Paint the purple dash lines going around the outline of each egg. Let the paint dry.

Thread a raffia piece through the front of one of the holes in any one the eggs and back out of the hole in the egg next to it. Pull the ends of the raffia even and tie a small bow. Continue this process around the basket until all of the raffia pieces are attached. Place a very small dot of glue on the knot of each bow to keep them from untying.

Pattern for 846: Six-Egg Basket

BASE

1/16" HOLE

EGG
CUT 6

HANDLE

These two patterns were reduced at 75%. Enlarge at 130%

Handle Pattern for 846: Six-Egg Basket

← 4 3/4" →

PATTERN 850A:
TOY BUNNY

SUPPLIES

6" x 4 ¼" Pine, ¾" to 1 ½" thick
3 ¼" x 9" Pine, ¾" thick
3 ½" x 3 ½" Pine, ¼" thick
2 ½" of ¼" wood dowel
Varnish (semi-gloss finish)
Wood glue

ACRYLIC PAINTS

Black
White
Brown
(Stain can be substituted for the brown paint.)

INSTRUCTIONS

Duplicate the pattern on a copier machine or with tracing paper. Transfer the body pattern onto the 6" x 4 ¼" piece of wood. Transfer the patterns for the front and the back legs onto the 3 ¼" x 9" piece of wood. Transfer the ear patterns onto the 3 ½" x 3 ½" piece of wood. Cut out the shapes with a scroll saw. It is important that each hole is in the correct position and drilled straight. Mark the drill holes as they are shown on the pattern. Carefully drill the holes. Round the edges of the pieces slightly with 100-grid sandpaper. Contour the shaded areas (where shown on the pattern) with sandpaper, to add depth and definition to the project design. Sand all surfaces with 100-grid and then 150-grid sandpaper. Remove the sanding dust with a tack cloth.

Mix 3 parts of brown paint with 1 part of water. Use this mixture to paint the body, ear and the leg pieces, continuing the color around the edges and onto the backs. Let the paint dry. Sand lightly to remove the "fuzz" raised by the paint. Remove the sanding dust with a tack cloth. Touch-up the paint if necessary.

Transfer the eye placement onto both sides of the head. Paint the black dots for the eyes using the eraser end of a pencil. Let the paint dry. Add a white highlight to each eye with a paintbrush handle. Let the paint dry. Varnish all surfaces of the body, ear and leg pieces. Let the varnish dry. Apply a second coat of varnish to all surfaces. Let the varnish dry.

If you have applied finish to the glue areas, sand the finish off where the pieces join. Glue the legs into position, making sure they are straight and even. Let the glue dry thoroughly.

To determine the length of dowel needed to attach the ears, add ¼" to the combined width of the 2 ears and the head. Cut the dowel to this length. Dip one end of the dowel into wood glue and push it into one of the ears. Push the other end of the dowel through the head and glue it on to the other ear. Make sure you only glue the dowel to the ears or they will not move.

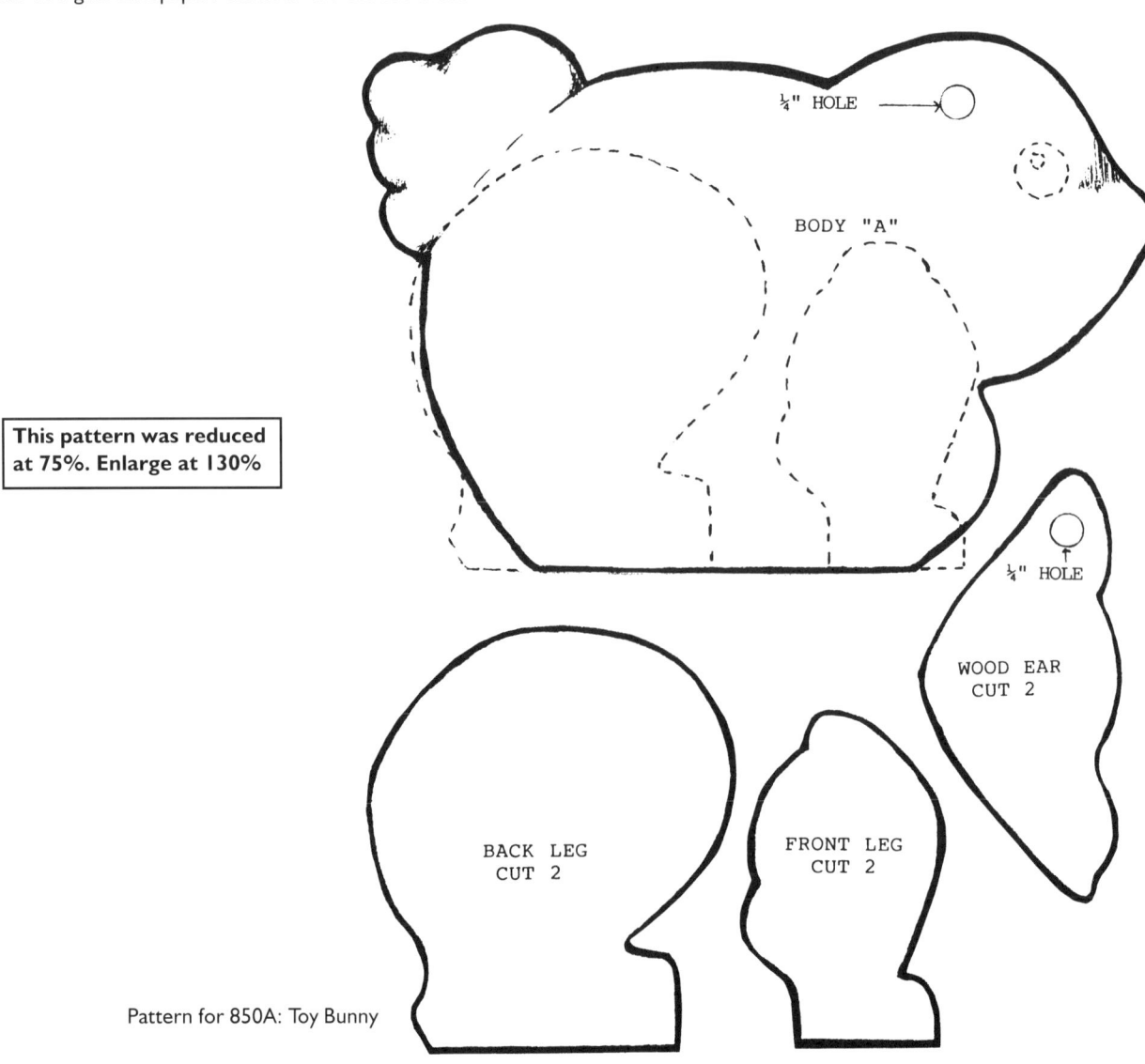

This pattern was reduced at 75%. Enlarge at 130%

¼" HOLE

BODY "A"

¼" HOLE

WOOD EAR
CUT 2

BACK LEG
CUT 2

FRONT LEG
CUT 2

Pattern for 850A: Toy Bunny

PATTERN 850B:
TOY BUNNY (FABRIC EARS)

SUPPLIES

5 1/2" x 4" Pine, 3/4" to 1 1/2" thick
3 1/4" x 9" Pine, 3/4" thick
9" of 1/4" wood dowel
4 – 1 1/2" wooden wheels
Varnish (semi-gloss finish)
Wood glue
3" x 8" piece of pink fabric
3" x 8" piece of print fabric
1 – 1 1/2" wooden ball for the tail

ACRYLIC PAINTS

Black
White
Brown
(Stain can be substituted for the brown paint.)

INSTRUCTIONS

Duplicate the pattern on a copier machine or with tracing paper. Transfer the body pattern onto the 5 1/2" x 4" piece of wood. Transfer the patterns for the legs onto the 3 1/4" x 9" piece of wood. Cut out the shapes with a scroll saw. It is important that each hole is in the correct position and drilled straight. Mark the drill holes, as they are shown on the pattern, and drill carefully. Round the edges of the pieces slightly with 100-grid sandpaper. Contour the shaded areas (where shown on the pattern) with sandpaper, to add depth and definition to the project design. Sand all surfaces with 100-grid and then 150-grid sandpaper. Drill a 1/4" hole, 1/2" deep into the wooden ball. Lightly sand the wheels and the tail with 150-grid sandpaper. Remove the sanding dust with a tack cloth.

Mix 3 parts of brown paint with 1 part of water. Use this mixture to paint the body, the wooden ball for the tail and the leg pieces, continuing the color around the edges and onto the backs. Let the paint dry. Sand lightly to remove the "fuzz" raised by the paint. Remove the sanding dust with a tack cloth. Touch-up the paint if necessary.

Transfer the eye placement onto both sides of the head. Paint the black dots for the eyes using the eraser end of a pencil. Let the paint dry. Add a white highlight to each eye with a paintbrush handle. Let the paint dry. Varnish the wheels and the tail. Varnish all surfaces of the body and leg pieces. Let the varnish dry. Apply a second coat of varnish to all surfaces. Let the varnish dry.

If you have applied finish to the glue areas, sand the finish off where the pieces join. Glue the legs into position, making sure they are straight and even and that the dowel holes line up. Cut a 1" piece of dowel. Dip one end of the dowel into glue and push it into the wooden tail ball. Dip the other end into glue and push it into the tail hole on the body. Let the glue dry thoroughly.

To determine the length of dowel needed to attach the wheels, add 1/4" to the combined width of the 2 wheels, the front legs and the body. Cut the dowel to this length. Dip one end of the dowel into glue and push it into the wheel. Push the other end of the dowel through the holes in the body and front legs and glue it into a second wheel. Measure and attach the back wheels in the same manner. Make sure you only glue the dowel to the wheels or they will not turn.

Transfer 1 ear pattern onto each piece of fabric. Cut out the fabric pieces. Place the ear pieces right sides together. Sew a 1/4" seam around the edge leaving the opening as shown on the pattern. Turn the ear right side out. Stitch the opening closed. Slide the ear through the ear hole, adjust and glue it in place.

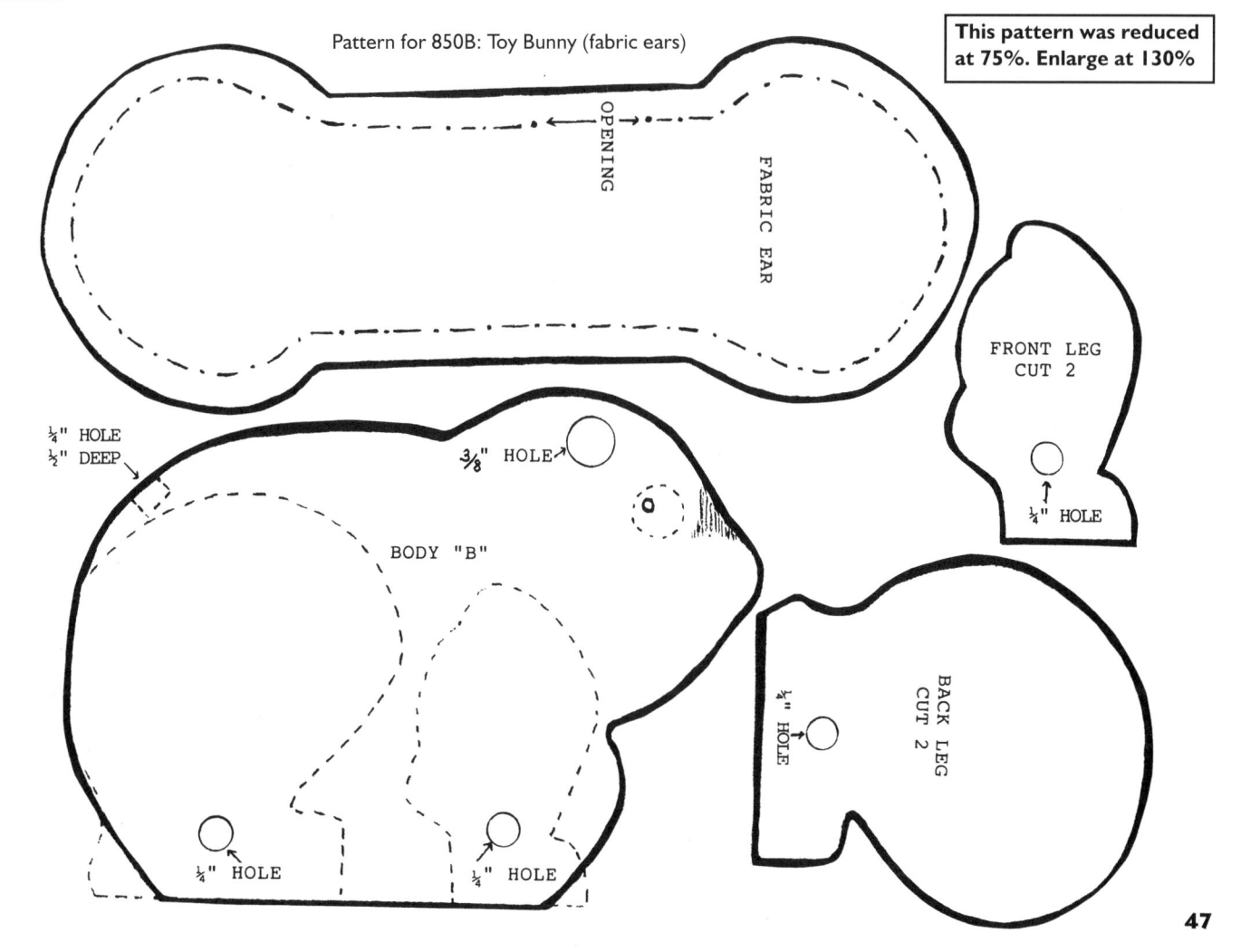

Pattern for 850B: Toy Bunny (fabric ears)

This pattern was reduced at 75%. Enlarge at 130%

PATTERN 851A:
TOY DOG
(FABRIC EARS)

SUPPLIES

6 ¼" x 4 ½" Pine, ¾" to 1 ½" thick
4" x 9" Pine, ¾" thick
8" of ¼" wood dowel
4 – 1 ½" wooden wheels
Varnish (semi-gloss finish)
Wood glue
6" x 7" piece of fabric
10" of ½" wide ribbon

ACRYLIC PAINTS

Black
White
Brown
(Stain can be substituted for the brown paint.)

INSTRUCTIONS

Duplicate the pattern on a copier machine or with tracing paper. Transfer the body pattern onto the 6 ¼" x 4 ½" piece of wood. Transfer the patterns for the front and back legs onto the 4" x 9" piece of wood. Cut out the shapes with a scroll saw. It is important that each hole is in the correct position and drilled straight or the wheels will not turn smoothly. Mark the drill holes, as they are shown on the pattern, and drill carefully. Round the edges of the pieces slightly with 100-grid sandpaper. Contour the shaded areas (where shown on the pattern) with sandpaper, to add depth and definition to the project design. Sand all surfaces with 100-grid and then 150-grid sandpaper. Lightly sand the wheels with 150-grid sandpaper. Remove the sanding dust with a tack cloth.

Mix 3 parts brown paint with 1 part water. Use this mixture to paint the body and the leg pieces, continuing the color around the edges and onto the backs. Let the paint dry. Sand lightly to remove the "fuzz" raised by the paint. Remove the sanding dust with a tack cloth. Touch-up the paint if necessary.

Transfer the eye and nose placement onto both sides of the head. Paint the black dots for the eyes using the eraser end of a pencil. Paint the nose black. Let the paint dry. Add a white highlight to each eye with a paintbrush handle. Let the paint dry. Varnish the wheels and set them aside. Varnish all surfaces of the body and leg pieces. Let the varnish dry. Apply a second coat of varnish to all surfaces. Let the varnish dry.

If you have applied finish to the glue areas, sand the finish off where the pieces join. Glue the legs into position, making sure they are straight and even and that the dowel holes line up. Let the glue dry thoroughly.

To determine the length of dowel needed to attach the wheels, add ¼" to the combined width of the 2 wheels, the 2 front legs and the body. Cut the dowel to this length. Dip one end of the dowel into wood glue and push it into a wheel. Push the other end of the dowel through the holes in the 2 front legs and glue it into a second wheel. Measure and attach the back wheels in the same manner. Make sure you only glue the dowel to the wheels or they will not turn.

Transfer 4 ear patterns and 2 tail patterns onto the fabric. Cut out the fabric pieces. Place 2 ear pieces right sides together. Sew a 1/8" seam around the edge leaving the opening, as shown on the pattern. Turn the ear right side out. Sew the second ear and the tail in the same manner. Tuck and glue one ear into each ear hole. Tuck and glue the tail into the tail hole. Tie the ribbon around the base of the tail and make a bow.

Pattern for 851A: Toy Dog (fabric ears)

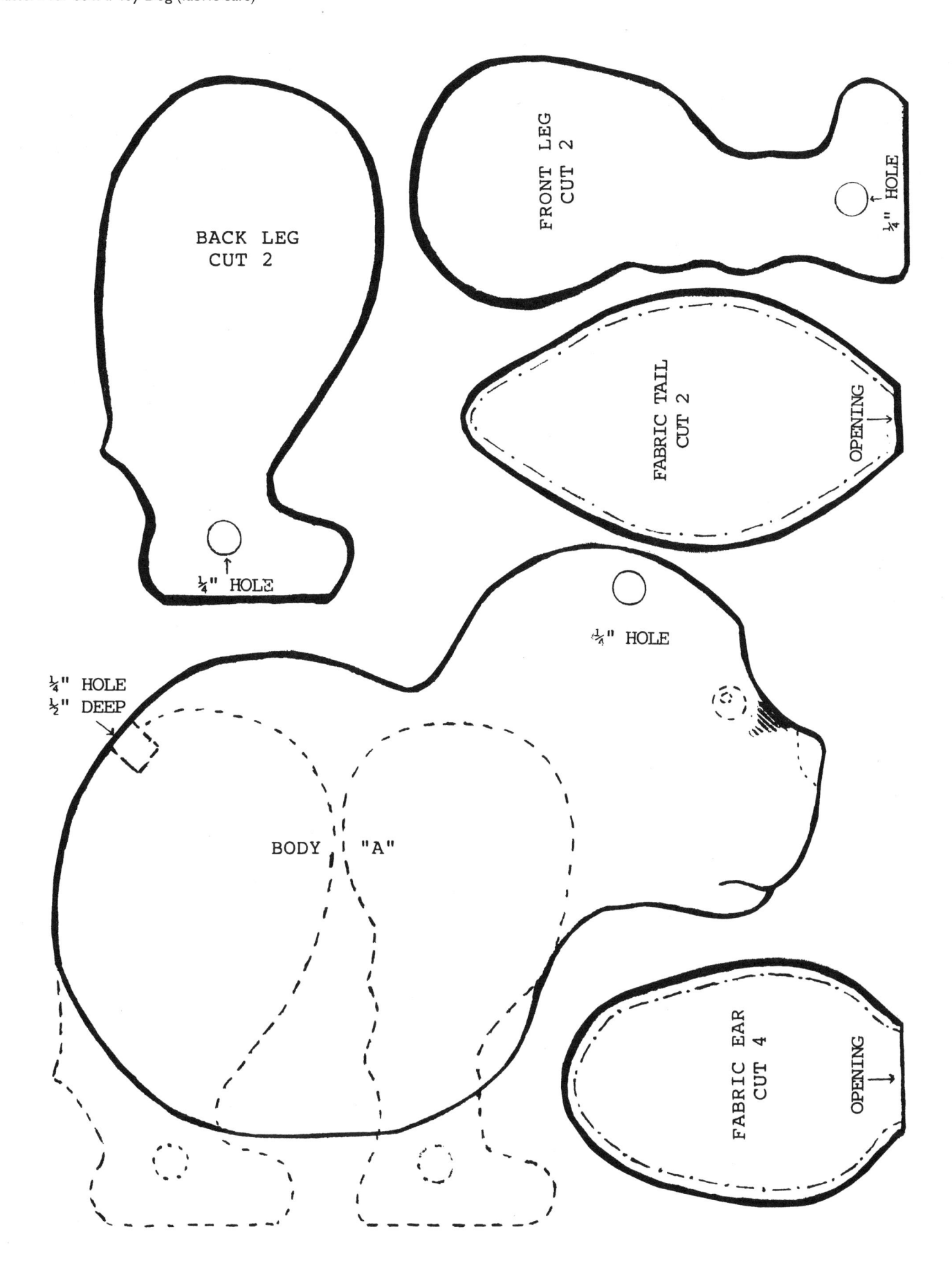

BACK LEG
CUT 2

FRONT LEG
CUT 2

¼" HOLE

FABRIC TAIL
CUT 2

OPENING

¼" HOLE

¼" HOLE
½" DEEP

BODY "A"

¼" HOLE

FABRIC EAR
CUT 4

OPENING

49

PATTERN 851B:
TOY DOG

SUPPLIES

7 ¼" x 4 ½" Pine, ¾" to 1 ½" thick
4" x 9" Pine, ¾" thick
2 ½" x 2 ½" Pine, ¼" thick
2 ½" of ¼" wood dowel
Varnish (semi-gloss finish)
Wood glue

ACRYLIC PAINTS

Black
White
Brown
(Stain can be substituted for the brown paint.)

INSTRUCTIONS

Duplicate the pattern on a copier machine or with tracing paper. Transfer the body pattern onto the 7 ¼" x 4 ½" piece of wood. Transfer the patterns for the front and the back legs onto the 4" x 9" piece of wood. Transfer the ear patterns onto the 2 ½" x 2 ½" piece of wood. Cut out the shapes with a scroll saw. It is important that each hole is in the correct position and drilled straight. Mark the drill holes as they are shown on the pattern. Carefully drill the holes. Round the edges of the pieces slightly with 100-grid sandpaper. Contour the shaded areas (where shown on the pattern) with sandpaper, to add depth and definition to the project design. Sand all surfaces with 100-grid and then 150-grid sandpaper. Remove the sanding dust with a tack cloth.

Mix 3 parts brown paint with 1 part water. Use this mixture to paint the body, ear and leg pieces, continuing the color around the edges and onto the backs. Let the paint dry. Sand lightly to remove the "fuzz" raised by the paint. Remove the sanding dust with a tack cloth. Touch-up the paint if necessary.

Transfer the eye and nose placement onto both sides of the head. Paint the black dots for the eyes using the eraser end of a pencil. Paint the nose black. Let the paint dry. Add a white highlight to each eye with a paintbrush handle. Let the paint dry. Varnish all surfaces of the body, ear and leg pieces. Let the varnish dry. Apply a second coat of varnish to all surfaces. Let the varnish dry.

If you have applied finish to the glue areas, sand the finish off where the pieces join. Glue the legs into position, making sure they are straight and even. Let the glue dry thoroughly.

To determine the length of dowel needed to attach the ears, add ¼" to the combined width of the 2 ears and the head. Cut the dowel to this length. Dip one end of the dowel into wood glue and push it into one of the ears. Push the other end of the dowel through the head and glue it on to the other ear. Make sure you only glue the dowel to the ears or they will not move.

Pattern for 851B: Toy Dog

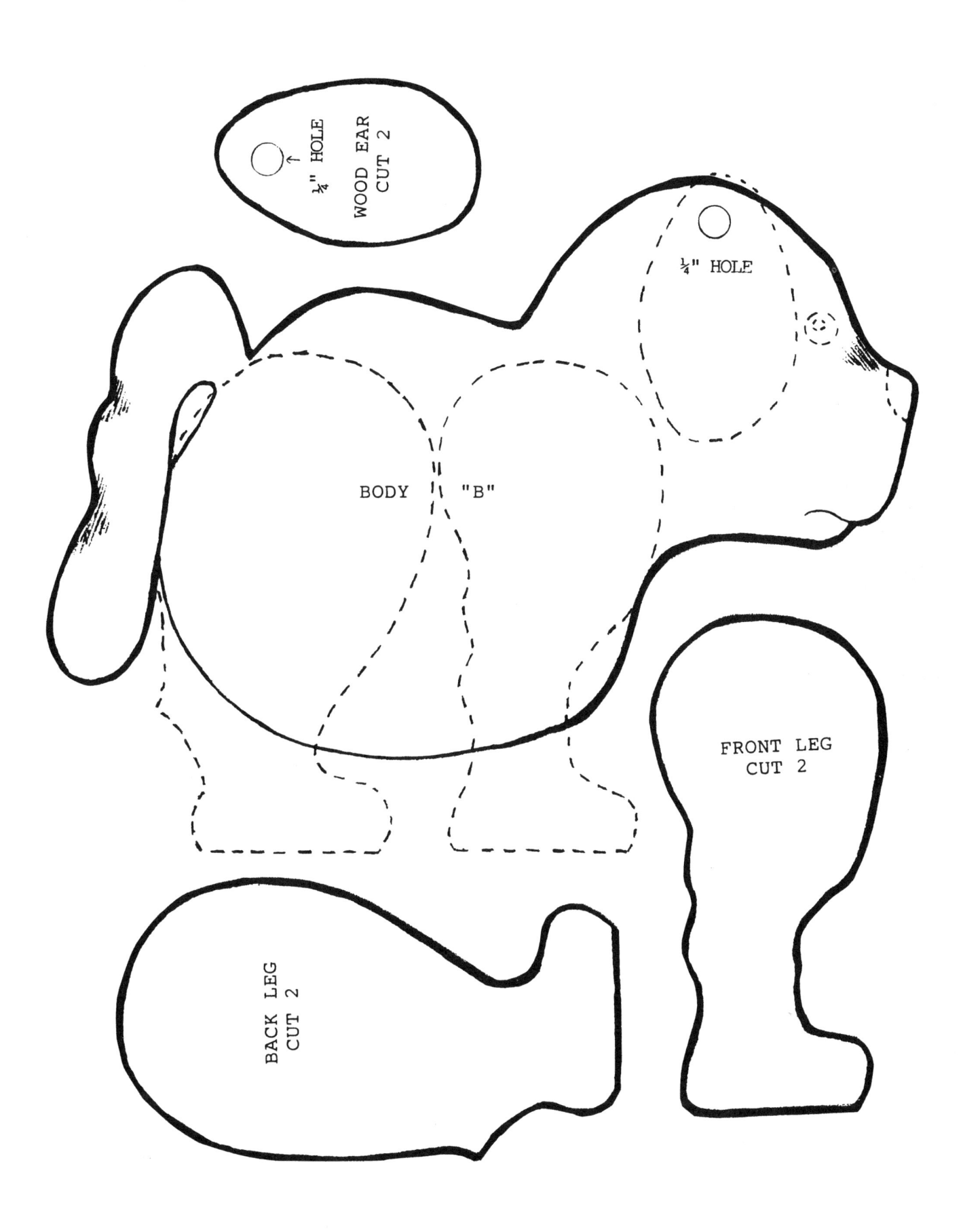

WOOD EAR
CUT 2
¼" HOLE

¼" HOLE

BODY "B"

FRONT LEG
CUT 2

BACK LEG
CUT 2

PATTERN 860:
APPLE PUZZLE

SUPPLIES

7 ½" x 8 ¼" Pine, ¾" to 1 ½" thick
Sea sponge
Varnish (Semi-gloss finish)

ACRYLIC PAINTS

Red
Green
Black
Yellow

NOTE: Using thicker wood will add stability to the puzzle. The puzzle pieces are small with many close turns; they must be cut slowly and carefully. Use the smallest blade that is recommended for the wood thickness you have chosen. As you are cutting, make sure the blade is not bending or your cuts will be slanted.

To increase the difficulty level in assembling the puzzle, sponge paint the front and the back the same. To decrease the difficulty, paint the edges and back a solid red and only sponge paint on the front of the puzzle pieces.

INSTRUCTIONS

Duplicate the pattern on a copier machine or with tracing paper. Transfer the main pattern lines onto the wood. Cut out the apple's shape. Cut out the stem/leaf piece and trim off the two open areas. Cut out piece "A" from the outer circle. Cut all the way around, following the pattern line between the outer circle and the middle circle. Then do the side cuts on the outer circle to form the individual pieces. Cut out piece "B" from the middle circle. Cut all the way around, following the pattern line between the middle circle and the inner circle. Do the side cuts for the middle circle. Cut down line "C" to the inside apple. Continue cutting all the way around the inside apple's pattern line and back out of line "C". Separate the inside apple from inner circle. Saw the three side cuts for the inner circle. Sand all surfaces with 100-grid and then 150-grid sandpaper. Remove the sanding dust with a tack cloth.

Varnish all surfaces of the inside apple and set aside. Base-coat the stem/leaf piece green (except for the puzzle knob), continuing the color around the edges and onto the back. Base-coat all remaining puzzle piece surfaces with yellow, including the puzzle knob on the stem/leaf piece. Let the paint dry. Sand lightly to remove "fuzz" raised by the paints. Remove the sanding dust with a tack cloth. Touch-up the paint if necessary.

Apply a second coat of varnish to the inside apple. Mix green with a small amount of black. Sponge paint the mixture over the stem and leaves. Be sure to leave some of the base-coat showing through. Let the paint dry. Sponge paint red on all of the remaining puzzle piece surfaces, leaving a yellow highlight area unpainted as shown on the color picture. Mix 3 parts red with 1 part green. Use this mixture to sponge paint shading on the outer circle and the inner circle.

Transfer the details onto the stem and leaves. Paint the details on the stem and leaves with black. Let the paint dry thoroughly before assembling the puzzle or the pieces will stick together.

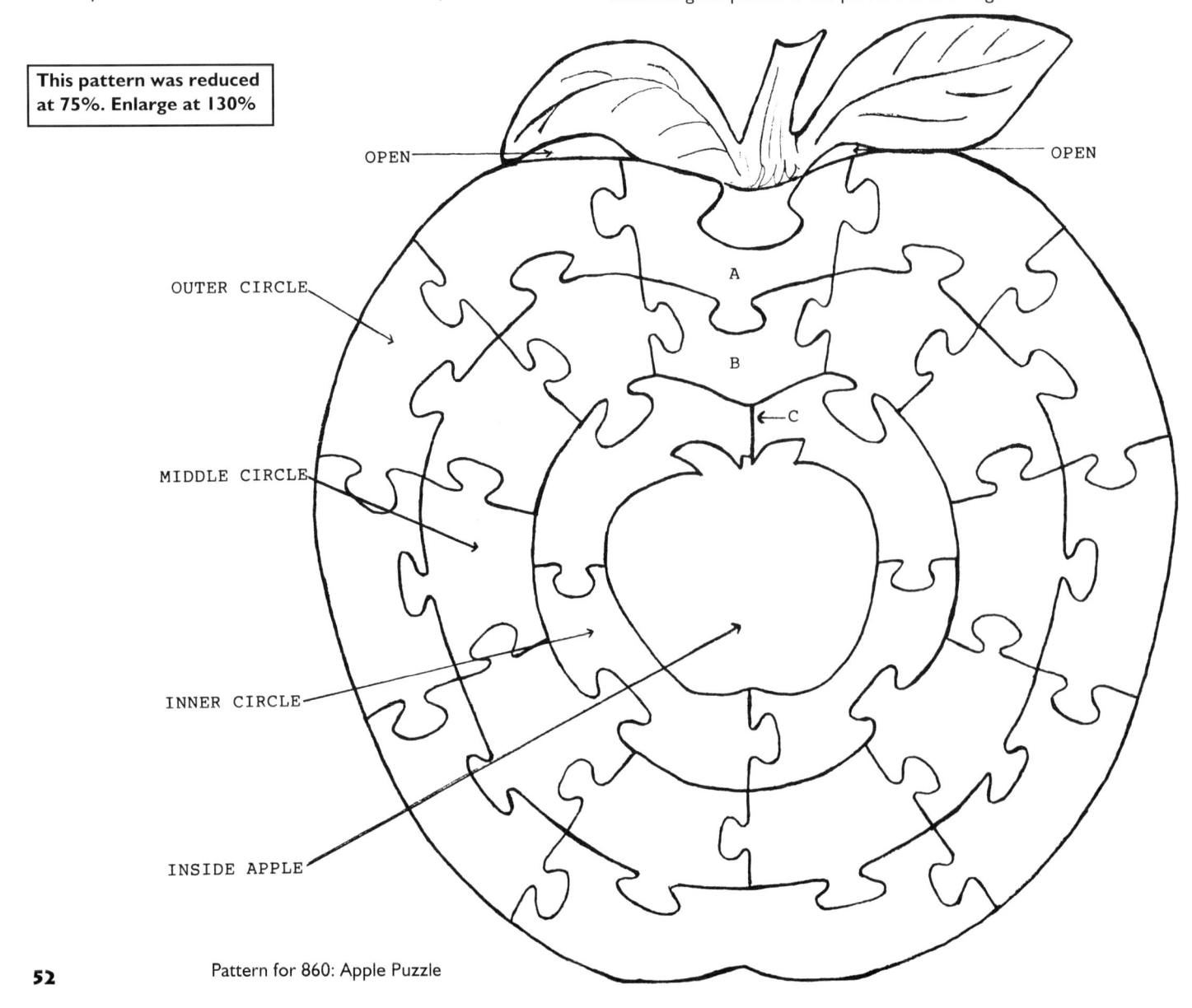

This pattern was reduced at 75%. Enlarge at 130%

Pattern for 860: Apple Puzzle

PATTERN 861: PEAR PUZZLE

SUPPLIES

6 ½" x 9 ¼" Pine, ¾" to 1 ½" thick
Sea sponge

ACRYLIC PAINTS

Green
Light Green
Black
Yellow

NOTE: Using thicker wood will add stability to the puzzle. The puzzle pieces are small with many close turns; they must be cut slowly and carefully. Use the smallest blade that is recommended for the wood thickness you have chosen. As you are cutting, make sure the blade is not bending or your cuts will be slanted.

To increase the difficulty level in assembling the puzzle, sponge paint the front and the back the same. To decrease the difficulty, paint the edges and back a solid light green and only sponge paint on the front of the puzzle pieces.

INSTRUCTIONS

Duplicate the pattern on a copier machine or with tracing paper. Transfer the main pattern lines onto the wood. Cut out the pear's shape. Starting at the top, cut out the stem/leaf piece. Cut out the next three pieces going down. Cut out piece "A" from the outer circle. Cut all the way around, following the pattern line between the outer circle and the middle circle. Then do the side cuts on the outer circle to form the individual pieces. Cut out piece "B" from the middle circle. Cut all the way around, following the pattern line between the middle circle and the center piece. Do the side cuts for the middle circle. Sand all surfaces with 100-grid and then 150-grid sandpaper. Remove the sanding dust with a tack cloth.

Base-coat the stem/leaf piece green (except for the puzzle knob), continuing the color around the edges and onto the back. Base-coat all remaining puzzle piece surfaces with yellow, including the puzzle knob on the stem/leaf piece. Let the paint dry. Sand lightly to remove the "fuzz" raised by the paints. Remove the sanding dust with a tack cloth. Touch-up the paint if necessary.

Mix green with a small amount of black. Sponge paint the mixture over the stem and leaves. Be sure to leave some of the base-coat showing through. Let the paint dry. Sponge paint light green on all of the remaining puzzle piece surfaces, leaving a yellow highlight area unpainted as shown on the color picture. Mix 3 parts light green with 1 part black. Use this mixture to sponge paint shading around the outer puzzle edge.

Transfer the pattern details onto the stem and leaves. Paint the details on the stem and leaves black. Let the paint dry thoroughly before assembling the puzzle or the pieces will stick together.

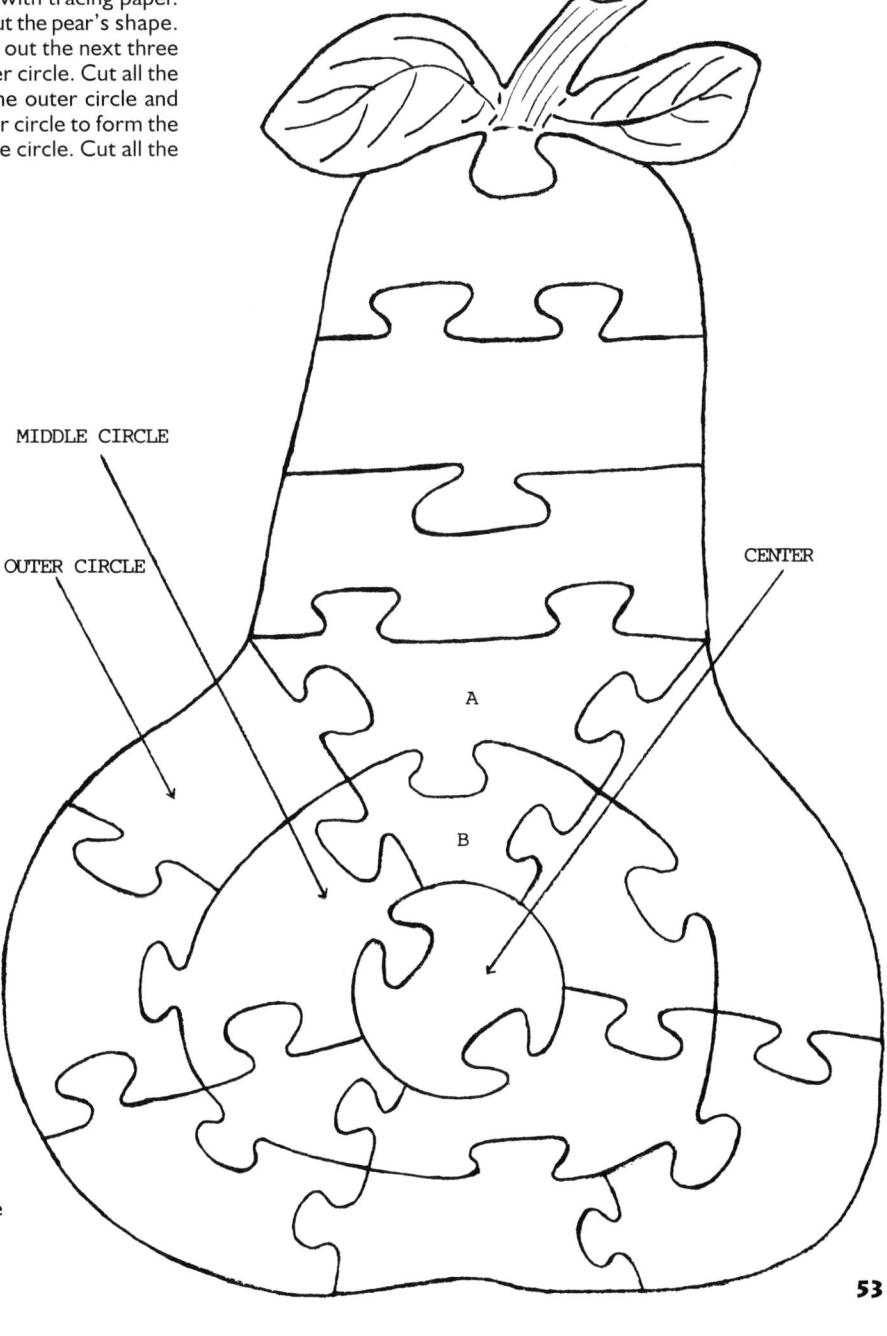

This pattern was reduced at 75%. Enlarge at 130%

Pattern for 861: Pear Puzzle

Pattern 862:
GRAPES PUZZLE

SUPPLIES

8 ¾" x 5" Pine, ¾" thick
Sea sponge

ACRYLIC PAINTS

Light green
Green
White
Purple
Red

NOTE: The puzzle pieces are small with many close turns; they must be cut slowly and carefully. Use the smallest blade that is recommended for the wood thickness. As you are cutting, make sure the blade is not bending or your cuts will be slanted.

To increase the difficulty level in assembling the puzzle, paint the front and the back the same. To decrease the difficulty, paint the edges and back a solid purple and only paint the details on the front of the puzzle pieces.

INSTRUCTIONS

Duplicate the pattern on a copier machine or with tracing paper. Transfer the main pattern lines onto the wood. Cut along the outline of the grape bunch. Cut the individual grape pieces out in numerical order. Trim off the open areas (shown as shaded areas on the pattern) as you go along. Sand all surfaces with 100-grid and then 150-grid sandpaper. Remove the sanding dust with a tack cloth.

Paint the stem/leaf piece with light green (except for the puzzle knob), continuing the color around the edges and on to the back. Mix equal parts red and purple paint together and add enough water to form a transparent wash. Use this mixture to base-coat all surfaces of the grape pieces including the puzzle knob on the stem/leaf piece. Let the paint dry. Sand lightly to remove "fuzz" raised by the paints. Remove the sanding dust with a tack cloth. Touch-up the paint if necessary. Add green shading to the stem and leaf. Let the paint dry.

Transfer the details onto the stem and leaf. Paint the green details on the stem and leaf. Deepen the color for the grapes by increasing the paint to water ratio of the red and purple mixture. Working from the outer edge of each grape, push the paint in toward the center of the grape. Deepen the color again and continue adding the shading effect to each grape. Use an undiluted red and purple paint mixture to define the outline of each grape. Let the paint dry. With the sea sponge, add a white highlight to each grape and to the leaf. Let the paint dry thoroughly before assembling the puzzle or the pieces will stick together.

Pattern for 862: Grape Puzzle

Pattern 867:
CAT

SUPPLIES

3 1/4" x 4 1/4" Pine, 1 1/2" thick
4" x 5" Pine, 1/4" thick
Wood glue
Black paint pen (fine-tip)
1" of 20-gauge wire

ACRYLIC PAINTS

Gray
White
Black
Red
Pink

INSTRUCTIONS

Duplicate the pattern on a copier machine or with tracing paper. Transfer the body pattern onto the 1 1/2" thick wood. Transfer the patterns for the body parts onto the 1/4" thick wood. Cut out the smallest pieces first, then the larger ones. Drill all holes where shown on the pattern. Sand all surfaces with 100-grid and then 150-grid sandpaper. Remove the sanding dust with a tack cloth.

Paint the pink area of each ear. Paint the hair tuft, face, paws and tummy pieces with white, continuing the color around the edges. Paint the body, tail and the rest of the ear pieces gray, continuing the color around the sides and onto the backs. Let the paint dry. Sand lightly to remove the "fuzz" raised by the paints. Remove the sanding dust with a tack cloth. Touch-up the paint if necessary.

Transfer the pattern details onto the pieces, as they are needed. Paint white ovals for the eyes. Paint the mouth red. Let the paint dry. Dot on the black eye pupils using a paintbrush handle. Paint the nose black. Let the paint dry. With the black paint pen, add the details on the ears, face, eyes and feet. Dot a white highlight on each eye with the tip of a round toothpick. Paint a white highlight on the nose.

If you have painted the glue areas, sand the paint off where the pieces join. Cut the 1" piece of wire in half. Dip one end of a piece of wire into glue and push it into the bottom of one of the ears. Run a thin line of glue across the bottom edge of the ear. Dip the other end of the wire into the glue and push it into the body. Make sure the ear is straight and glued tightly. Glue the second ear on in the same manner. Glue the hair tuft, face, tummy and feet in place on the body. Let the glue dry. Glue the tail on to the back of the body, starting it at the bottom center.

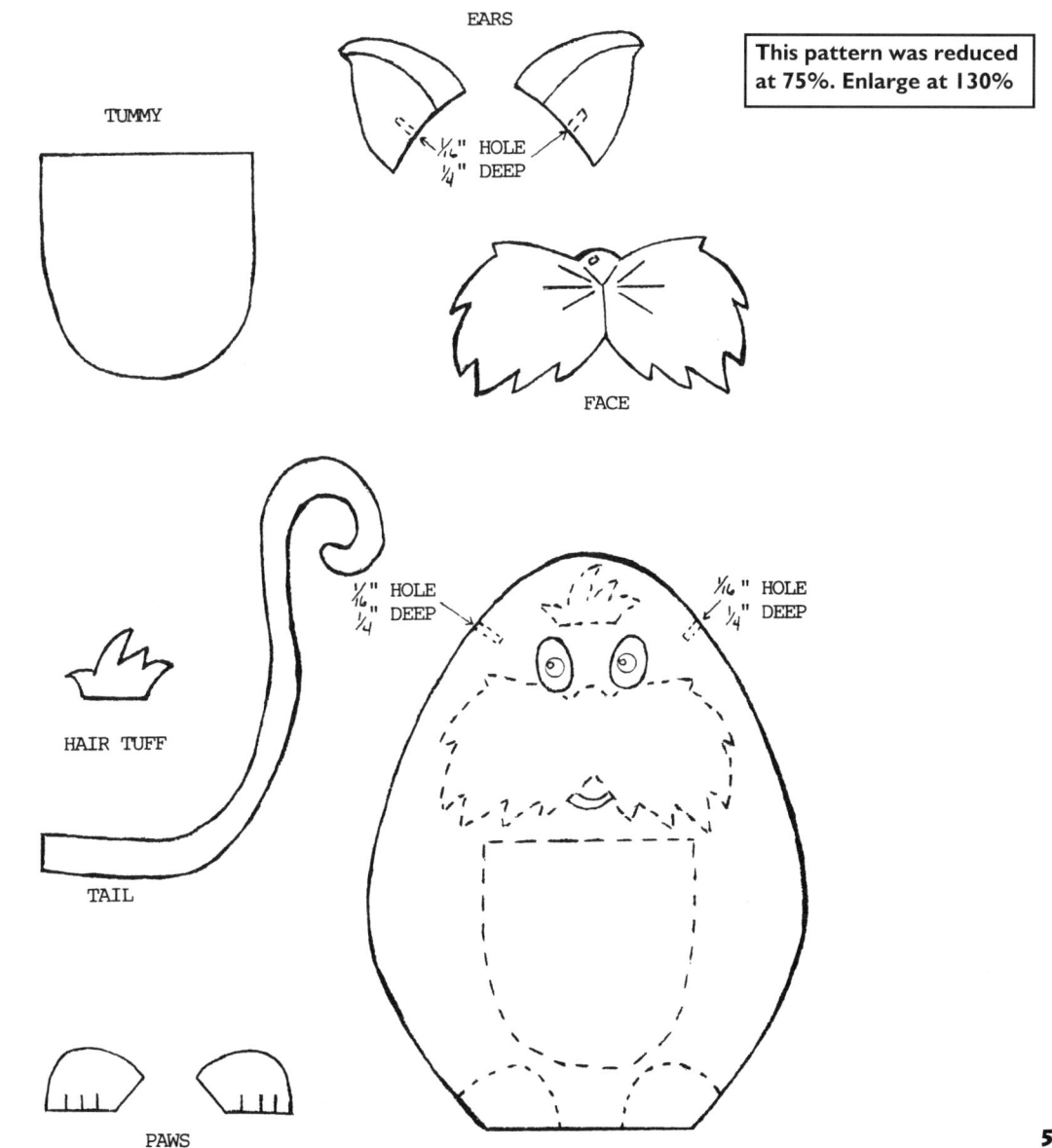

This pattern was reduced at 75%. Enlarge at 130%

TUMMY

EARS
1/16" HOLE
1/4" DEEP

FACE

HAIR TUFF

TAIL

1/16" HOLE
1/4" DEEP

1/16" HOLE
1/4" DEEP

Pattern for 867: Cat

PAWS

Pattern 868:
DOG

SUPPLIES

3 ¼" x 4 ¼" Pine, 1 ½" thick
4" x 5" Pine, ¼" thick
Black paint pen (fine-tip)
Small piece of red felt
Wood glue

ACRYLIC PAINTS

Brown
White
Black
Pink
Cream

INSTRUCTIONS

Duplicate the pattern on a copier machine or with tracing paper. Transfer the body pattern onto the 1 ½" thick wood. Transfer the patterns for the body parts, except for the tongue, onto the ¼" thick wood. Cut out the smallest pieces first, then the larger ones. Sand all surfaces with 100-grid and then 150-grid sandpaper. Remove the sanding dust with a tack cloth.

Paint the front of the ears, heart and tail brown. Paint the face cream, continuing the color around the edges. Let the paint dry. Mix equal parts brown and cream together. Use this mixture to paint all of the remaining surfaces. Let the paint dry. Sand the pieces lightly to remove the "fuzz" raised by the paints. Remove the sanding dust with a tack cloth. Touch-up the paint if necessary.

Transfer the pattern details onto the pieces, as they are needed. Paint the white ovals for the eyes. Swirl pink paint onto the front of the ears and the front of the heart. Let the paint dry. Swirl cream paint onto the front of the heart. Dot on the black for the eye pupils using a paintbrush handle. Paint the nose black. Let the paint dry. With the black paint pen, add the details to the face, eyes and feet. Dot a white highlight on each eye with the tip of a round toothpick. Paint the white highlight on the nose.

If you have painted the glue areas, sand the paint off where the pieces join. Transfer the tongue pattern onto the red felt. Cut the tongue out and glue it onto the back of the face piece. Glue the face onto the body. Glue the ears, heart and feet in place on the body. Let the glue dry. Glue the tail onto the back of the body, starting it at the bottom center.

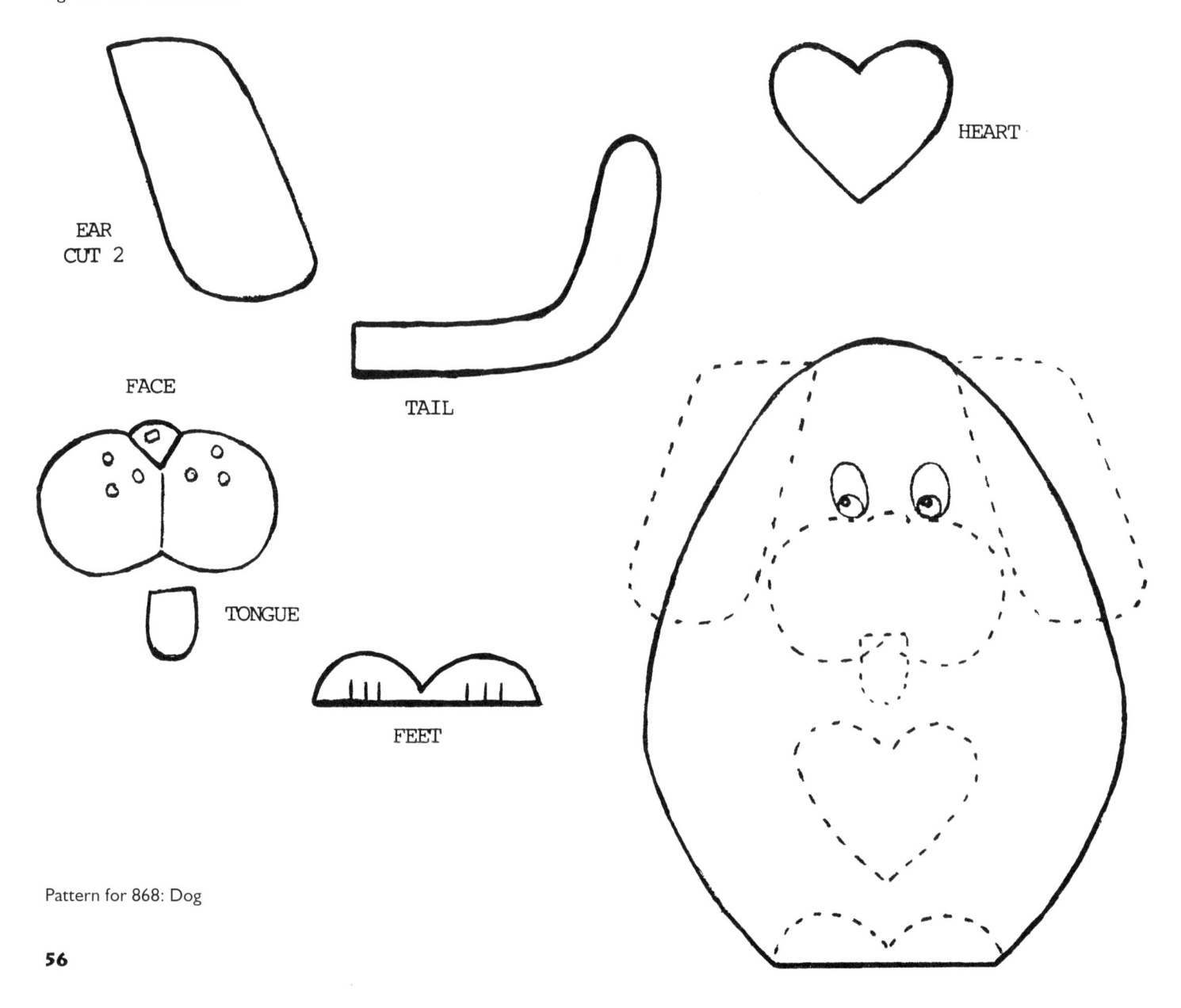

EAR
CUT 2

HEART

FACE

TAIL

TONGUE

FEET

Pattern for 868: Dog

Pattern 869:
BUNNY

SUPPLIES

3 1/4" x 4 1/4" Pine, 1 1/2" thick
4" x 5" Pine, 1/4" thick
Wood glue
Black paint pen (fine-tip)
1" White pom-pom

ACRYLIC PAINTS

Gray
White
Black
Pink
Red

INSTRUCTIONS

Duplicate the pattern on a copier machine or with tracing paper. Transfer the body pattern onto the 1 1/2" thick wood. Transfer the patterns for the body parts onto the 1/4" thick wood. Cut out the smallest pieces first, then the larger ones. Sand all surfaces with 100-grid and then 150-grid sandpaper. Remove the sanding dust with a tack cloth.

Paint the pink area of each ear. Paint the face white, continuing the color around the edges. Paint the heart red, continuing the color around the edges. Let the paint dry. Paint the body, the bottom ear pieces and the rest of the top ear pieces gray, continuing the color around the sides and onto the backs. Paint the feet gray, continuing the color around the edges. Let the paint dry. Sand lightly to remove the "fuzz" raised by the paints. Remove the sanding dust with a tack cloth. Touch-up the paint if necessary.

Transfer the pattern details onto the pieces, as they are needed. Paint the white ovals for the eyes. Let the paint dry. Dot on the black eye pupils with a paintbrush handle. Paint the nose black. With the black paint pen, add the details to the face, ears, eyes and feet. Paint the white dots on the heart with a paintbrush handle. Let the paint dry. Dot a white highlight on each eye with the tip of a round toothpick.

If you have painted the glue areas, sand the paint off where the pieces join. Glue the bottom piece of each ear onto the top piece of each ear. Let the glue dry. Run a line of glue along the bottom edge of the top ear piece and on the back of the bottom ear piece (where they will be attached to the body). Position the ears on the body. Glue the face, heart and feet in place on the body. Let the glue dry. Glue on the pom-pom for the tail at the bottom center of the back.

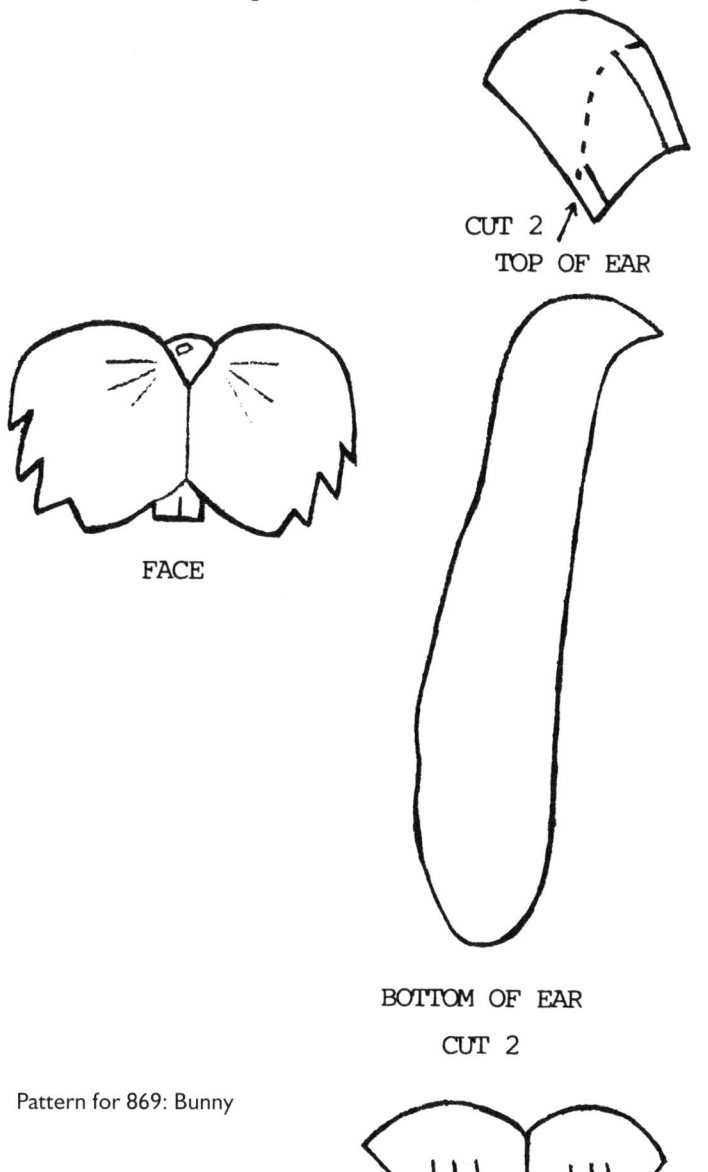

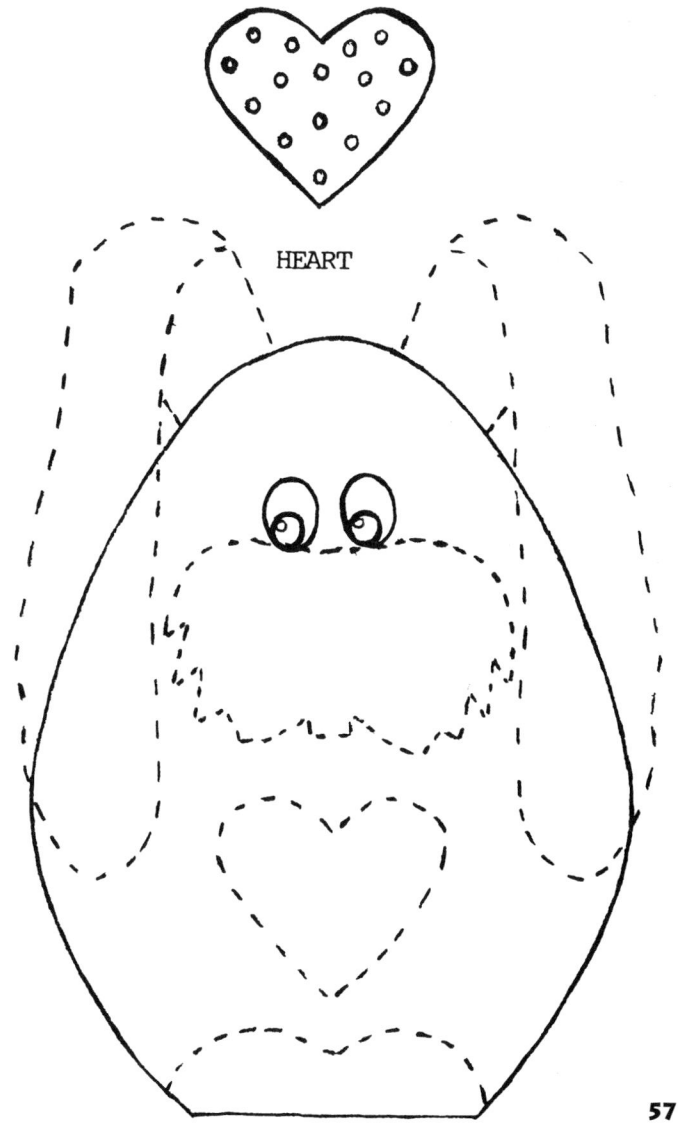

CUT 2
TOP OF EAR

FACE

HEART

BOTTOM OF EAR
CUT 2

Pattern for 869: Bunny

FEET

PATTERN 870:
ANGEL WITH FLOWER

SUPPLIES

3 ¼" x 4 ¼" Pine, 1 ½" thick
5" x 5" Pine, ¼" thick
5 ½" of 20-gauge wire
Green floral tape
Black paint pen (fine-tip)
Varnish (semi-gloss finish)
Wood glue

ACRYLIC PAINTS

Burgundy
Brown
White
Black
Light Yellow

INSTRUCTIONS

Duplicate the pattern on a copier machine or with tracing paper. Transfer the body pattern onto the 1 ½" thick wood. Transfer the remaining pattern outlines onto the ¼" thick wood. With a scroll saw, slowly cut out the flower first, and then the arms and wings. Cut out the body. Drill the hole for the halo. Sand all surfaces with 100-grid and then 150-grid sandpaper. Remove the sanding dust with a tack cloth.

Mix 2 parts white with 1 part brown. Use this mixture to paint the wings, continuing the color around the edges and onto the back. Transfer the main pattern lines onto the pieces. Varnish the face. Varnish the hands, continuing the varnish around the edges. Base-coat the light yellow for the hair, continuing the color around the edges and onto the back. Base-coat the flower light yellow, continuing the color around the edges. Mix burgundy with enough water to make a transparent wash. Use this mixture to base-coat the dress, continuing the color around the edges and onto the back. Use the same mixture to base-coat the sleeves, continuing the color around the edges. Let the paint and varnish dry. Sand lightly to remove the "fuzz" raised by the paints. Remove the sanding dust with a tack cloth. Touch-up the paint if necessary.

Mix burgundy with a small amount of water. Shade the dress and sleeves with this mixture. Mix light yellow with a small amount of brown and add enough water to form a transparent wash. Use this mixture to shade the hair. Let the paint dry.

Transfer the pattern details onto the pieces. Paint the hair detail lines brown. With a small paintbrush handle dot on the eyes, nose and the wing design with black. Draw on the mouth and add the details to the dress, sleeves and flower with the black paint pen. Dot on white for the dress collar using a paintbrush handle. Let the paint dry. Blush the cheeks with red. Dot a white highlight on each eye with the tip of a round toothpick. Dot on the freckles and add the detail to the dress collar with the black paint pen.

If you have painted the glue areas, sand the paint off where the pieces will join. Glue the arms and wings in place. Cut a 1 ½" piece of wire, wrap it in green floral tape and glue it in-between the hands. Glue the flower on. Bend the remaining piece of wire to a 90-degree angle, approximately 1" from the end. Bend the longer end of the wire into a circle for the halo. Dip the straight end of the wire into the glue and push it into the hole on the top of the angel's head.

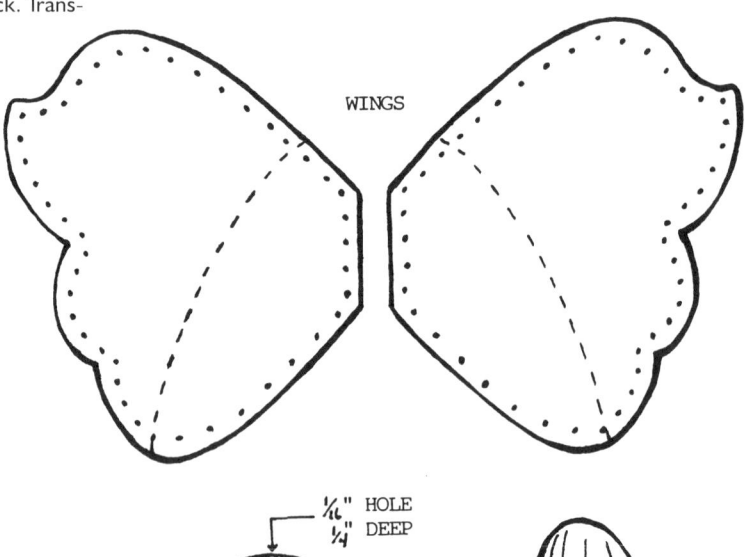

This pattern was reduced at 75%. Enlarge at 130%

Pattern for 870: Angel with Flower

PATTERN 871:
SANTA WITH HAT

SUPPLIES

3 ¼" x 4 ¼" Pine, 1 ½" thick
1" x 3 ½" Basswood, 1/8" thick
2" x 4" piece of red felt
1" x 9" strip of polyester batting
3 ¾" of 20-gauge wire
Varnish (semi-gloss finish)
Wood glue
1 Wood button (plug)
Small piece of holly (or green felt and 3 – 5mm pom-poms)

ACRYLIC PAINTS

White
Red
Brown
Black

INSTRUCTIONS

Duplicate the pattern on a copier machine or with tracing paper. Transfer the head pattern onto the 1 ½" thick wood. Transfer the 2 mustache patterns onto the 1/8" thick wood. Cut out the shapes with a scroll saw. Sand all surfaces with 100-grid and then 150-grid sandpaper. Remove the sanding dust with a tack cloth.

Transfer the main pattern lines onto the head. Varnish the wood button nose and the face portion of Santa's head. Let the varnish dry. Base-coat the rest of Santa's head white, continuing the color around the edges and onto the back. Base-coat the two mustache pieces white, continuing the color around the edges and onto the back areas where they stick out from the head. Let the paint dry. Sand lightly to remove the "fuzz" raised by the paint. Remove the sanding dust with a tack cloth. Touch-up the white paint if necessary.

Transfer the pattern details onto the pieces. Paint the mouth red. Paint the eyes and the outline of the mouth black. Glue on the nose. Let the paint and glue dry. Lightly blush the cheeks and nose with red. Add a white highlight to each eye using the handle of a paintbrush. Mix 3 parts white and 1 part brown together with an equal amount of water to form a wash. Use this mixture to add shading to the beard and to the mustache pieces. Let the paint dry. Mix 3 parts white and 1 part brown with water, until it is an ink consistency. Use this mixture to add the details to the beard and the mustache pieces.

If you have painted the glue areas, sand the paint off where the pieces join. Glue the mustache pieces in place. Fold and glue the felt hat piece into a cone shape. Let the glue dry. Cut a small piece of batting and roll it into a ball. Glue it onto the top of the hat. Glue the hat onto Santa's head. Glue the remaining length of batting around the bottom of the hat. Clip off any excess. Glue the piece of holly onto the hat (or cut 3 holly leafs from the green felt and use with the pom-poms to make a holly design). Bend the wire to form the eyeglasses, using the pattern as a guide. Attach the glasses with a small amount of glue.

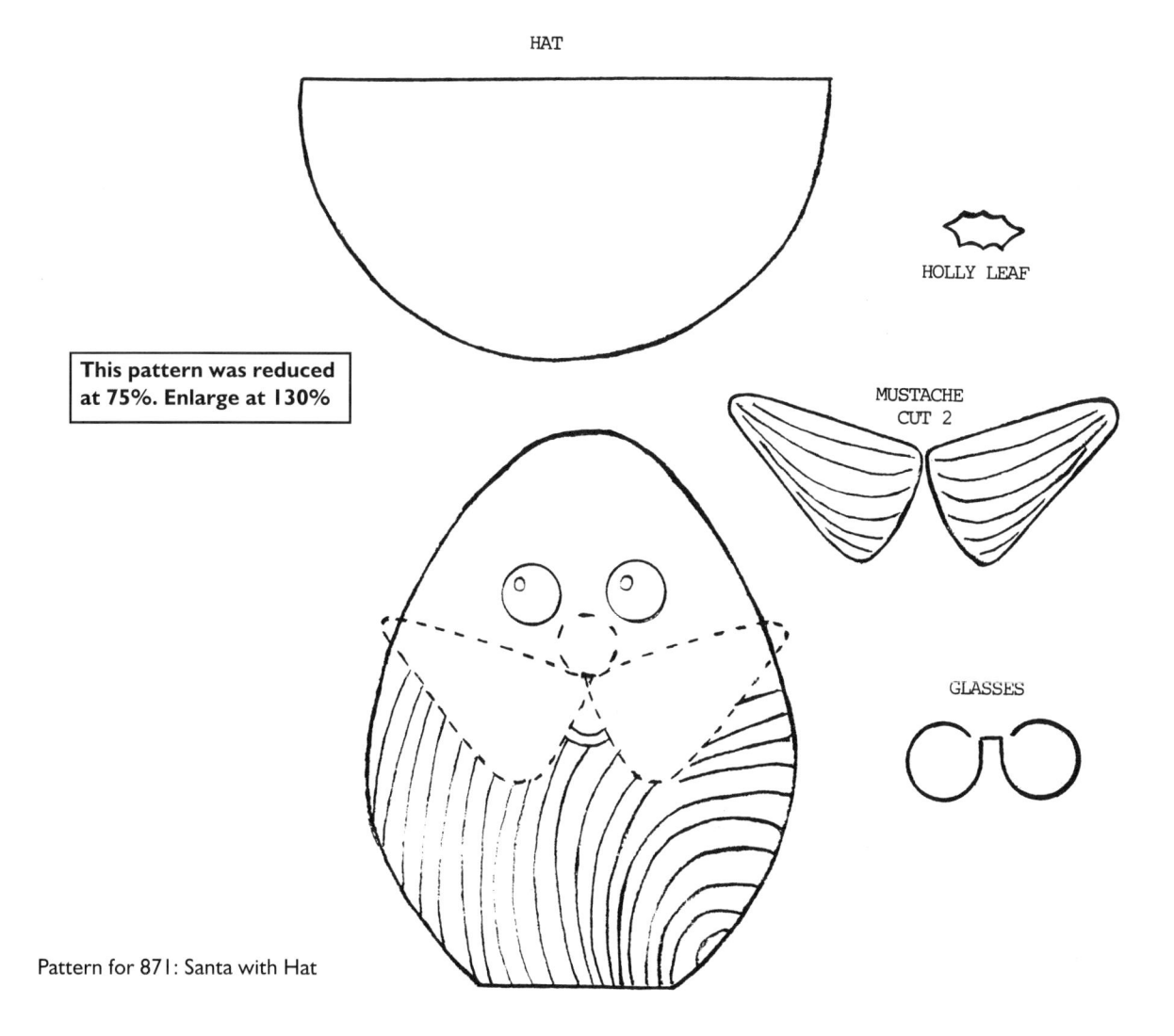

HAT

HOLLY LEAF

MUSTACHE
CUT 2

This pattern was reduced at 75%. Enlarge at 130%

GLASSES

Pattern for 871: Santa with Hat

PATTERN 872:
SNOWMAN WITH SCARF

SUPPLIES

3 ¼" x 4 ¼" Pine, 1 ½" thick
2 ½" x 3" Basswood, 1/8" thick
2" of 5/16" wood dowel
2 ½" of 20-gauge wire
1 ½" x 3" scrap of fabric
1 cotton ball
Wood glue
Black paint pen (fine-tip)

ACRYLIC PAINTS

White
Black
Orange
Light green
Green

INSTRUCTIONS

Duplicate the pattern on a copier machine or with tracing paper. Transfer the body outline onto the 1 ½" thick wood. Transfer the scarf outline onto the 1/8" thick wood. Cut out the shapes with a scroll saw. Using a pencil sharpener, sharpen one end of the dowel to form the pointed nose. Cut off the sharpened end to approximately ¾ of an inch in length. Sand all surfaces with 100-grid and then 150-grid sandpaper. Remove the sanding dust with a tack cloth.

Paint the nose orange. Base-coat the scarf light green, continuing the color around the edges. Base-coat the body white, continuing the color around the edges and onto the back. Let the paint dry. Sand lightly to remove the "fuzz" raised by the paints. Remove the sanding dust with a tack cloth. Touch-up the paint if necessary. Shade the scarf with a green wash (3 parts green mixed with 1 part water). Let the paint dry.

Transfer the pattern details onto the body and the scarf. Paint the eyes, mouth and buttons with black. Dilute green paint with water to an ink consistency. Using a small detail brush, paint the plaid design on the scarf. Let the paint dry. Add a small white highlight to each eye using the tip of a round toothpick. With the black paint pen, add the details to the scarf.

Transfer 2 earmuff patterns onto the fabric. Cut the fabric earmuff circles out. Sew a running stitch around each circle, 1/8" in from the edge. Cut the cotton ball in half. Roll each half into a ball. Place one ball in the middle of each earmuff circle. Pull the thread to tighten it around the cotton ball. Stitch the circles closed and flatten the bottoms. Bend the wire over the top of the snowman's head to shape it.

If you have painted the glue areas, sand the paint off where the pieces will join. Glue one of the earmuff pieces on each side of the snowman's head, placing them over the wire ends to form the earmuffs. Glue the nose and scarf in place.

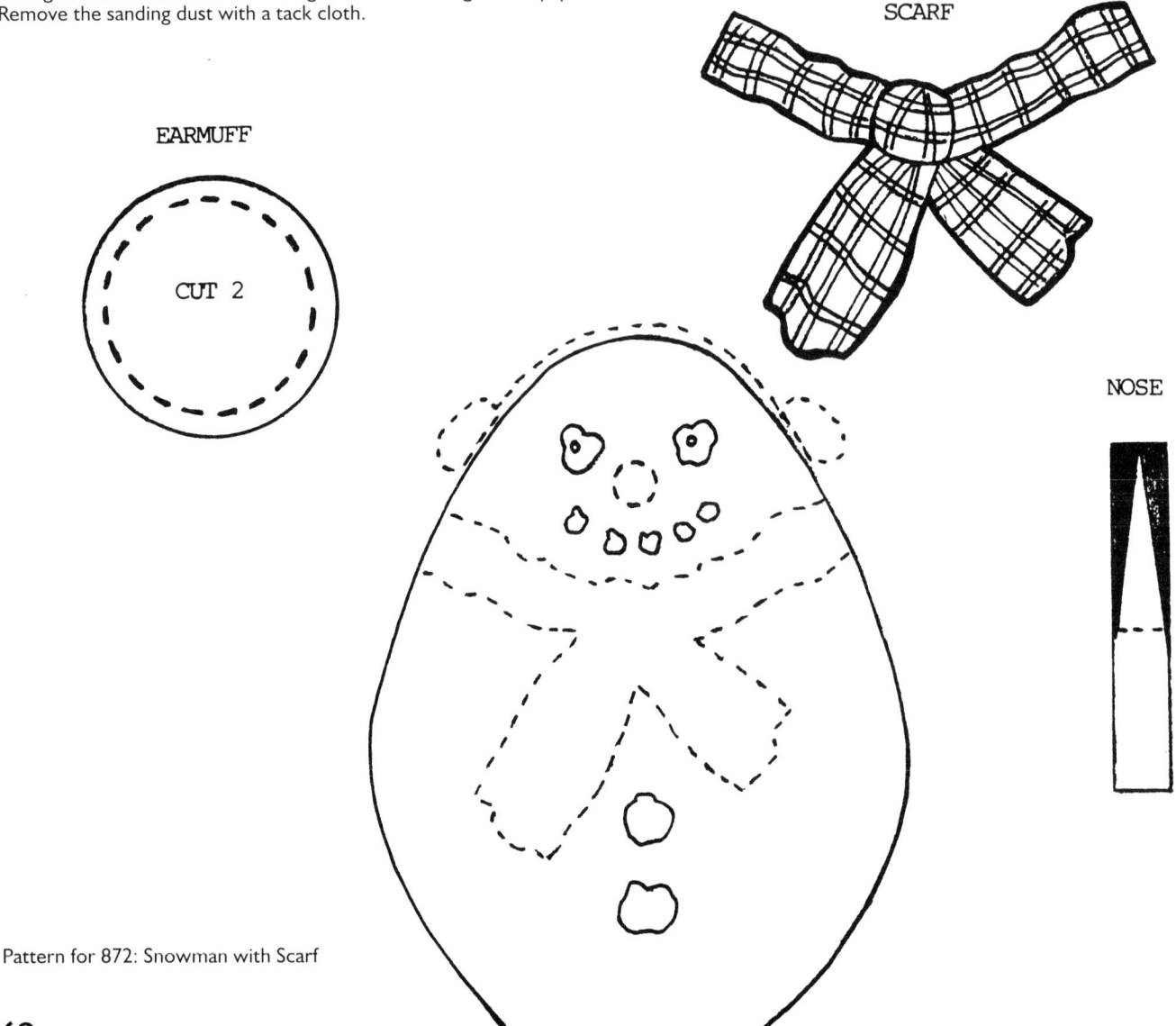

EARMUFF — CUT 2

SCARF

NOSE

Pattern for 872: Snowman with Scarf

Pattern 873:
REINDEER

SUPPLIES

3 ¼" x 4 ¼" Pine, ¾" thick
4" x 6" Pine, ¼" thick
4" x 5" piece of fabric
Wood glue

ACRYLIC PAINTS

Beige
Brown
Black
White

INSTRUCTIONS

Duplicate the pattern on a copier machine or with tracing paper. Transfer the head pattern onto the 3/4" thick wood. Transfer the patterns for the nose, muzzle and antlers onto the 1/4" thick wood. Cut out all of the shapes. Drill the holes as shown on the pattern. Sand all surfaces with 100-grid and then 150-grid sandpaper. Remove the sanding dust with a tack cloth.

Base-coat the nose black, continuing the color around the edges. Paint the antlers beige, continuing the color around the edges and onto the back. Paint the head and muzzle with a brown wash (3 parts brown to 1 part water), continuing the color around the edges and onto the back of each piece. Let the paint dry. Sand lightly to remove the "fuzz" raised by the paints. Remove the sanding dust with a tack cloth. Touch-up the paint if necessary.

Transfer the pattern details onto the pieces, as they are needed. Paint on the white ovals for the eyes. Paint the white highlight on the nose. With black, add the detail line to the muzzle and paint the mouth. Dot on the black whiskers using a paintbrush handle. Let the paint dry. Paint on the brown for the eyes. Let the paint dry. Dot on the black eye pupils using the eraser end of a pencil. Let the paint dry. Add a white highlight to each eye using a paintbrush handle.

Transfer 4 ear patterns onto the fabric. Cut the ear pieces out. Place 2 ear pieces right sides together. Sew a 1/8" seam around the edge leaving the opening as shown on the pattern. Turn the ear right side out. Sew and turn the second ear in the same manner. Tuck and glue one ear into each ear hole.

If you have painted the glue areas, sand the paint off where the pieces join. Glue the nose in place on the muzzle. Glue the muzzle onto the head. Let the glue dry. Glue the antlers onto the back of the head. Let the glue dry.

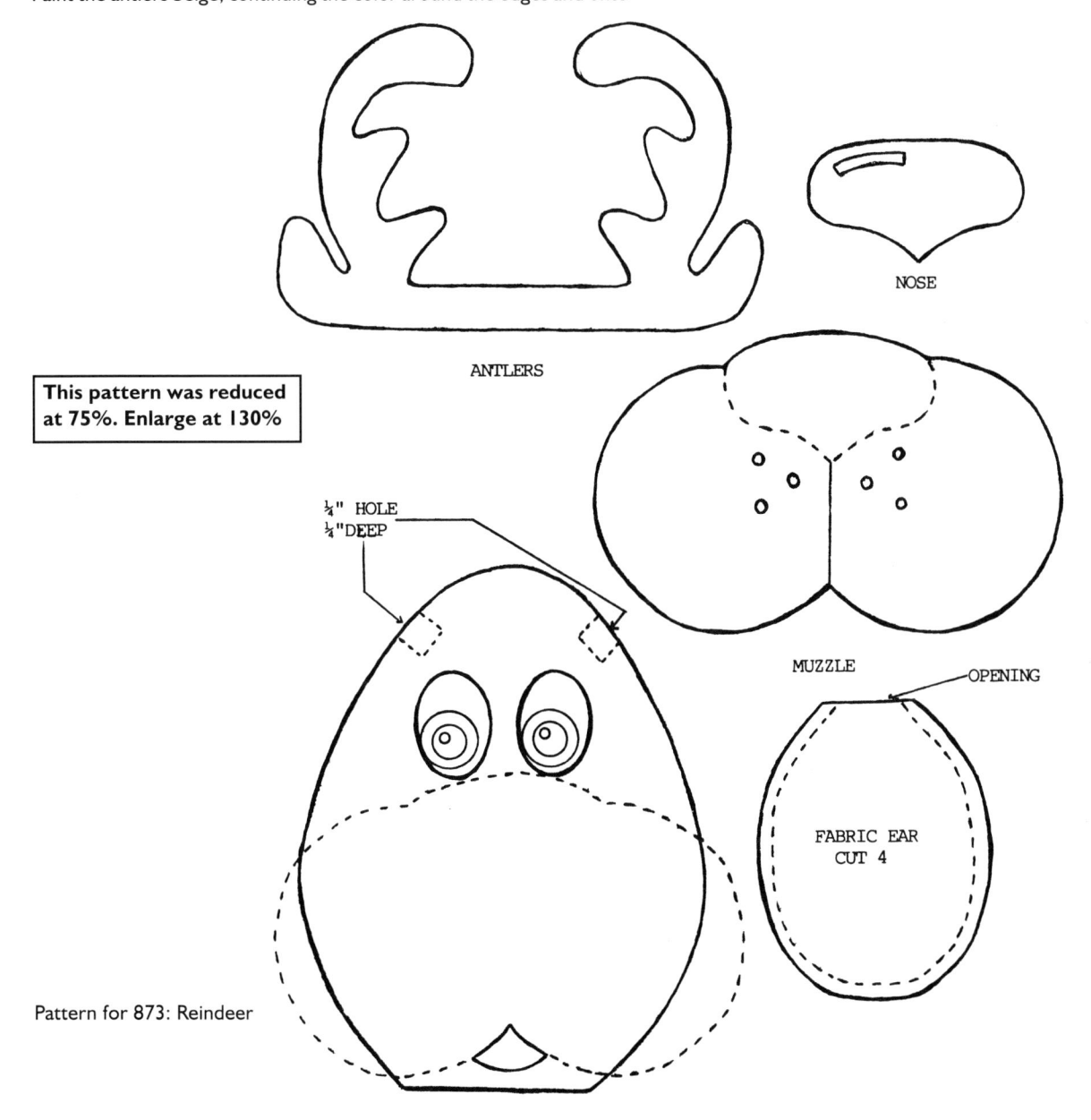

ANTLERS

NOSE

MUZZLE

OPENING

FABRIC EAR
CUT 4

This pattern was reduced at 75%. Enlarge at 130%

¼" HOLE
¼" DEEP

Pattern for 873: Reindeer

PATTERN 874:
HOLIDAY TREE

SUPPLIES

3 ¼" x 4 ¼" Pine, 1 ½" thick
1 1/8" x 2" Pine, ½" thick
1 ¼" x 1 ¼" Pine, ¼" thick
1 ¼" of ¼" dowel
Varnish (semi-gloss finish)
4 ½" of 20-gauge wire
Sea sponge
Wood glue

ACRYLIC PAINTS

Black
Green
Yellow

INSTRUCTIONS

Duplicate the pattern on a copier machine or with tracing paper. Transfer the tree pattern onto the 1 ½" thick wood. Transfer the star pattern onto the ¼" thick wood. Cut out the shapes with a scroll saw. Cut the base from the ½" thick wood. Drill all holes where shown on pattern. Sand all surfaces with 100-grid and then 150-grid sandpaper. Remove the sanding dust with a tack cloth.

Paint the star yellow, continuing the color around the edges and onto the back. Varnish the dowel. Varnish the base, continuing the varnish around the edges and onto the bottom. Base-coat all surfaces of the tree yellow. Let the paint and varnish dry. Sand the pieces lightly to remove the "fuzz" raised by the paint and varnish. Remove the sanding dust with a tack cloth. Touch-up paint if necessary.

Sponge paint all surfaces of the tree with green (be sure to leave some of the base-coat showing through). Apply a second coat of varnish to the base. Let the paint and varnish dry. Mix green with a small amount of black. Sponge this mixture onto all surfaces of the tree to add a shading effect. Let the paint dry.

Transfer the pattern details onto both sides of the tree. With a brush handle, apply the small yellow dot lines onto the front and back of the tree. Continue the dots around the sides to connect each of the front and back line of dots together. Let the paint dry. Add the large yellow ornament dots using the eraser end of a pencil. Let the paint dry.

Dip one end of the wood dowel into glue and push it into the hole in the base. Dip the other end into the glue and push it into the bottom of the tree. Make sure the tree is straight. Let the glue dry. Wrap the wire piece around a small paintbrush handle six or seven times. Dip one end of the wire into glue and push it into the star. Dip the other end into the glue and push it into the hole on the top of the tree. Adjust the wire, bending slightly.

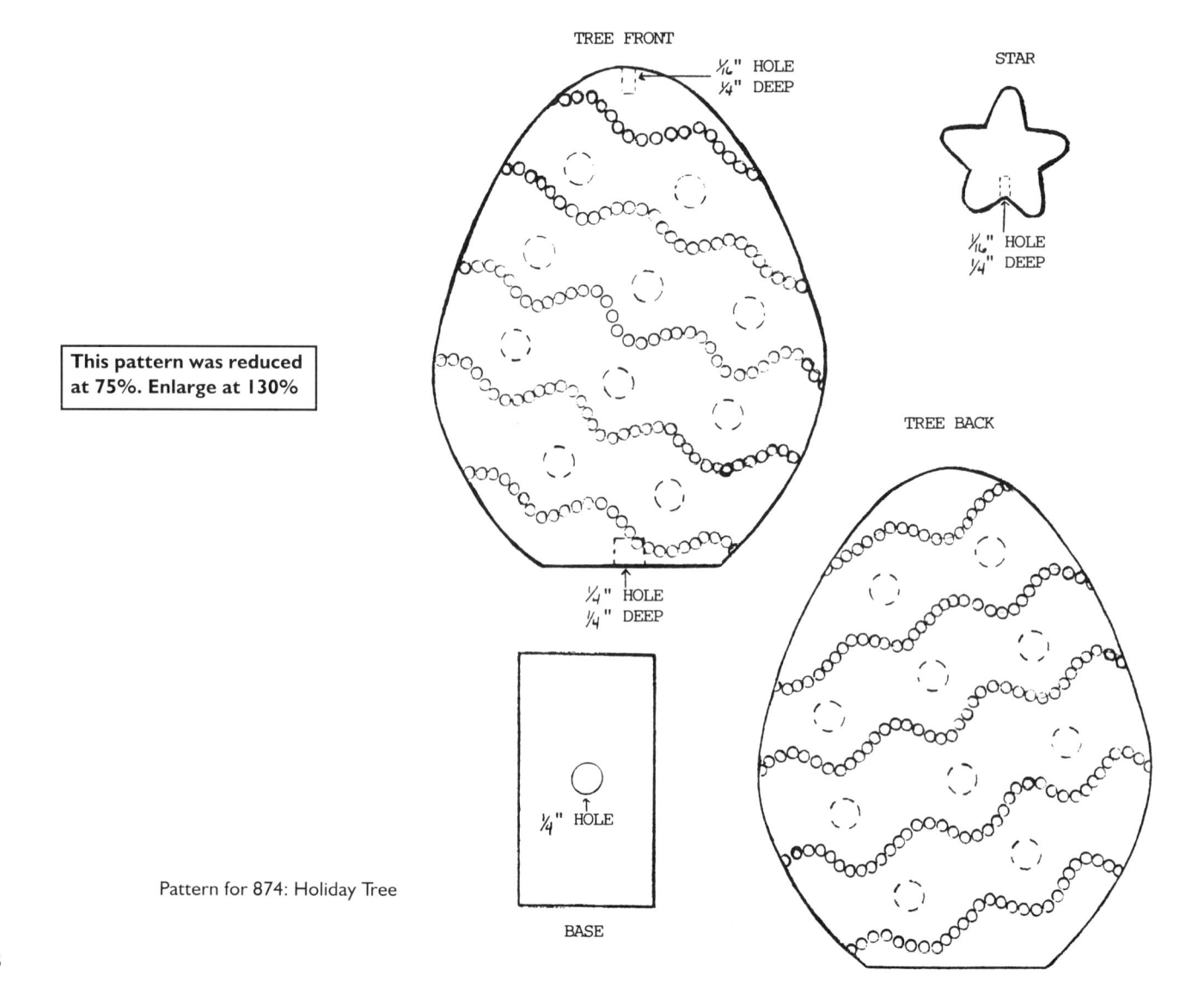

This pattern was reduced at 75%. Enlarge at 130%

Pattern for 874: Holiday Tree

PATTERN 875:
HOLIDAY TURKEY

SUPPLIES

3 ¼" x 4 ¼" Pine, 1 ½" thick for body
6" x 6" Pine, ¼" thick for tail
1 ½" x 2" Pine, ¼" thick for feet
2" of 5/16" Wood dowel
1 ¼" x 2" Red felt
Wood glue

ACRYLIC PAINTS

White
Brown
Black
Orange

INSTRUCTIONS

Duplicate the pattern on a copier machine or with tracing paper. Transfer the body pattern onto the 1 ½" thick wood. Transfer the tail pattern, including the feather separation lines, onto the larger piece of ¼" thick wood. Transfer the pattern for the feet onto the smaller piece of ¼" thick wood. Cut the shapes out with a scroll saw. Cut in along each of the pattern lines that form the feather separations on the tail and back the blade out. Make the beak by sharpening one end of the wood dowel with a pencil sharpener. Round the tip slightly. Cut the sharpened end off to approximately ¾ of an inch in length. Sand all surfaces with 100-grid and then 150-grid sandpaper. Remove the sanding dust with a tack cloth.

The front and back of the tail are painted the same. Transfer the main pattern lines onto the tail. Paint the outer stripe of the tail orange, continue the color around the edges, and then paint the outer stripe on the back. Paint the beak orange. Paint the feet orange, continuing the color around the edges. Mix equal parts of orange and brown together. Use this mixture to paint the inner stripe on both sides of the tail and to base-coat all surfaces of the body shape. Paint the middle circle on both sides of the tail brown. Let the paint dry. Sand the pieces lightly to remove the "fuzz" raised by the paint and varnish. Remove the sanding dust with a tack cloth. Touch-up paint if necessary.

Add a transparent brown wash over the orange tail stripe to mute the color. Let the paint dry. Paint thin white stripes, on both sides of the tail, near the edge and in-between the wide stripes, as shown on the color picture.

Transfer the pattern details onto the body shape. Dot on the white for the eyes with the eraser end of a pencil. Let the paint dry. Add the black dot for each eye pupil with a paintbrush handle. Let the paint dry. Dot a white highlight on each eye using the tip of a round toothpick.

If you have painted the glue areas, sand the paint off where the pieces join. Glue the feet, tail and beak in place. Let the glue dry. Transfer the wattle pattern onto the red felt. Cut the wattle out and glue it onto the beak.

This pattern was reduced at 75%. Enlarge at 130%

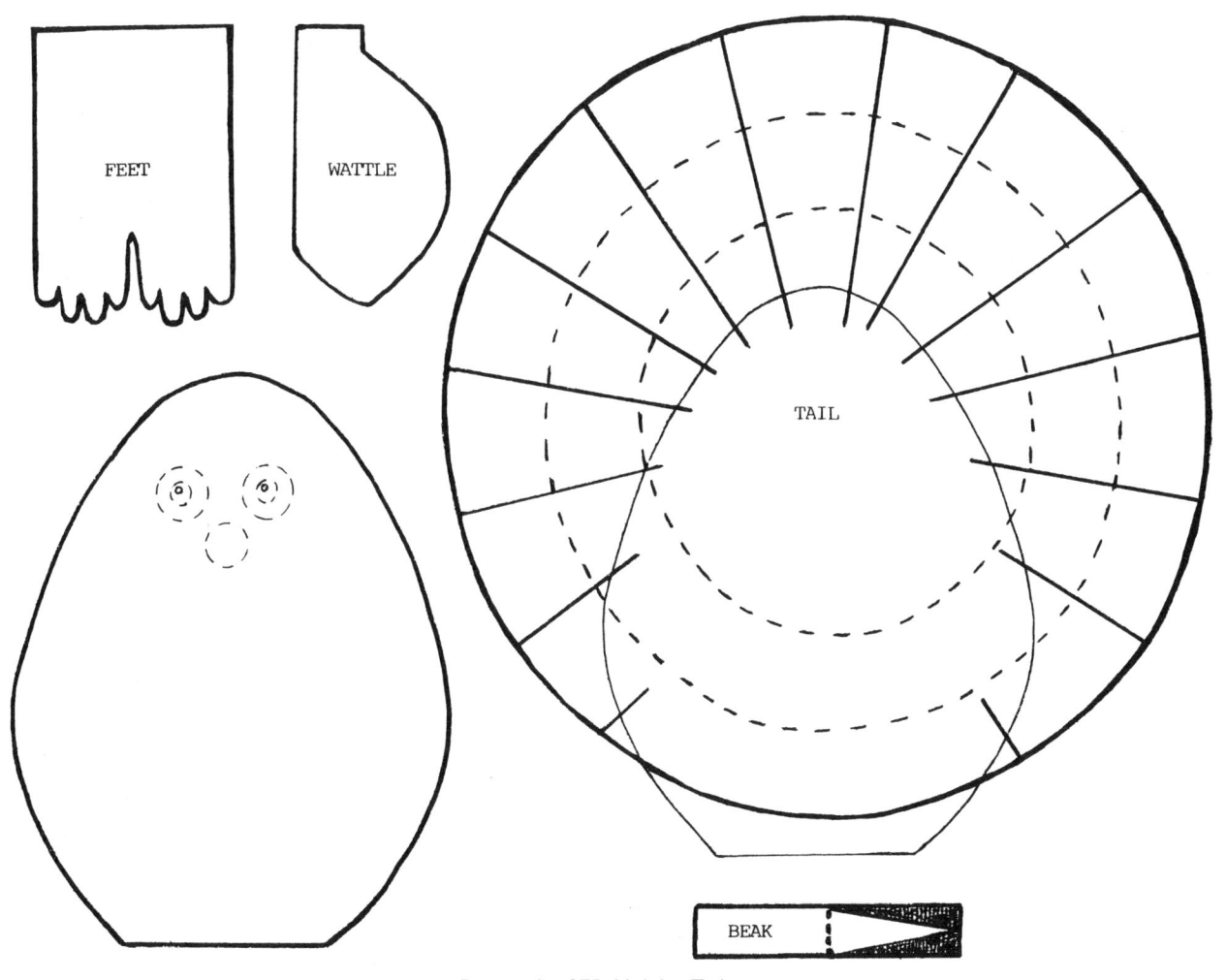

FEET

WATTLE

TAIL

BEAK

Pattern for 875: Holiday Turkey

PATTERN 876:
HOLIDAY EAGLE

SUPPLIES

3 ¼" x 4 ¼" Pine, 1 ½" thick
4" x 6 ½" Pine, ¼" thick
Black paint pen (fine-tip)
Wood glue
6 – ¼" White stick-on stars (optional)

ACRYLIC PAINTS

Blue
Orange
Brown
White
Red

INSTRUCTIONS

Duplicate the pattern on a copier machine or with tracing paper. Transfer the body pattern onto the 1 ½" thick wood. Transfer 2 wing patterns, including the feather separation lines, onto the ¼" thick wood. Transfer the star, feet and beak patterns onto the same piece of wood. Cut out the shapes with a scroll saw. Cut in along each of the pattern lines that form the feather separations on the wings and back the blade out. Sand all surfaces with 100-grid and then 150-grid sandpaper. Remove the sanding dust with a tack cloth.

Transfer the main pattern lines onto the shapes. Paint the blue on the front of each wing; continuing the color around the edges. Paint the back of both wings blue. Paint the blue on the front of the star. Paint the white for the top of the eagle's body, continuing the color around the edges and onto the back. Paint on the brown for the bottom of the eagle's body, continuing the color around the edges and onto the back. Paint the edges of the star brown. Paint the feet and the beak pieces orange, continuing the color around the edges. Let the paint dry. Sand the pieces lightly to remove the "fuzz" raised by the paint. Remove the sanding dust with a tack cloth. Touch-up paint if necessary.

Transfer the pattern details onto the shapes. Paint the red stripes on the wings and the star. Let the paint dry. Paint the white stripes on the wings and the star. With the handle of a paintbrush, make the small white dots on the blue area of the star. Paint the back beak area on the body orange. Let the paint dry. With the black paint pen, draw the oval outlines for the eyes and add the detail to the back beak area. Dot on the black eye pupils using a large paintbrush handle. Let the paint dry. Add a white highlight to each eye using a small paintbrush handle. Glue the white stars in place on the wings, OR paint them on using the following directions.

To paint the stars on the wings, put a drop of white paint in the spot where you want the center of the star, then pull the paint out from the center of the dot, with the tip of a round toothpick, to form each point. Try a few practice stars on scrap wood before doing your good ones on the wings.

If you have painted the glue areas, sand the paint off where the pieces join. Glue the beak, feet and star in place. Let the glue dry. Glue the wings onto the back of the body.

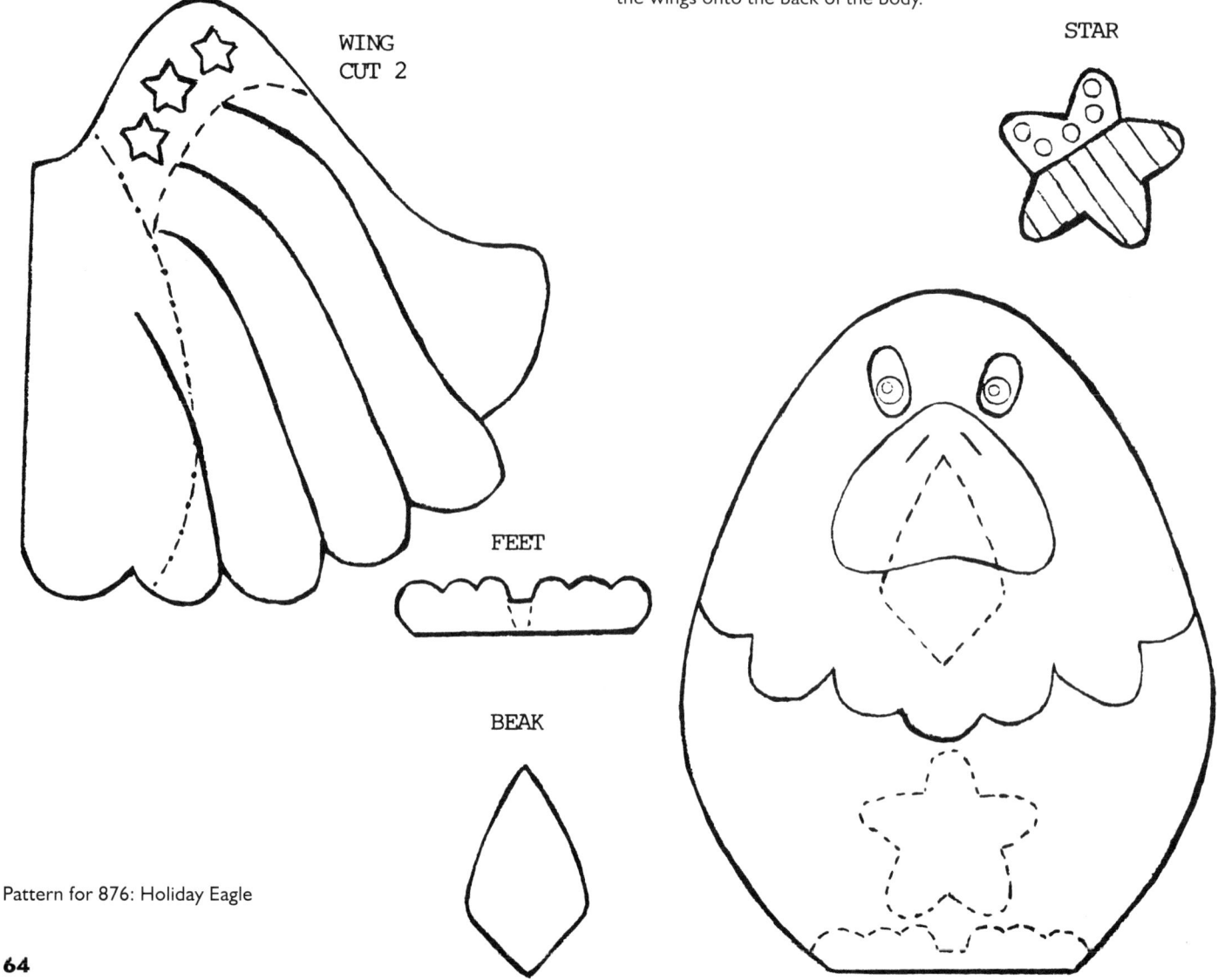

WING
CUT 2

STAR

FEET

BEAK

Pattern for 876: Holiday Eagle

PATTERN 877:
THREE BEARS

SUPPLIES

10" x 4 ½" Pine, ¾" thick
3" x 7" Pine, ¼" thick
1" x 2 ½" Pine, 1/16" thick
3" of 20-gauge wire
9" of lace ½" wide
12" of ribbon ½" wide
Black paint pen (fine tip)
Wood glue

ACRYLIC PAINTS

White
Black
Red
Rose
Orange
Yellow
Brown
Beige
Blue

INSTRUCTIONS

Duplicate the patterns on a copier machine or with tracing paper. Transfer a body pattern for each bear onto the ¾" thick wood. Transfer three muzzles, three right ear and three left ear patterns onto the ¼" thick wood. Transfer three nose patterns onto the 1/16" thick wood. With a scroll saw, cut out the shapes. Drill the holes where shown on the patterns. Sand all surfaces with 100-grid and then 150-grid sandpaper. Remove the sanding dust with a tack cloth.

Base-coat the muzzles beige, continuing the color around the edges. Base-coat the inner ear area on the front of each ear beige. Base-coat the noses black, continuing the color around the edges. Let the paint dry.

Transfer the main pattern lines onto the bodies. Paint the following base-coat colors on the front, around the edges and onto the back of the shapes. Base-coat the bear heads brown. Base-coat the ears brown. Base-coat the father's shirt white. Base-coat the baby's shirt white. Base-coat the mother's dress rose. Base-coat the baby's overalls blue. Let the paint dry. Sand lightly to remove the "fuzz" raised by the paints. Remove the sanding dust with a tack cloth. Touch-up paint if necessary.

Transfer the pattern details onto the shapes, as they are needed. Paint the eyes white. Paint a white highlight on each nose. Paint the red for the mouths. Paint the brown lines on the inner ears. Let the paint dry. Paint the black dot for each eye pupil using the eraser end of a pencil. Let the paint dry. With the black paint pen add the details on the mouths, the muzzles, and the ears and the eyelashes on the mother bear. With a paintbrush handle, add a small white highlight to each eye. Paint the father's tie yellow. Shade the tie using an orange wash. Paint the red stripes on the baby's shirt. With a paintbrush handle, dot the red flowers onto the mother's dress. Let the paint dry. Paint the orange stripes on the father's tie. Glue the lace on for the mother's dress collar. Using the black paint pen, add the details on the father's shirt and tie and on baby's shirt and overalls. Dot white buttons on the baby's overalls using a paintbrush handle.

If you have painted the glue areas, sand the paint off where the pieces join. Glue a nose on each muzzle. Glue a muzzle on each bear. Cut the wire into 6 – ½" pieces. Dip one end of a wire into the wood glue and push it into the bottom of an ear. Run a line of glue along the bottom edge of the ear. Dip the other end of the wire into the wood glue and push it into the bear's head. Repeat until all 6 ears are attached. Let the glue dry. Tie the ½" wide ribbon around the mother's right ears and make a bow.

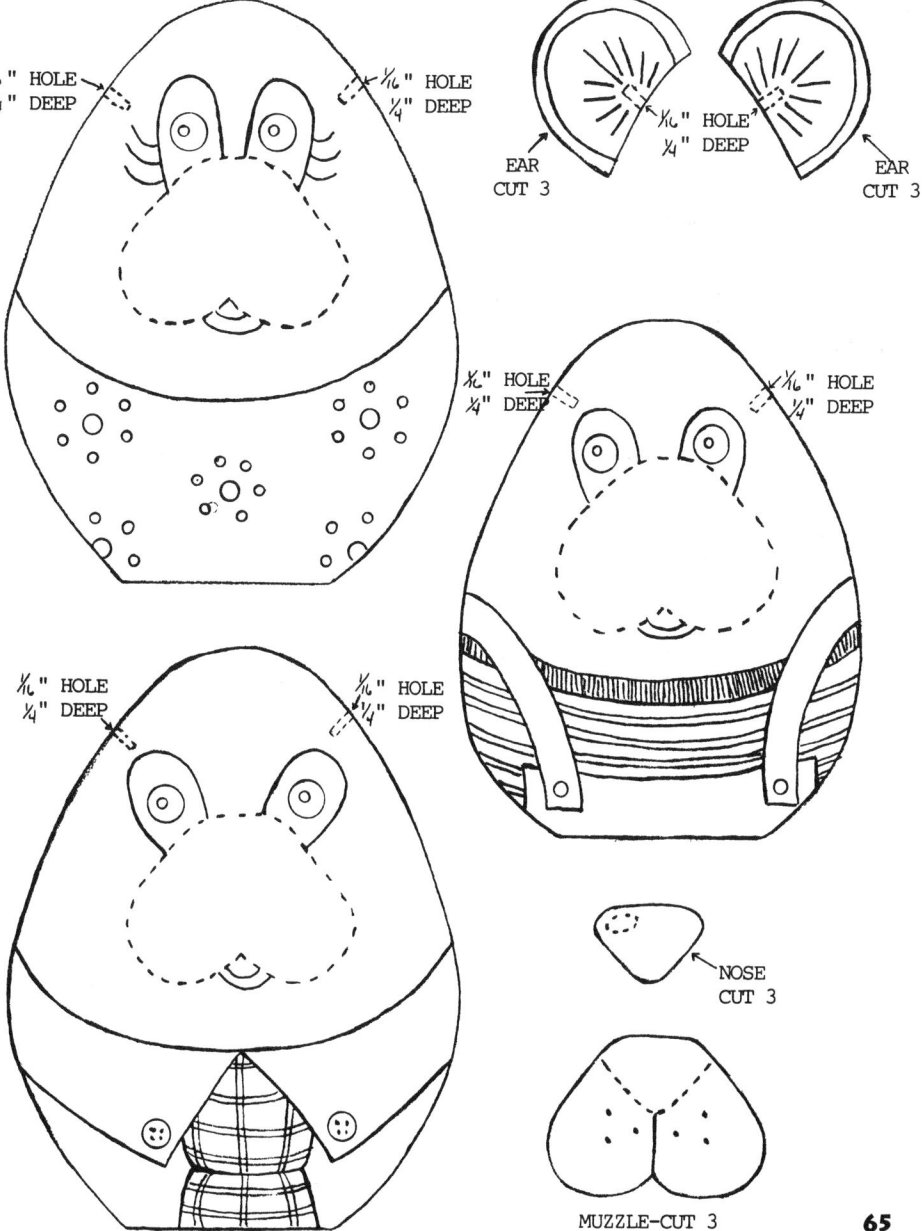

This pattern was reduced at 75%. Enlarge at 130%.

Pattern for 877: Three Bears

PATTERN 878:
GOLDIE

SUPPLIES

3 ¼" x 3 ¾" Pine, ¾" thick
2" x 2" Pine, 1/8" thick
5" of ¼" Wide Ribbon
Wood glue
Black paint pen (extra-fine tip)

ACRYLIC PAINTS

Blue
Light blue
Light brown
Brown
Light Yellow
Red
White
Green
Black
Flesh

INSTRUCTIONS

Duplicate the pattern on a copier machine or with tracing paper. Transfer the body pattern onto the ¾" thick wood. Transfer arm patterns onto the 1/8" thick wood. With a scroll saw, cut out the shapes. Sand all surfaces with 100-grid and then 150-grid sandpaper. Remove the sanding dust with a tack cloth.

Transfer the main pattern lines onto the bodies. Paint the face and hands flesh, continuing the color around the edges of the hands. Base-coat the dress light blue, continuing the color around the edges and onto the back. Base-coat the sleeves light blue, continuing the color around the edges. Let the paint dry. Base-coat the hair light yellow, continuing the color around the edges and onto the back. Let the paint dry. Sand lightly to remove the "fuzz" raised by the paints. Remove the sanding dust with a tack cloth. Touch-up paint if necessary.

Mix light yellow with a small amount of brown and add enough water to form a wash. Use this mixture to add shading to the hair. Let the paint dry.

Transfer the pattern details onto the shapes, as they are needed. Paint the white for the eyes. Add the white dots for the dress collar using a paintbrush handle. Let the paint dry. Dot on green for the eyes with a paintbrush handle. Shade the dress and sleeves with a blue wash. Let the paint dry. Paint the blue stripes on the dress and sleeves. Add the black dots for the nose and eye pupils using a small paintbrush handle. Paint the hair curls using light brown. Draw on the mouth with the black paint pen. Blush the cheeks with red. Paint the teddy bear's shape with light brown. Add shading to the teddy bear using a brown wash. Let the paint dry. Add the white dots for the teddy bear's eyes using a small paintbrush handle. Add a white highlight to each of Goldie's eyes using the tip of a round toothpick. With the black paint pen, add the details to the dress, sleeves and the teddy bear.

Tie the ¼" wide ribbon into a bow and glue it in place (as shown on the color picture). If you have painted the glue areas, sand the paint off where the pieces join. Glue the arms in place.

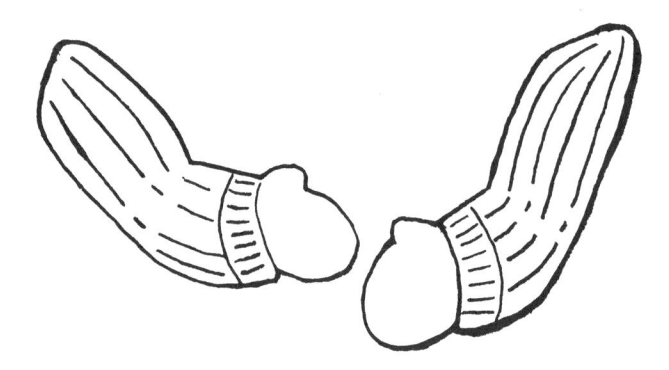

Pattern for 878: Goldie

PATTERN 880:
BOY BUNNY WITH SUCKER

SUPPLIES
4 ½" x 8" Pine, ¾" thick
2" x 3" Basswood, ¼" thick
Black paint pen (extra-fine tip)
Wood glue
Sucker

ACRYLIC PAINTS
Gray
Charcoal Gray
Pink
Rose
White
Blue
Black
Light Green

INSTRUCTIONS
Duplicate the pattern on a copier machine or with tracing paper. Transfer the body outline onto the ¾" thick wood. Transfer the arm and floppy-ear outlines onto the ¼" thick wood. Cut out the shapes with a scroll saw. Drill the hole where shown on the pattern (the size is determined by the diameter of the sucker stick). Sand all surfaces with 100-grid and then 150-grid sandpaper. Remove the sanding dust with a tack cloth.

Transfer the main pattern lines onto the body. Base-coat the gray areas on the body piece, continuing the color around the edges and onto the back. Base-coat the arm piece and the floppy-ear piece gray, continuing the color around the edges and onto the back (only in the areas where they will stick out from the body). Let the paint dry. Base-coat the overalls blue, continuing the color around the edges and onto the back. Let the paint dry. Sand the pieces lightly to remove the "fuzz" raised by the paints. Remove the sanding dust with a tack cloth. Touch-up the paint if necessary.

Shade the gray areas on the body, the arm piece and the floppy-ear piece with charcoal gray. Mix blue with a small amount of black. Use this mixture to shade the overall. Let the paint dry.

Transfer the pattern details onto the pieces. Base-coat the nose and inner ears pink. Let the paint dry. Shade the nose and inner ears with rose and then highlight them with white. Base-coat the eyes and teeth white. Paint the buttons on the overalls and the center dot of the flower on the pocket white using the handle of a paintbrush. Paint the flower petal dots pink using a smaller paintbrush handle. Paint the light green design on the pocket. Let the paint dry. Mix equal parts of blue and white together. Use this mixture to paint the iris for each eye using the eraser end of a pencil. Let the paint dry. Paint the eye pupils black with a paintbrush handle. Let the paint dry. Paint a white highlight on each eye with the handle of a small paintbrush. Add the remaining details with the black paint pen.

If you have painted the glue areas, sand the paint off where the pieces join. Glue the floppy-ear piece and the arm piece in place on the bunny. Push the sucker stick into the drilled hole in the arm.

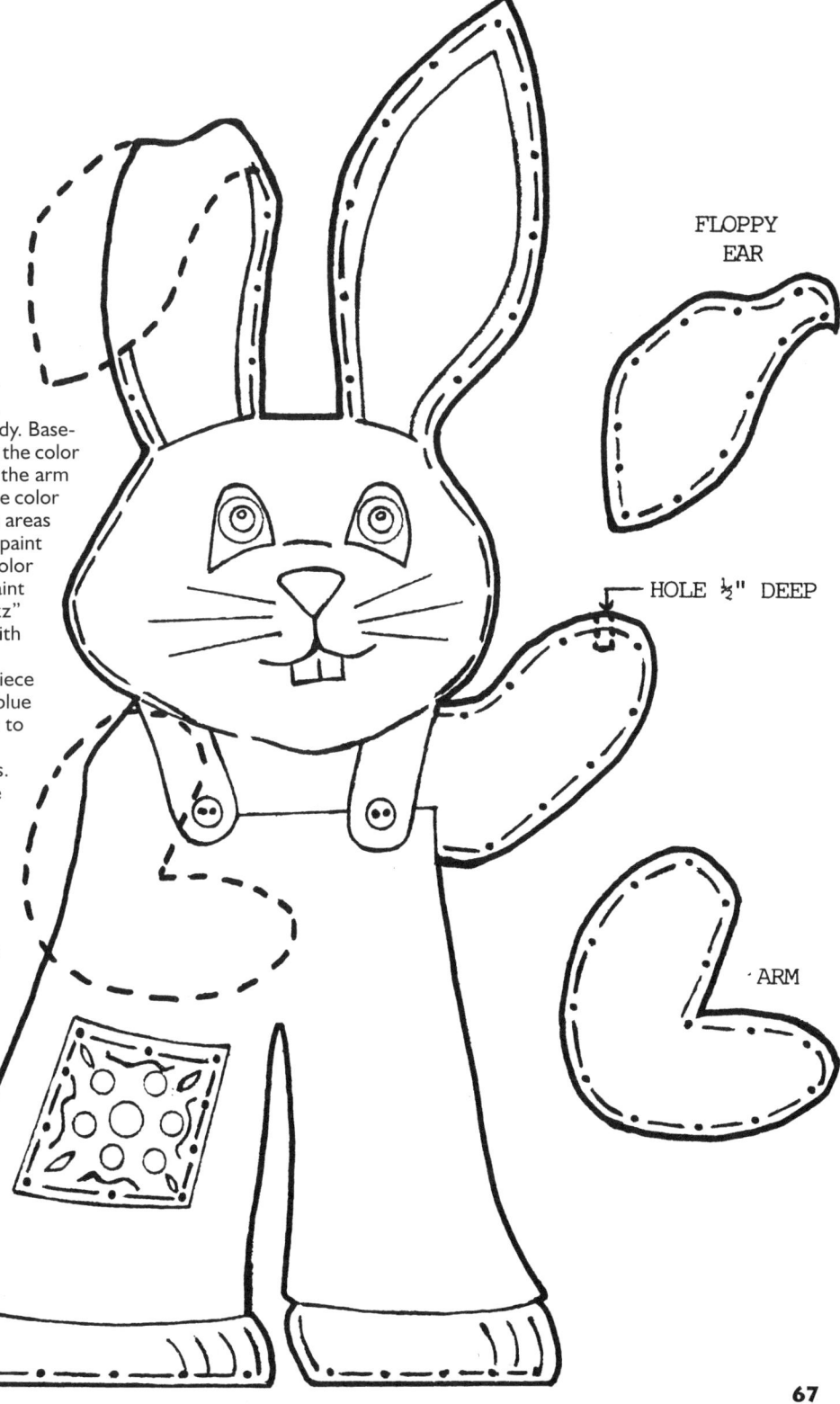

Pattern for 880: Boy Bunny with Sucker

FLOPPY EAR

HOLE ½" DEEP

ARM

PATTERN 881:
GIRL BUNNY WITH BALLOON

SUPPLIES

4 ½" x 8" Pine, ¾" thick
2" x 5" Basswood, ¼" thick
Black paint pen (extra-fine tip)
Wood glue
5" of 20-gauge wire

ACRYLIC PAINTS

Beige
Pink
Rose
White
Blue
Light Blue
Black
Light Green
Brown

INSTRUCTIONS

Duplicate the pattern on a copier machine or with tracing paper. Transfer the body outline onto the ¾" thick wood. Transfer the arm, balloon and floppy-ear outlines onto the ¼" thick wood. Cut out the shapes with a scroll saw. Drill the hole where shown on the pattern. Sand all surfaces with 100-grid and then 150-grid sandpaper. Remove the sanding dust with a tack cloth.

Transfer the main pattern lines onto the body and the arm piece. Base-coat the blouse and belt areas on the body white, continuing the color around the edges and onto the back. Base-coat the sleeve area on the arm piece white, continuing the color around the edges and onto the back (only in the area where it will stick out from the body). Let the paint dry. Base-coat the beige areas on the body, continuing the color around the edges and onto the back. Base-coat the arm piece and floppy-ear piece beige, continuing the color around the edges and onto the back (only in the areas where they will stick out from the body). Let the paint dry. Base-coat the jumper blue, continuing the color around the edges and onto the back. Base-coat the balloon light blue, continuing the color around the edges and onto the back. Let the paint dry. Sand the pieces lightly to remove the "fuzz" raised by the paints. Remove the sanding dust with a tack cloth. Touch-up the paint if necessary.

Shade the beige areas on the body, the arm piece and the floppy-ear piece with brown. Mix blue with a small amount of black and use to shade the jumper. Mix light blue with a small amount of black and use to shade the balloon. Mix light blue with a small amount of white and use to highlight the balloon. Let the paint dry.

Transfer the pattern details onto the pieces. Base-coat the nose and inner ears pink. Let the paint dry. Shade the nose and inner ears with rose and then highlight them with white. Base-coat the eyes and teeth white. Paint the buttons on the jumper and the center dot of the flower on the pocket white using the handle of a paintbrush. Paint the flower petal dots pink using a smaller paintbrush handle. Paint the light green design on the pocket. Let the paint dry. Paint the iris for each eye light blue using the eraser end of a pencil. Let the paint dry. Paint the eye pupils black with a paintbrush handle. Let the paint dry. Paint a white highlight on each eye with the handle of a small paintbrush. Add the remaining details to the pieces with the black paint pen.

If you have painted the glue areas, sand the paint off where the pieces join. Glue the floppy-ear piece and the arm piece in place. Wrap one end of the wire tightly around the balloon stem, twisting it together in the back. Dip the other end of the wire into glue and push it into the drilled hole in the arm.

ARM

1/16" HOLE 1/2" DEEP

FLOPPY EAR

BALLOON

Pattern for 881: Girl Bunny with Balloon

69

PATTERN 886:
IRISH SHAMROCK HEART

SUPPLIES

6 ½" x 5" Pine, ¾" thick
Black paint pen (medium tip)
Wood glue
Wood filler
Varnish (semi-gloss finish)

ACRYLIC PAINTS

Green
Light Green
Red

INSTRUCTIONS

Duplicate the pattern on a copier machine or with tracing paper. Transfer the main pattern lines onto the wood. Cut out the shamrock shape with a scroll saw. Cut out the inside shamrock shape along the pattern line. Separate the two pieces.

The middle heart is cut out using the piercing technique. Drill the blade-threading (pierce) hole, where shown on the pattern. Using the smallest blade recommended for the wood thickness, thread the blade through the hole and attach it to the saw. Slowly cut all the way around the heart pattern line until the blade is back to the pierce hole. Turn the saw off, remove the blade and separate the pieces. Fill the drill hole in the heart with wood filler and let the filler dry. Sand the front, face edges of the pieces with 100-grid sandpaper until they are well-rounded. It isn't necessary to sand the inside edges where the pieces will be glued back together, but sand all other surfaces with 100-grid and then 150-grid sandpaper. Remove the sanding dust with a tack cloth.

Paint the front and back surfaces of the heart red, allowing the paint to go slightly around the edges. Paint the front and back surfaces of the inside shamrock light green, allowing the paint to go slightly around the edges. Paint all the surfaces of the shamrock green, except for the inside glue edge. Let the paint dry. Sand the pieces lightly to remove the "fuzz" raised by the paints. Remove the sanding dust with a tack cloth. Touch-up the paints if necessary.

If you have painted the glue areas, sand the paint off where the pieces will join. Glue the shamrock and the inside shamrock back together. Wrap a rubber band around the 2 pieces to hold them tightly until the glue dries. Glue the heart back in place. Let the glue dry.

Transfer the pattern details onto the pieces. To paint the small green shamrocks: using a small paintbrush handle, paint 2 uniform green dots next to each other with their edges slightly touching. Add a third uniform dot centered on top of them (as shown in the enlarged shamrock illustration on the pattern page). With the tip of a round toothpick pull some of the paint down from the center of the shamrock to form the stem. Let the paint dry. Paint the lettering and the stitching details on with the black paint pen. Let the paint dry. Apply a thin topcoat of varnish to all surfaces. Let the varnish dry. Apply a second thin topcoat and let it dry.

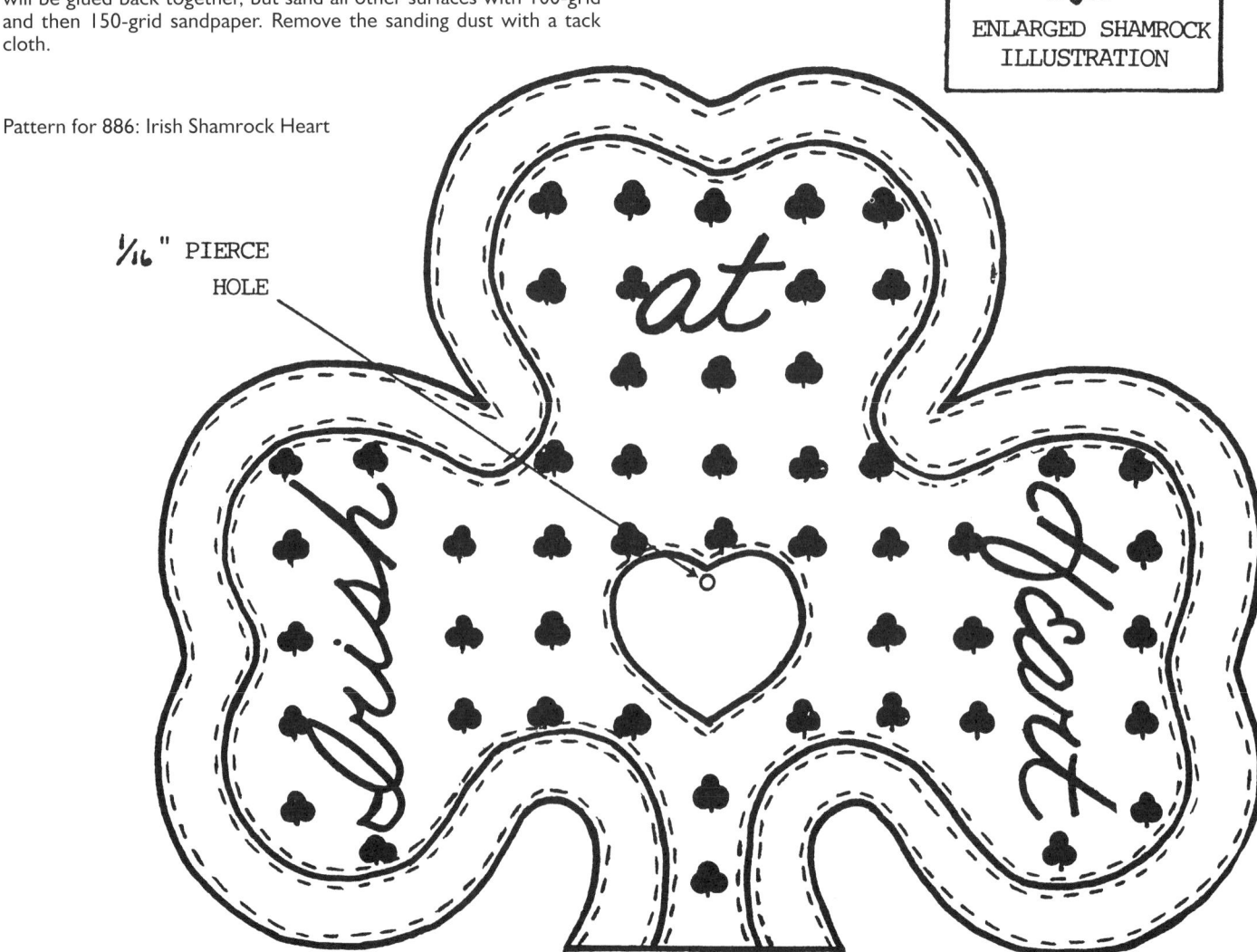

ENLARGED SHAMROCK ILLUSTRATION

Pattern for 886: Irish Shamrock Heart

1/16" PIERCE HOLE

PATTERN 887:
IRISH AT HEART BEAR

SUPPLIES

4 ¾" x 8 ½" Pine, 1 ½" thick
1 ½" x 3 ½" Pine, ¾" thick
1 ¼" x 1 ½" Basswood, ¼" thick
¾" x 1" Basswood, 1/16" thick
11/16" x 4 ¾" White paper
Black permanent marker (extra-fine tip)
Wood glue

ACRYLIC PAINTS

Light Green
Beige
Pink
Brown
Black
White

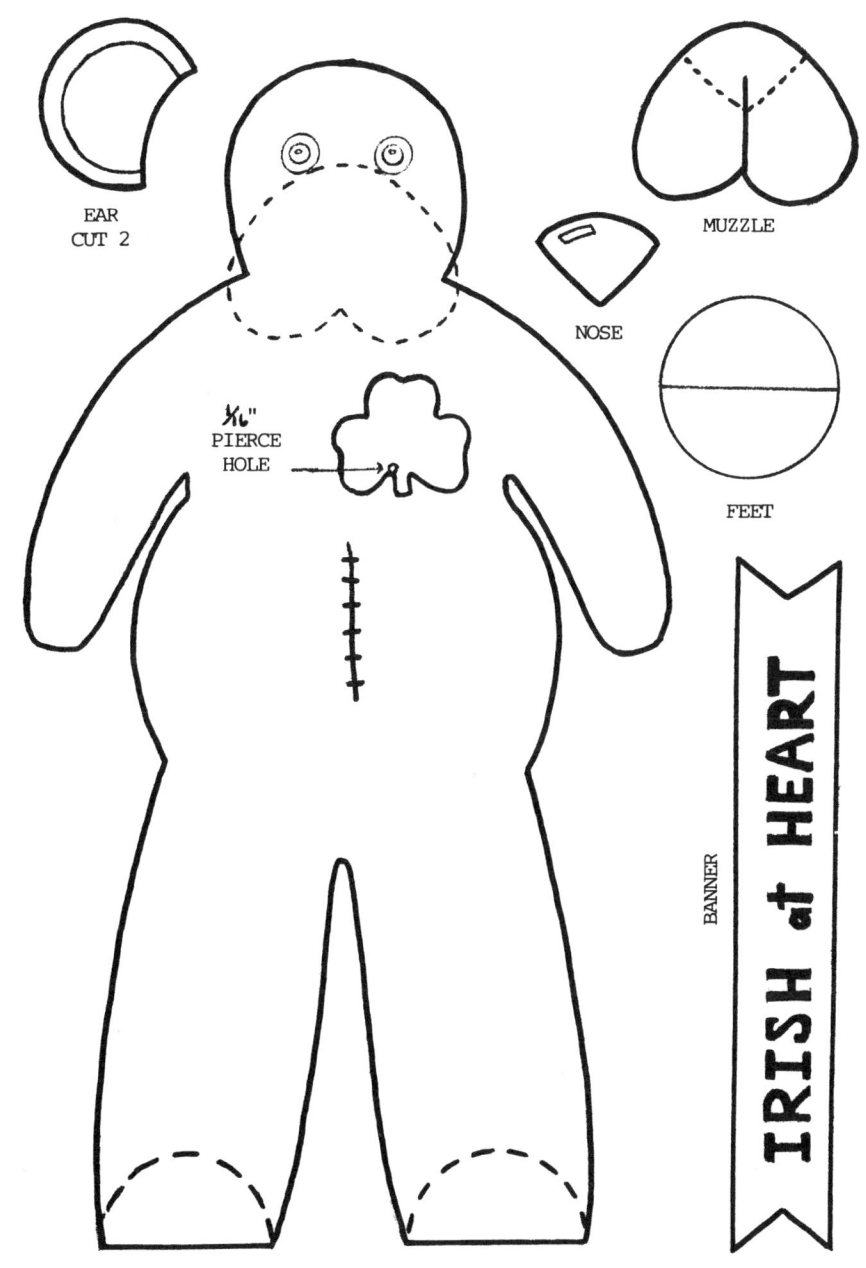

INSTRUCTIONS

Duplicate the pattern on a copier machine or with tracing paper. Transfer the body outline onto the 1 ½" thick wood. Transfer the feet circle and the 2 ear outlines onto the ¾" thick wood. Transfer the muzzle outline onto the ¼" thick wood. Transfer the nose outline onto the 1/16" thick wood. Cut out the shapes. The circle for the feet is cut out and then cut in half to make the 2 feet.

The piercing technique is used to cut out the shamrock-heart opening. Drill the blade-threading (pierce) hole, where shown on the pattern. Using the smallest blade recommended for the wood thickness, thread the blade through the hole and attach it to the saw. Slowly cut all the way around the shamrock-heart pattern line until the blade is back to the pierce hole. Remove the blade from the saw and separate the pieces. Sand all surfaces with 100-grid and then 150-grid sandpaper. Remove the sanding dust with a tack cloth.

Paint the inside edges of the shamrock-heart light green. Paint the inner ears pink. Paint the muzzle beige. Paint the nose black. Let the paint dry. Sand off any light green paint that has spilled over onto the front or back surfaces of the body. Paint the bear's body brown, continuing the color around the edges and onto the back. Paint the feet brown, continuing the color around the edges. Paint the rest of the ears brown, except for the bottom glue areas. Let the paint dry. Sand the pieces lightly to remove the "fuzz" raised by the paints. Remove the sanding dust with a tack cloth. Touch-up the paint if necessary. Mix 3 parts brown with 1 part black and use to shade the body, feet and ears. Let the paint dry.

Transfer the pattern details onto the pieces. Paint the eyes white with the eraser end of a pencil. Let the paint dry. Paint the eye pupils black with a paintbrush handle. Mix black with water until it is the consistency of ink. Use this mixture to paint the details on the muzzle, ears and tummy. Let the paint dry. Paint a white highlight on each eye with the tip of a round toothpick. Paint the white highlight on the nose. Let the paint dry. Cut the white paper to the correct size and shape and do the lettering with the black permanent marker or if you used a copier machine, you can cut the banner out and use it instead.

If you have painted the glue areas, sand the paint off where the pieces join. Glue the nose onto the muzzle. Glue the muzzle onto the bear. Glue the feet on. Glue the ears on, so that the backs of the ears are even with the back surface of the bear's body. Glue one end of the banner onto the end of each arm.

This pattern was reduced at 75%. Enlarge at 130%

Pattern for 887: Irish at Heart Bear

Pattern 888:
SITTING BEAR

SUPPLIES

4" x 4" Pine, ½" thick
1" x 1" Pine, ¼" thick
2" Wooden half-egg
Varnish
Wood Glue
Black paint pen (extra-fine tip)
Small bunch of silk flowers (optional)

ACRYLIC PAINTS

Beige
Brown
Black
White

INSTRUCTIONS

Duplicate the pattern on a copier machine or with tracing paper. Transfer the body pattern onto the ½" thick wood. Transfer the leg patterns onto the same piece of wood. Transfer the muzzle pattern onto the ¼" thick wood. Slowly and carefully cut out the shapes with a scroll saw. Sand all surfaces with 100-grid and then 150-grid sandpaper. Lightly sand the front of the wooden half-egg with 150-grid sandpaper. Remove the sanding dust with a tack cloth.

Base-coat the muzzle beige, continuing the color around the edges. Base-coat all surfaces of the legs brown. Base-coat the body brown, continuing the color around the edges and onto the back. Varnish the front of the wooden half-egg. Let the paint and varnish dry. Sand the pieces lightly to remove the "fuzz" raised by the paint. Remove the sanding dust with a tack cloth. Touch-up the paint if necessary. Apply a second coat of varnish to the wooden half-egg. Let the varnish dry.

Transfer the pattern details onto the shapes. Paint the inner ears beige. Paint the beige area on the bottom of each foot. Paint a black dot for each eye using the handle of a paintbrush. Paint the nose black. Let the paint dry. Add a white highlight to each eye using the tip of a round toothpick. Paint the white highlight on the nose. Add the stitch line detail to the wooden half-egg using the black paint pen. Add the details to the muzzle, the ears and the bottom of the feet with the black paint pen. Let the paint dry.

If you have painted the glue areas, sand the paint off where the pieces join. Glue the muzzle and the wooden half-egg in place on the bear. Let the glue dry. Glue one leg onto each side of the bear, make sure they are even and that the bear sits straight. Let the glue dry. Glue the flowers in place.

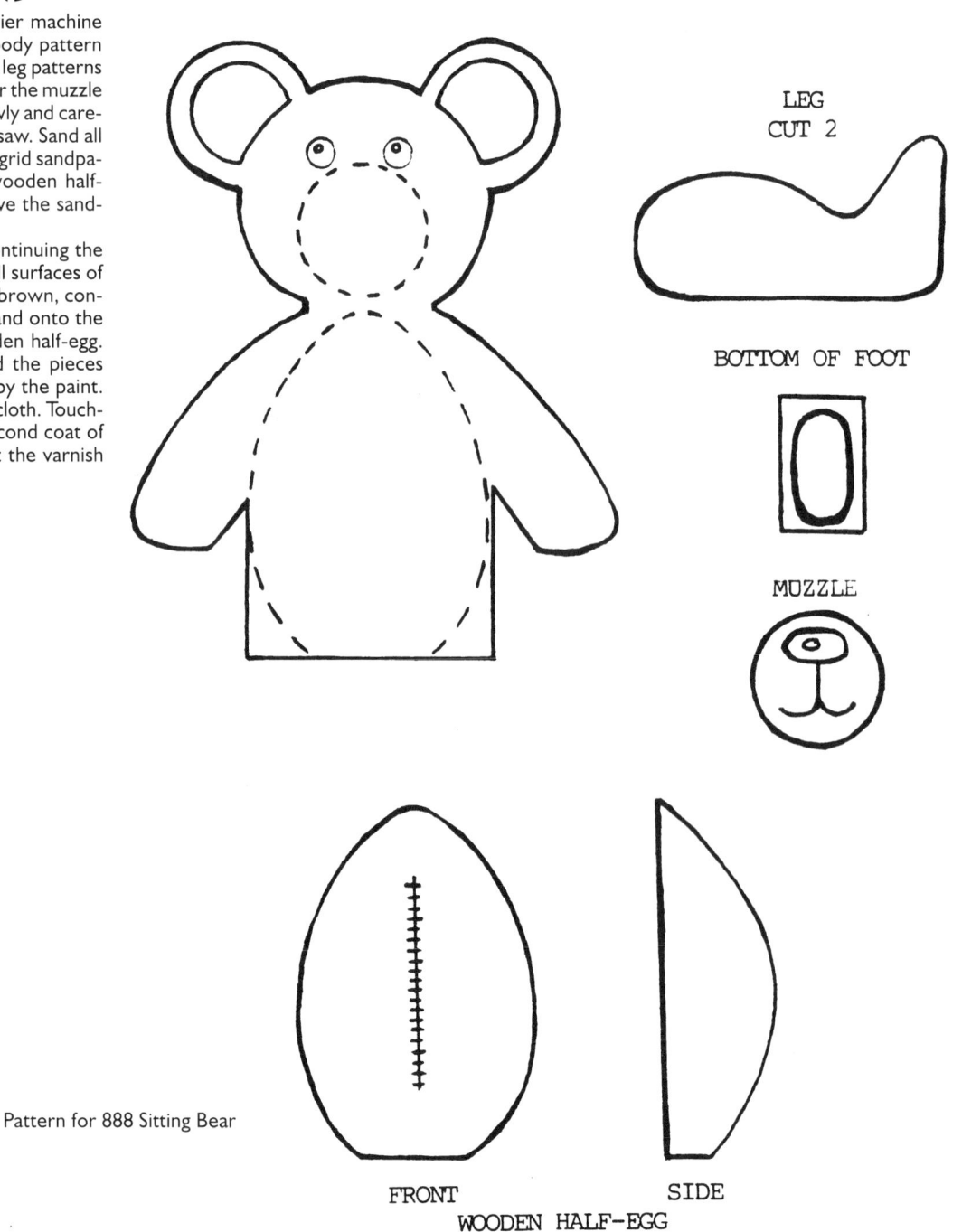

LEG
CUT 2

BOTTOM OF FOOT

MUZZLE

Pattern for 888 Sitting Bear

FRONT   SIDE
WOODEN HALF-EGG
for TUMMY

PATTERN 890:
SINGLE BOW

SUPPLIES

4" x 5" Pine, ¼" thick
Wood glue
Varnish (semi-gloss finish)
Stencil – 1/8" circle pattern (optional)

ACRYLIC PAINTS

Blue
White
Black

INSTRUCTIONS

Duplicate the pattern on a copier machine or with tracing paper. Transfer the pattern outlines onto the wood. Cut out the pieces with a scroll saw. Sand all surfaces with 100-grid and then 150-grid sandpaper. Remove the sanding dust with a tack cloth.

Base-coat the bow piece blue, continuing the color around the edges and onto the back. Base-coat the knot piece blue, continuing the color around the edges. Let the paint dry. Sand lightly to remove the "fuzz" raised by the paint. Remove the sanding dust with a tack cloth. Touch-up the paint if necessary.

Apply the white dots using the stencil OR transfer the dot placement from the pattern onto the pieces and apply the white dots with a paintbrush handle. Let the paint dry. Mix blue with a small amount of black. Use this mixture to shade the bow and knot pieces on the front and around the edges. Let the paint dry. Varnish all surfaces of the bow piece. Varnish the knot piece, continuing the varnish around the edges. Let the varnish dry. Apply a second coat of varnish and let it dry.

If you have applied finish to the glue areas, sand the finish off where the pieces join. Glue the knot onto the bow.

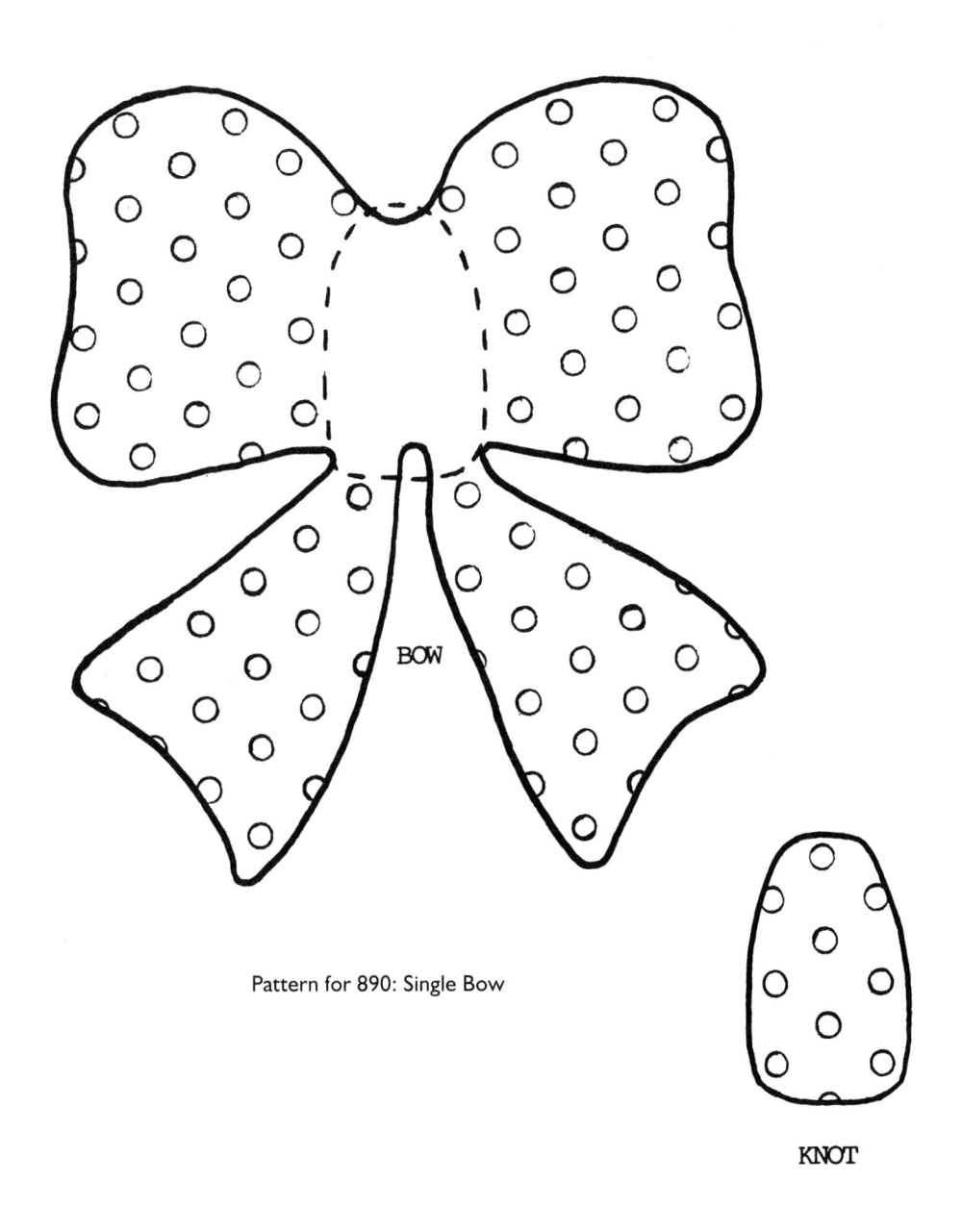

Pattern for 890: Single Bow

BOW

KNOT

Pattern 891:
DOUBLE BOW

SUPPLIES

4" x 5" Pine, ¾" thick
2" x 3" Pine, ½" thick
Wood glue
Varnish (semi-gloss finish)

ACRYLIC PAINTS

Red
Burgundy

INSTRUCTIONS

Duplicate the pattern on a copier machine or with tracing paper. Transfer the pattern outline for the bow onto the ¾" thick wood. Transfer the knot pattern onto the same piece of wood. Cut out the bow and knot pieces. Make a 45 degree angle cut in the ½" thick wood, as shown in illustration (1) on the pattern sheet. Place the 2 pieces together as shown in illustration (2) on the pattern sheet. Tape the pieces together so that they will not separate as you are sawing. Transfer the double bow pattern onto the wood. Make sure it is positioned correctly with the straight edge of the pattern toward the slanted cuts. Stack cut the workpieces with the scroll saw, using the smallest blade recommended for the combined wood thickness. Remove the tape and separate the pieces. Sand all surfaces with 100-grid and then 150-grid sandpaper. Remove the sanding dust with a tack cloth.

Base-coat the bow piece red, continuing the color around the edges and onto the back. Base-coat all surfaces of the 2 double bow pieces red, except for the slanted edge glue areas. Base-coat all surfaces of the knot piece red, except for the back glue area. Let the paint dry. Sand lightly to remove the "fuzz" raised by the paint. Remove the sanding dust with a tack cloth. Touch-up the paint if necessary.

Float burgundy shading onto all surfaces (except in the glue areas) of the bow, knot and 2 double bow pieces. Let the paint dry. Varnish the bow piece, continuing the varnish around the edges and onto the back. Varnish all surfaces of the 2 double bow pieces and the knot piece, except for the glue areas. Let the varnish dry. Apply a second coat of varnish and let it dry.

If you have applied finish to the glue areas, sand the finish off where the pieces join. Glue the knot onto the bow. Let the glue dry. Apply a line of glue along the slanted edge of each double bow piece. Set them in place on the bow, propping them up until the glue is thoroughly dry.

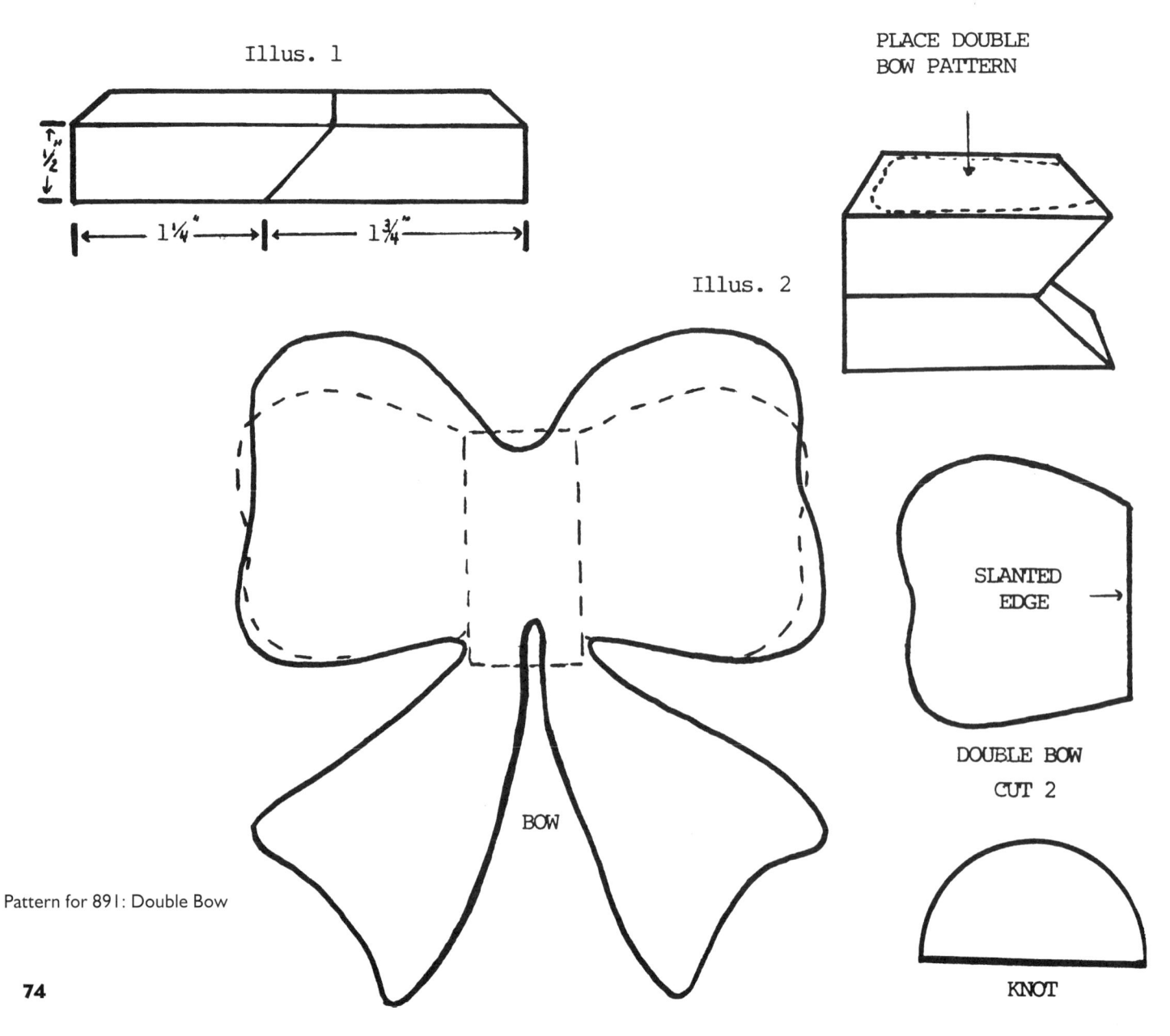

Illus. 1

Illus. 2

PLACE DOUBLE BOW PATTERN

SLANTED EDGE

DOUBLE BOW
CUT 2

BOW

KNOT

Pattern for 891: Double Bow

PATTERN 898:
BUTTERFLY WREATH

SUPPLIES

2 ½" x 3 ¾" Basswood, ¼" thick
1 ¾" of ¼" wood dowel
Grapevine Bow (approx. 7" across x 8" long)
Raffia – 8 or 9 strands
Silk flowers – Yellow
4" 20-gauge wire
Wood glue
Hot glue gun

ACRYLIC PAINTS

Orange
Yellow
Black

INSTRUCTIONS

Duplicate the pattern on a copier machine or with tracing paper. Make a 45 degree angle cut in the ¼" thick wood, as shown in illustration (1) on the pattern page. Place the 2 pieces together as shown in illustration (2) on the pattern page. Tape the pieces together so they will not separate as you are sawing. Carefully position the wing pattern on the wood with the straight edge of the pattern toward the slanted cuts. Transfer the wing outline onto the wood. Stack cut the workpieces with a scroll saw, using the smallest blade recommended for the combined wood thickness. Remove the tape and separate the pieces. Sand both ends of the wood dowel until they are well-rounded. Sand all surfaces of the wings with 100-grid and then 150-grid sandpaper. Remove the sanding dust with a tack cloth.

Transfer the main pattern lines onto the front of both wings, as shown in illustration (3) on the pattern page. Paint the edges of the wings, except for the slanted glue areas, with black. Paint the back of both wings black. Paint the wood dowel black. Let the paint dry. Paint the black areas on the front of both wings. Let the paint dry. Sand lightly to remove the "fuzz" raised by the paints. Remove the sanding dust with a tack cloth. Touch-up the paint if necessary.

Paint the orange areas on the front of the wings. Paint the yellow dots on the wings with the tip of a round toothpick. Let the paint dry.

If you have painted the glue areas, sand the paint off where the pieces join. Prop each wing up on its slanted cut edge, as shown in illustration (4) on the pattern page. Glue the wood dowel in place. It should stick out approximately ¼" on each end. Let the glue dry thoroughly.

Tie the raffia strands together into a large bow (not quite as wide as the grapevine bow). Hot glue it in place on the grapevine bow. Hot glue the silk flower onto the bow in a pleasing arrangement. Hot glue the butterfly onto the bow. Thread the wire through the back of the grapevine bow, near the center top and twist the ends together to form a hanger.

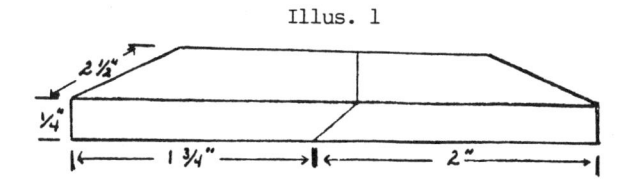

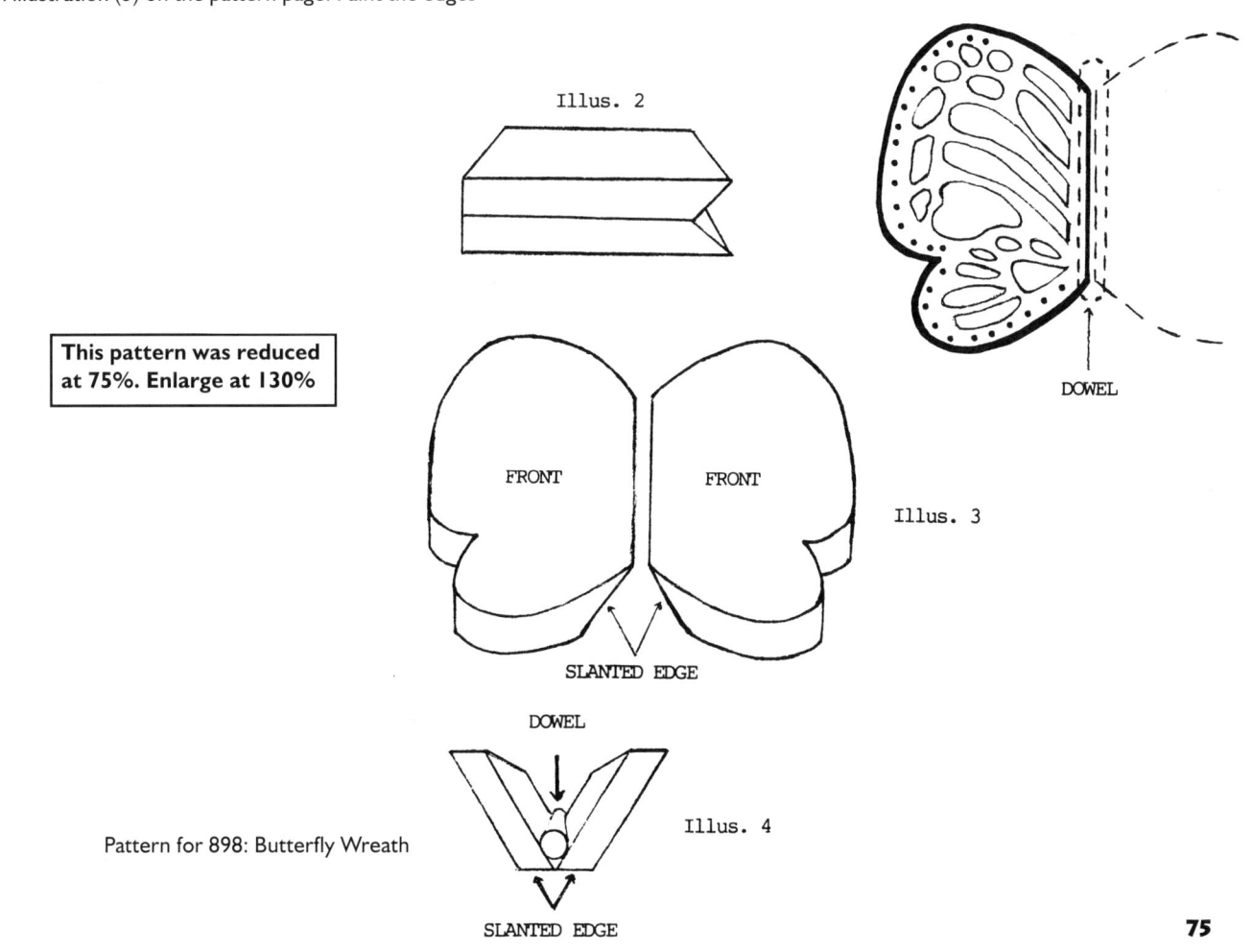

Illus. 1

Illus. 2

This pattern was reduced at 75%. Enlarge at 130%

Illus. 3

DOWEL

SLANTED EDGE

DOWEL

Illus. 4

SLANTED EDGE

Pattern for 898: Butterfly Wreath

PATTERN 899:
BUTTERFLY WALL OR LAWN ORNAMENT (3-D)

SUPPLIES

6" x 5 ¾" Pine, ¾" thick
5 ¼" of 5/16" wood dowel
Wood glue
Hanger or Wood stake
Spar varnish
Acrylic medium and varnish (optional)

OUTDOOR PAINTS

Orange
Black
White

INSTRUCTIONS

Duplicate the pattern on a copier machine or with tracing paper. Make a 45 degree angle cut in the ¾" thick wood, as shown in illustration (1) on the pattern page. Carefully position a wing pattern on each piece of wood, placing the straight edge of each pattern toward the slanted cut edge. Transfer the wing outlines onto the pieces of wood. Cut out the 2 wings. Cut in along the pattern line on each wing that defines the separation of the front and the back wings. Sand one end of the wood dowel until it is well-rounded. Sharpen the other end of the wood dowel with a pencil sharpener and then round the sharpened tip slightly with sandpaper. Sand all surfaces of the wings with 100-grid and then 150-grid sandpaper. Remove the sanding dust with a tack cloth.

Transfer the main pattern lines onto the front and back of the wings. Mix orange with enough acrylic medium and varnish or water to give it a slightly transparent finish. Paint the orange areas on the back of each wing. Let the paint dry. With the same mixture used on the back of the wings, paint the orange areas on the front of each wing. Paint the edges of the wings black. Paint the black areas on the back of both wings. Paint the wood dowel black. If you are making the lawn ornament, paint all surfaces of the wood stake black. Let the paint dry. Paint the black areas on the front of both wings. Let the paint dry. Sand lightly to remove the "fuzz" raised by the paints. Remove the sanding dust with a tack cloth. Touch-up the paint if necessary.

Paint the white dots on the front and back of each wing with a paintbrush handle. Let the paint dry. Apply a coat of spar varnish to all surfaces of the project. Let the varnish dry. Sand the pieces lightly with very fine sandpaper. Remove the sanding dust with a tack cloth. Apply a second coat of varnish and let it dry.

If you have applied finish to the glue areas, sand the finish off where the pieces join. Prop each wing up on its slanted cut edge, as shown in illustration (2) on the pattern page. Glue the wood dowel in place. It should stick out approximately ¾" on each end. Let the glue dry thoroughly. For the lawn ornament, attach the butterfly to the stake with small screws. For the wall ornament, attach the hanger onto the back of the butterfly, centered near the top.

Illus. 1

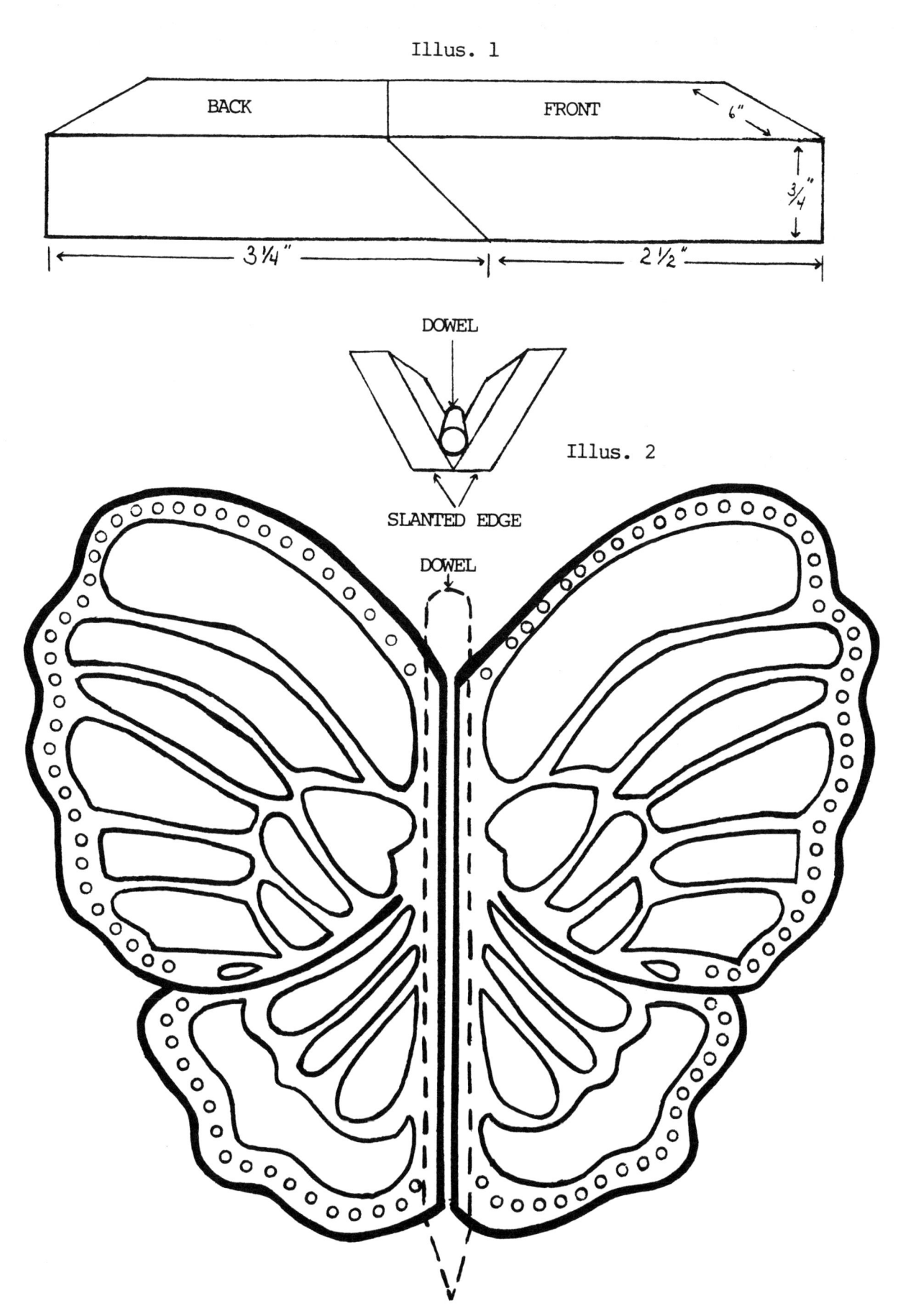

| BACK | FRONT |

6"
3/4"
3 1/4"
2 1/2"

DOWEL

Illus. 2

SLANTED EDGE

DOWEL

Pattern for 899: Butterfly Wall or Lawn Ornament (3-D)

PATTERN 900:
BUTTERFLY WALL OR LAWN ORNAMENT (FLAT)

SUPPLIES

6 ¾" x 5 ½" Pine, ¾" thick
4 ½" of 5/16" wood dowel
Wood glue
Hanger or Wood stake
Spar varnish

OUTDOOR PAINTS

Yellow
Black
Orange

INSTRUCTIONS

Duplicate the pattern on a copier machine or with tracing paper. Make a 45 degree angle cut in the ¾" thick wood, as shown in illustration (1) on the pattern page. Carefully position a wing pattern onto the **back** of each piece of wood, placing the straight edge of each pattern toward the slanted cut edge. Transfer the wing outlines onto the wood pieces. Cut out the 2 wings. Cut in along the pattern line on each wing that defines the separation of the front and the back wings. Sand one end of the wood dowel until it is well-rounded. Sharpen the other end of the wood dowel with a pencil sharpener and then round the sharpened tip slightly with sandpaper. Sand all surfaces of the wings with 100-grid and then 150-grid sandpaper. Remove the sanding dust with a tack cloth.

If you are making the lawn ornament, transfer the main pattern lines onto the front and back of the wings. Paint the yellow design areas on the back of each wing (do not paint the yellow dots that go around the wings outline). Let the paint dry. Add orange shading to the yellow design areas. Let the paint dry. Paint the edges of the wings black. Paint the black areas on the back of each wing. Paint all surfaces of the wood stake black. Let the paint dry.

If you are making the wall ornament, transfer the main pattern lines only onto the **front** of the wood pieces. Paint the edges of the wings black. Paint the back of both wings black. Let the paint dry.

The remaining painting instructions are used for either project. Paint the yellow design areas on the front of each wing (do not paint the yellow dots that go around the wings outline). Let the paint dry. Add orange shading to the yellow design areas. Let the paint dry. Paint the wood dowel black. Paint the black areas on the front of both wings. Let the paint dry. Sand lightly to remove the "fuzz" raised by the paints. Remove the sanding dust with a tack cloth. Touch-up the paint if necessary. Paint the yellow dots on with the tip of a round toothpick. Let the paint dry.

Apply a coat of spar varnish to all surfaces of the project. Let the varnish dry. Sand the pieces lightly with very fine sandpaper. Remove the sanding dust with a tack cloth. Apply a second coat of varnish and let it dry.

If you have applied finish to the glue areas, sand the finish off where the pieces join. Place the wings together, as shown in illustration (2) on the pattern page. Glue the wood dowel in place. Let the glue dry thoroughly. For the lawn ornament, attach the butterfly to the stake with small screws. For the wall ornament, attach the hanger onto the back of the butterfly, centered near the top.

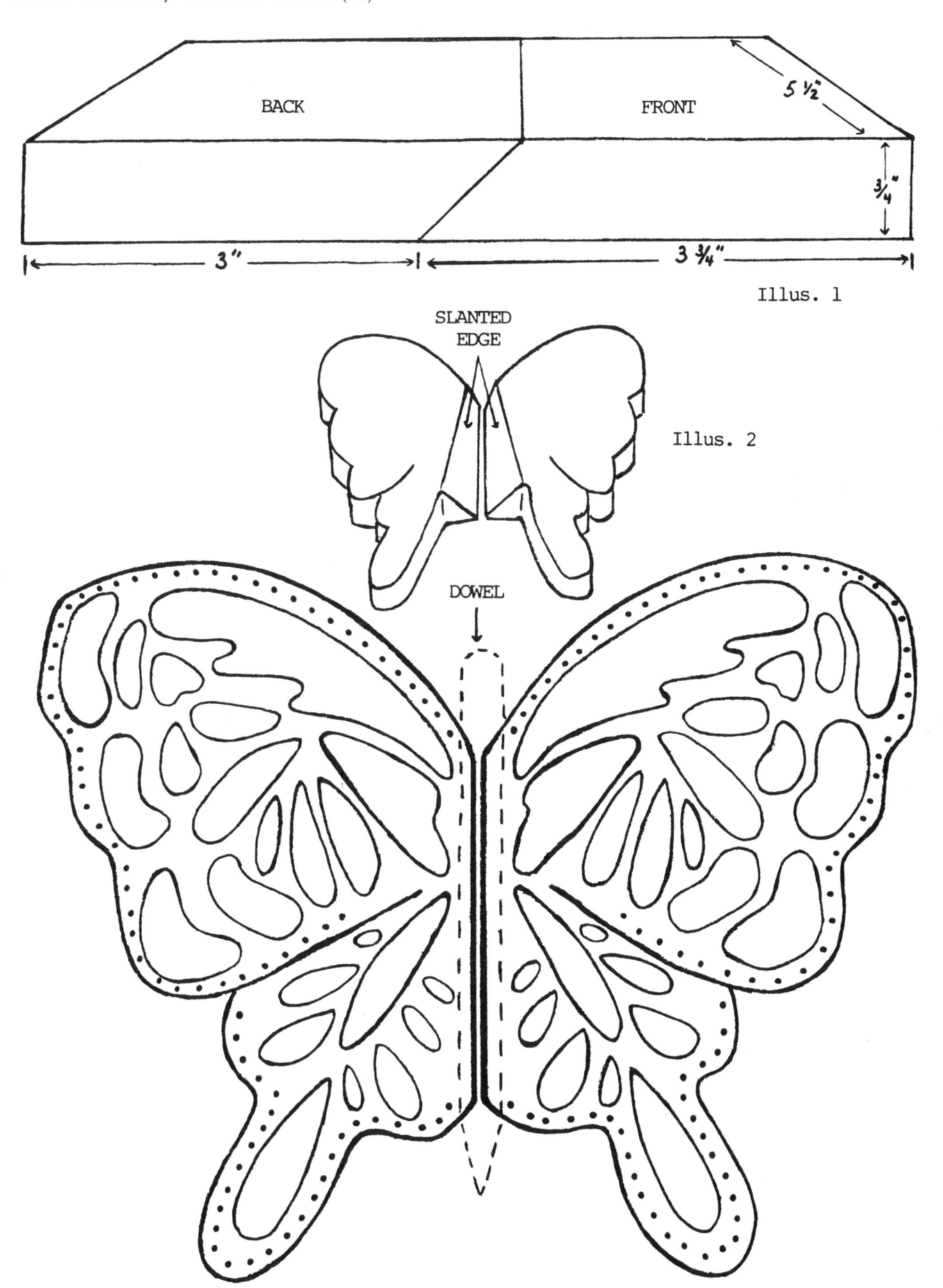

Pattern for 900: Butterfly Wall or Lawn Ornament (flat)

| BACK | FRONT |

5 ½"

¾"

3"   3 ¾"

Illus. 1

SLANTED EDGE

Illus. 2

DOWEL

79

PATTERN 901:
INNER/OUTER PUMPKIN

SUPPLIES

7 ½" x 9 ¼" Pine, ¾" thick
2" of 20-gauge wire
Brown paint pen (fine-tip)
Wood glue

ACRYLIC PAINTS

Orange
Pale Yellow
Brown
Black

INSTRUCTIONS

Duplicate the pattern on a copier machine or with tracing paper. Transfer the pumpkin pattern and the hanging nose pattern onto the wood. With scroll saw, cut along the outline of the outer pumpkin. Cut in at line "A" to the inner pumpkin pattern line. Continue cutting around, following the inner pumpkin's pattern line. (This will be one continuous cut, taking you all the way around the inner pumpkin shape and exiting back out at line "A".) Separate the two pumpkins. Cut out the hanging nose piece. Glue line "A" back together. Let the glue dry. Drill all holes where shown on the pattern. If you prefer, instead of drilling the nose hole, a 1" black circle can be painted on later. Sand all surfaces with 100-grid and then 150-grid sandpaper. Remove the sanding dust with a tack cloth.

FOR OUTER PUMPKIN

Paint the inside edges of the outer pumpkin pale yellow. Paint the edges of the hanging nose pale yellow. Let the paint dry. Paint the remaining surfaces of the pumpkin orange. Paint the front and back of the hanging nose orange. Let the paint dry. Sand lightly to remove the "fuzz" raised by the paints. Remove the sanding dust with a tack cloth. Touch-up the paint if necessary.

Curl one end of the wire piece with needle nose pliers. Insert the other end through the hole between the pumpkin's eyes. Dip the straight end of the wire into a dot of glue and push it into the hanging nose piece. Make sure the nose is straight. Let the glue dry.

FOR INNER PUMPKIN

Paint the inside edges of the inner pumpkin with pale yellow. Let the paint dry. Paint the front of the eyes black. Paint the stem brown, continuing the color around the edges and onto the back. Paint the remaining surfaces of the pumpkin orange. Let the paint dry. Sand lightly to remove the "fuzz" raised by the paints. Remove the sanding dust with a tack cloth. Touch-up the paint if necessary.

Transfer the pumpkin section lines (shown as dotted lines on the pattern) onto the pumpkin. Mix three parts orange and one part brown with enough water to form a transparent wash. Use this mixture to shade around the outline and along the section lines. Let the paint dry. Use the brown paint pen to define the section lines. If you did not drill the nose hole, paint a 1" black circle on for the nose.

Pattern for 901: Inner/Outer Pumpkin

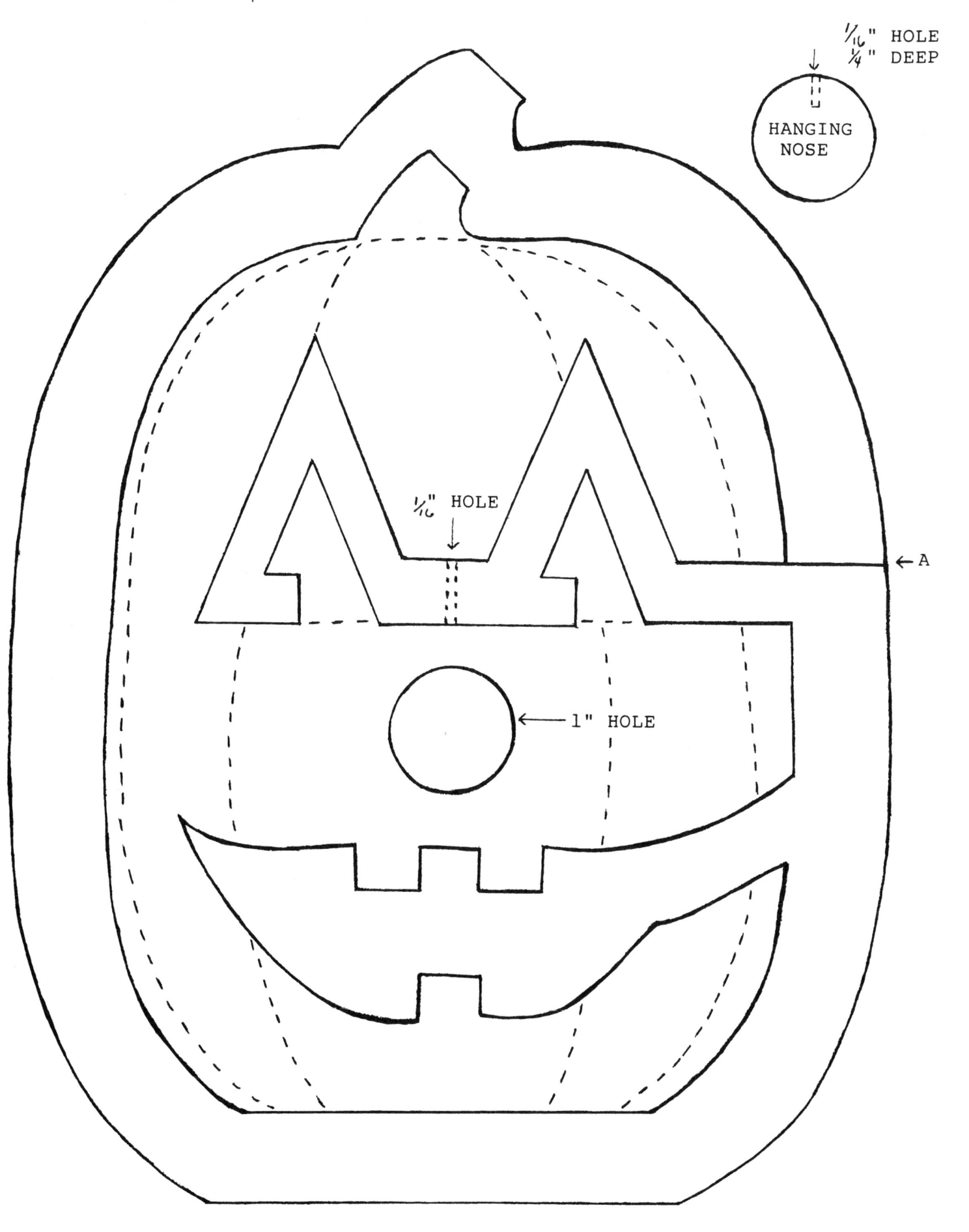

1/16" HOLE
1/4" DEEP

HANGING NOSE

1/16" HOLE

1" HOLE

← A

81

PATTERN 902:
THREE PUMPKINS

SUPPLIES

7" x 7" Pine, ¾" to 1 ½" thick…Small pumpkin
8 ½" x 7" Pine, ¾" to 1 ½" thick…Medium pumpkin
9 ¼" x 7" Pine, ¾" to 1 ½" thick…Large pumpkin
Brown paint pen (fine-tip)

ACRYLIC PAINTS

Orange
Brown
Green
Black

Notes: Using thicker wood will add stability to the puzzle. Cut slowly and carefully, using the smallest blade recommended for the wood thickness you have selected. As you are cutting, make sure the blade is not bending or your cuts will be slanted.

To increase the difficulty level in assembling the puzzle, paint the front and the back the same. To decrease the difficulty, paint the edges and back with an orange wash and only paint the details on the front.

INSTRUCTIONS

Decide which size pumpkin you want to make. Duplicate the pattern on a copier machine or with tracing paper. Transfer the main pattern lines onto the appropriate size wood. Cut out the pumpkin shape with a scroll saw. Cut along pattern line "A", all the way across the pumpkin shape. Cut line "B" up to the top point, than back the blade out. Cut line "C" up to the point to finish the left eye. Cut line "D" up to the top point, than back the blade out. Cut line "E" up to point to finish the right eye. Cut line "F" across to form the top of the mouth. Cut line "G" to finish the mouth. Cut line "H" to complete puzzle. Sand all surfaces with 100-grid and than 150-grid sandpaper. Remove the sanding dust with a tack cloth.

Base-coat the stem green, continuing the color around the edges and onto the back. Use an orange wash (approximately 3 parts orange to 1 part water) to paint all the remaining surfaces of the puzzle pieces. Let the paint dry. Sand lightly to remove the "fuzz" raised by the paints. Remove the sanding dust with a tack cloth. Touch up the paint if necessary. Paint the front of the eyes and the front of the mouth black. Let the paint dry.

Transfer the pattern details onto the pumpkin. With undiluted orange, add shading around the outline and along the section lines (shown as dotted lines on the pattern). Mix three parts orange with one part brown. Use this mixture to darken the shading around the outline and along the section lines. Let the paint dry. Use the brown paint pen to define the section lines. Paint the details on the stem with black. Paint a 7/8" black circle for the nose. Let the paint dry thoroughly before assembling the puzzle or the pieces will stick together.

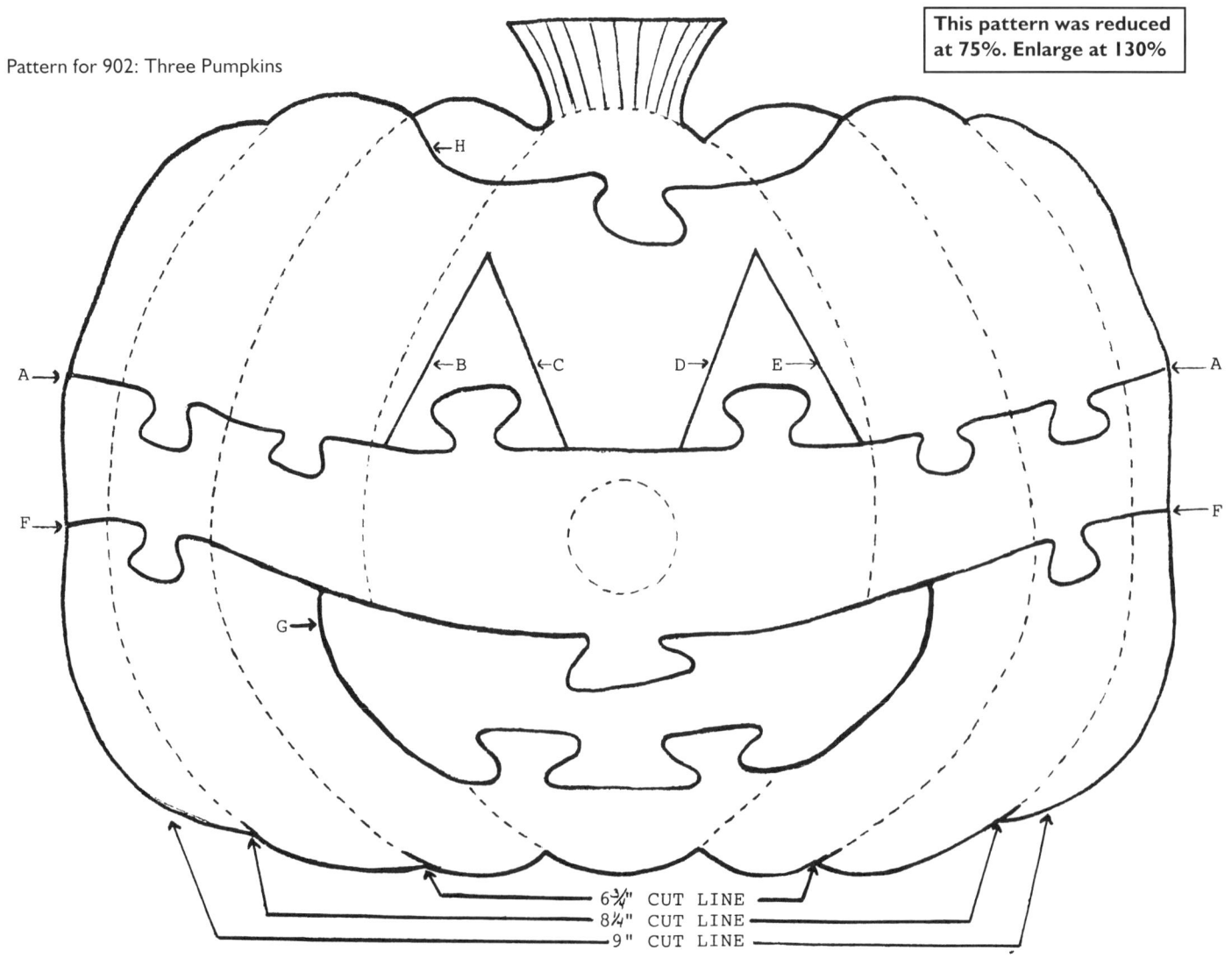

This pattern was reduced at 75%. Enlarge at 130%

Pattern for 902: Three Pumpkins

6¾" CUT LINE
8¼" CUT LINE
9" CUT LINE

PATTERN 903 A AND B:
TALL PUMPKIN

SUPPLIES

7 ¼" x 9 ½" Pine, ¾" to 1 ½" thick
Brown Paint Pen (fine-tip)

ACRYLIC PAINTS

Orange
Brown
Green
Black
Yellow (optional)

Notes: Using thicker wood will add stability to the puzzle. Cut slowly and carefully, using the smallest blade recommended for the wood thickness you have selected. As you are cutting, make sure the blade is not bending or your cuts will be slanted.

To increase the difficulty level in assembling the puzzle, paint the front and the back the same. To decrease the difficulty, paint the edges and back with an orange wash and only paint the details on the front.

INSTRUCTIONS

Decide which pumpkin design you want to make. Duplicate the pattern on a copier machine or with tracing paper. Transfer the main pattern lines onto the workpiece. Cut out the pumpkin shape with a scroll saw. Cut along pattern line "A", all the way across the pumpkin shape. Cut line "B" up to the top point, than back the blade out. Cut line "C" up to the point to finish the left eye. Cut line "D" up to the top point, then back the blade out. Cut line "E" up to point to finish the right eye. Cut line "F" across to form the top of the mouth. Cut line "G" to finish the mouth. Cut line "H" to complete puzzle. Sand all surfaces with 100-grid and than 150-grid sandpaper. Remove the sanding dust with a tack cloth.

Base-coat the stem green, continuing the color around the edges and onto the back. Use an orange wash (approximately 3 parts orange

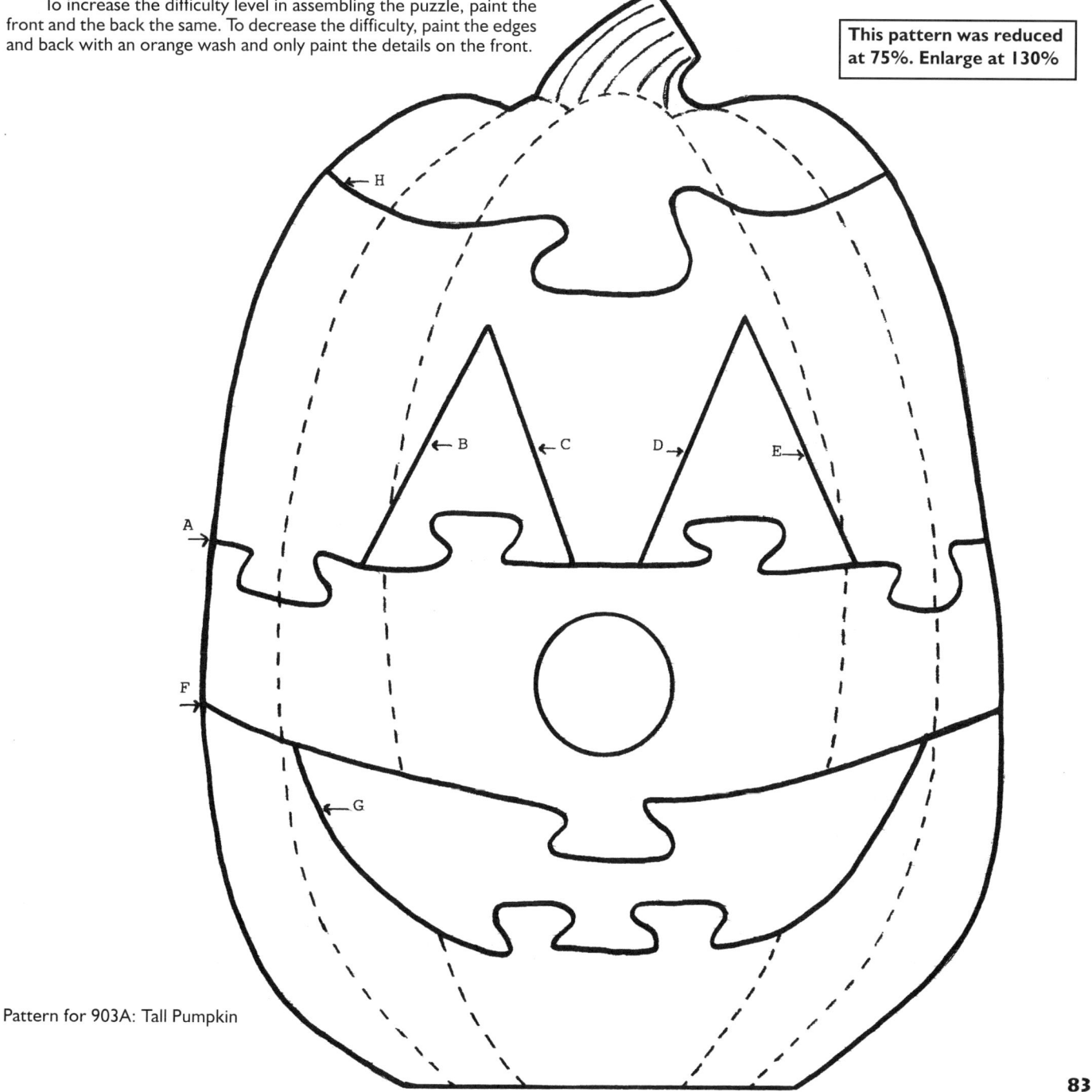

> **This pattern was reduced at 75%. Enlarge at 130%**

Pattern for 903A: Tall Pumpkin

83

to 1 part water) to paint all the remaining surfaces of the puzzle pieces. Let the paint dry. If a darker orange shade is desired, apply a second orange wash and let it dry. Sand lightly to remove the "fuzz" raised by the paints. Remove the sanding dust with a tack cloth. Touch up the paint if necessary. Paint the front of the eyes and the front of the mouth black. Let the paint dry.

Transfer the pattern details onto the pumpkin. With undiluted orange, add shading around the outline and along the section lines (shown as dotted lines on the pattern). Mix three parts of orange with one part brown. Use this mixture to darken the shading around the outline and along the section lines. Let the paint dry thoroughly. Assemble the puzzle.

Optional steps: Cover the stem area with masking tape. Remove the mouth and the 2 eye pieces. Mix yellow with water to an ink consistency. Lightly splatter the mixture onto the orange areas of the pumpkin with an old toothbrush or a splatter brush. Let the paint dry. Mix orange with water to an ink consistency. Lightly splatter the mixture onto the orange areas of the pumpkin with an old toothbrush or a splatter brush. Remove the tape. Let the paint dry.

Use the brown paint pen to define the section lines. Paint the details on the stem with black. Paint the nose black.

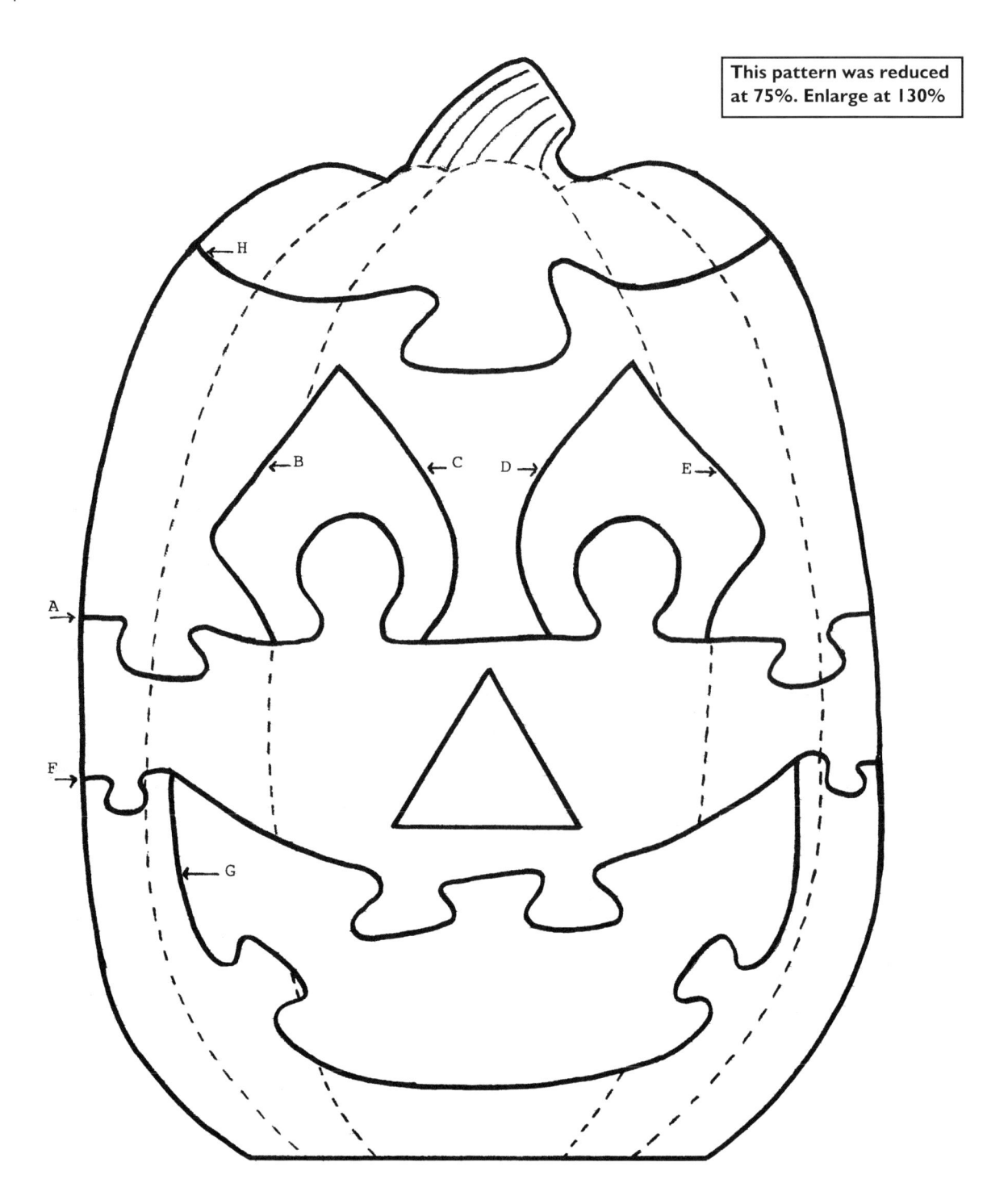

This pattern was reduced at 75%. Enlarge at 130%

Pattern for 903B: Tall Pumpkin

PATTERN 904:
GHOSTS AND PUMPKIN

SUPPLIES

5 ½" x 7 ½" Pine, ¾" thick
1 ¼" x 1 ¼" Basswood, 1/8" thick
2 ½" of 20-gauge wire
Wood glue

ACRYLIC PAINTS

Ivory
Black
Pumpkin
Brown
Green

INSTRUCTIONS

Duplicate the pattern on a copier machine or with tracing paper. Transfer the pattern lines for the ghosts and the pumpkin onto the ¾" thick pine. Transfer the leaf pattern outline onto the 1/8" thick basswood. Carefully cut the leaf shape out with a scroll saw. Cut out the shape of the larger ghost. Cut out the shape of the smaller ghost. Cut out the pumpkin shape. Cut out the center section of the pumpkin. Drill the hole, where shown on the pattern. Sand all surfaces with 100-grid and than 150-grid sandpaper. Remove the sanding dust with a tack cloth.

Base-coat the leaf green, continuing the color around the edges. Base-coat the pumpkin's stem brown, continuing the color around the edges and onto the back. Base-coat the front and back of the center section of the pumpkin with pumpkin (DO NOT paint the edges). Base-coat the outer pumpkin piece pumpkin, continuing the color around the outside edges and onto the back (DO NOT paint the inside edges where the center section of the pumpkin fits). Base-coat both ghosts ivory, continuing the color around the edges and onto the backs. Let the paint dry thoroughly. Sand the pieces lightly to remove the "fuzz" raised by the paints. Remove the sanding dust with a tack cloth. Touch-up the paint if necessary.

Sand the paint off of the front face edges of the outer pumpkin piece, the center section of the pumpkin and both of the ghost pieces.

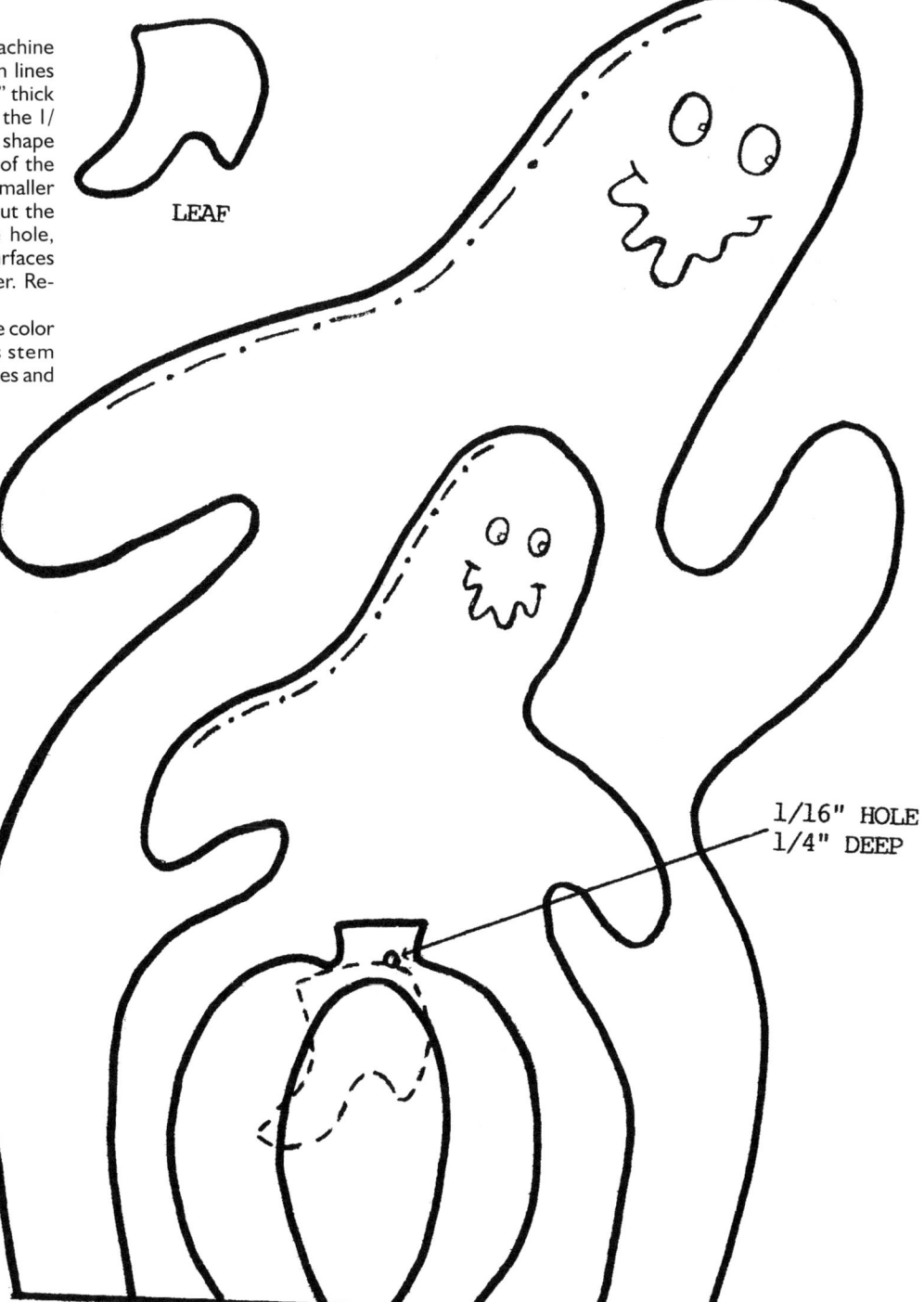

Wood glue the pumpkin pieces back together. Place a rubber band around the pieces, to hold them tightly together, until the glue dries. Glue the leaf in place on the pumpkin. Curl the wire piece around a small paintbrush handle. Dip one end of the wire in glue and push it in the drilled hole on the pumpkin.

Transfer the pattern details onto both of the ghost pieces. Paint the eyes and mouths black. Paint the dot/dash details brown. Let the paint dry. Dot an ivory highlight on each eye with the tip of a round toothpick.

LEAF

1/16" HOLE
1/4" DEEP

Pattern for 904: Ghosts and Pumpkin

PATTERN 905:
BOO-GHOST

SUPPLIES

5" x 6 ¼" Pine, ¾" thick
5" x 2 ¼" Pine, ¾" thick
Black paint pen (fine-tip)
Wood glue (optional)

ACRYLIC PAINTS

White
Black
Orange
Brown

Notes: The ghost and the "BOO" can be used as two separate pieces or they can be glued together to form one project. If you decide to glue them, do not apply paint to the glue area on the front of the ghost or the back of the "BOO" where the pieces will be joined together. The circles in the centers of the B and the O's in "BOO" can be drilled or painted on.

INSTRUCTIONS

Duplicate the pattern on a copier machine or with tracing paper. Transfer the pattern outline of the ghost onto the 5" x 6 ¼" piece of pine. Transfer the "BOO" outline onto the 5" x 2 ¼" piece of pine. Cut the pieces out with a scroll saw. Drill the holes where shown on the pattern or if you prefer you can paint the center circles of the letters on later with black paint. Sand all surfaces with 100-grid and than 150-grid sandpaper. Remove the sanding dust with a tack cloth.

Base-coat the ghost white, continuing the color around the edges and onto the back. Paint the outer edges of the "BOO" with black, continuing the color onto the back. If you have drilled the holes in the center of the letters, paint the inner edges of the holes black. Let the paint dry. Sand lightly to remove the "fuzz" raised by the acrylic paints. Remove the sanding dust with a tack cloth. Touch-up the paint if necessary.

Transfer the pattern details onto the ghost. Base-coat the tie orange. Paint the front of the "BOO" piece orange. Let the paint dry. Transfer the pattern details onto the "BOO". Shade the tie with brown. Float brown shading onto the "BOO". Let the paint dry. Paint the ghost's mouth black. Paint the black checks on the tie using a small detail brush. Paint the eyebrows and the ovals for the eyes with the black paint pen. Paint the detail lines on the "BOO" with the black paint pen. Dot on a black eye pupil for each eye using a small paintbrush handle.

If you did not drill the holes, paint the center circles of the B and both O's of the "BOO" piece black. Glue the pieces together if desired.

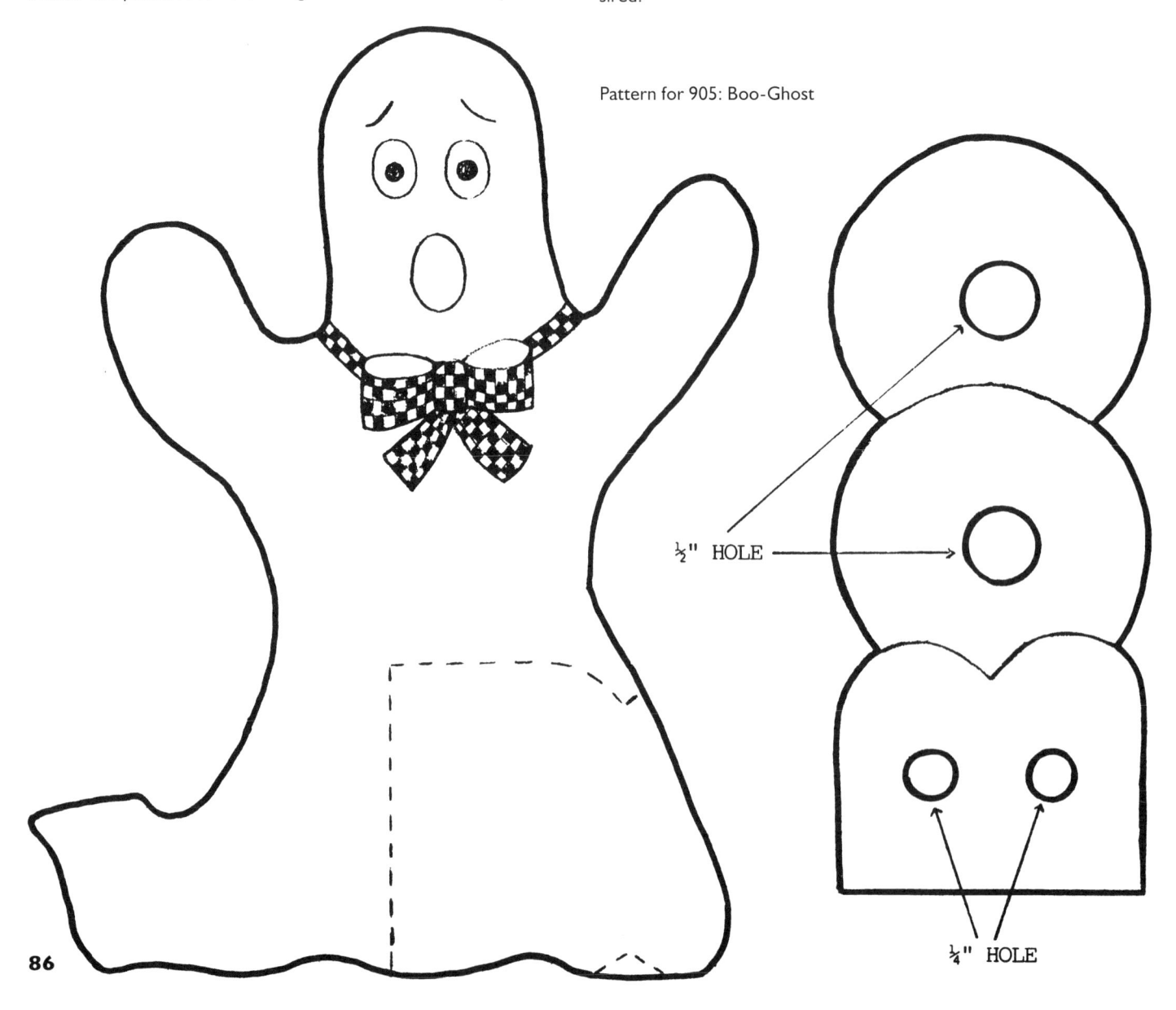

Pattern for 905: Boo-Ghost

½" HOLE

¼" HOLE

PATTERN 906:
SPECKLED BUNNY

SUPPLIES

7" x 5" Pine, ¾" thick

ACRYLIC GLOSS ENAMEL

Chocolate Brown
Beige
White
Pink
Rose

INSTRUCTIONS

Duplicate the pattern on a copier machine or with tracing paper. Transfer the pattern outline and the kerf cut lines onto the workpiece. Cut the shape out with a scroll saw. Cut in along the defining kerf lines that form the front of the ear, the nose, the back foot and the tail. Drill the eye hole where shown on the pattern. Remove the blade from the saw. Thread the saw blade though the drilled hole and re-attach it to the saw. Adjust the saw tension. Cut along the eye pattern kerf line to the end. Stop the saw and remove the blade from the saw and the workpiece. Sand all surfaces with 100-grid and than 150-grid sandpaper. Remove the sanding dust with a tack cloth.

Base-coat the bunny chocolate brown, continuing the color around the edges and onto the back. Let the paint dry thoroughly. Sand lightly to remove the "fuzz" raised by the paint. Remove the sanding dust with a tack cloth. Touch-up the paint if necessary.

Transfer the pattern lines for the nose, inner ear and chest onto the workpiece. Base-coat the chest white. Base-coat the nose and inner ear pink. Let the paint dry. Shade the nose and inner ear with rose. Apply a coat of beige over the remaining chocolate brown painted area on the front of the bunny. Let the paint dry. Apply a second coat of beige. Let the paint dry thoroughly.

Transfer the remaining pattern details onto the workpiece. Shade around the bunny's outline, the eyehole and the eye kerf cut line with chocolate brown. Float Chocolate Brown shading along the pattern detail lines and the kerf cut lines that define the tail, legs, feet and inner ear. Let the paint dry. Mix chocolate brown with water to an ink consistency. Splatter the mixture onto the front of the bunny with a splatter brush or an old toothbrush. Let the paint dry. Mix white with water to an ink consistency. Splatter the mixture onto the front of the bunny with a splatter brush or an old toothbrush. Let the paint dry thoroughly.

To give the project an aged look, carefully sand around the eye hole all of the kerf cut lines and the bunny's outline with 150-grid sandpaper removing only the top-coats of beige. Very lightly sand a few areas along the bunny's shaded detail lines. If you happen to sand an area too deeply, touch it up with diluted chocolate brown paint.

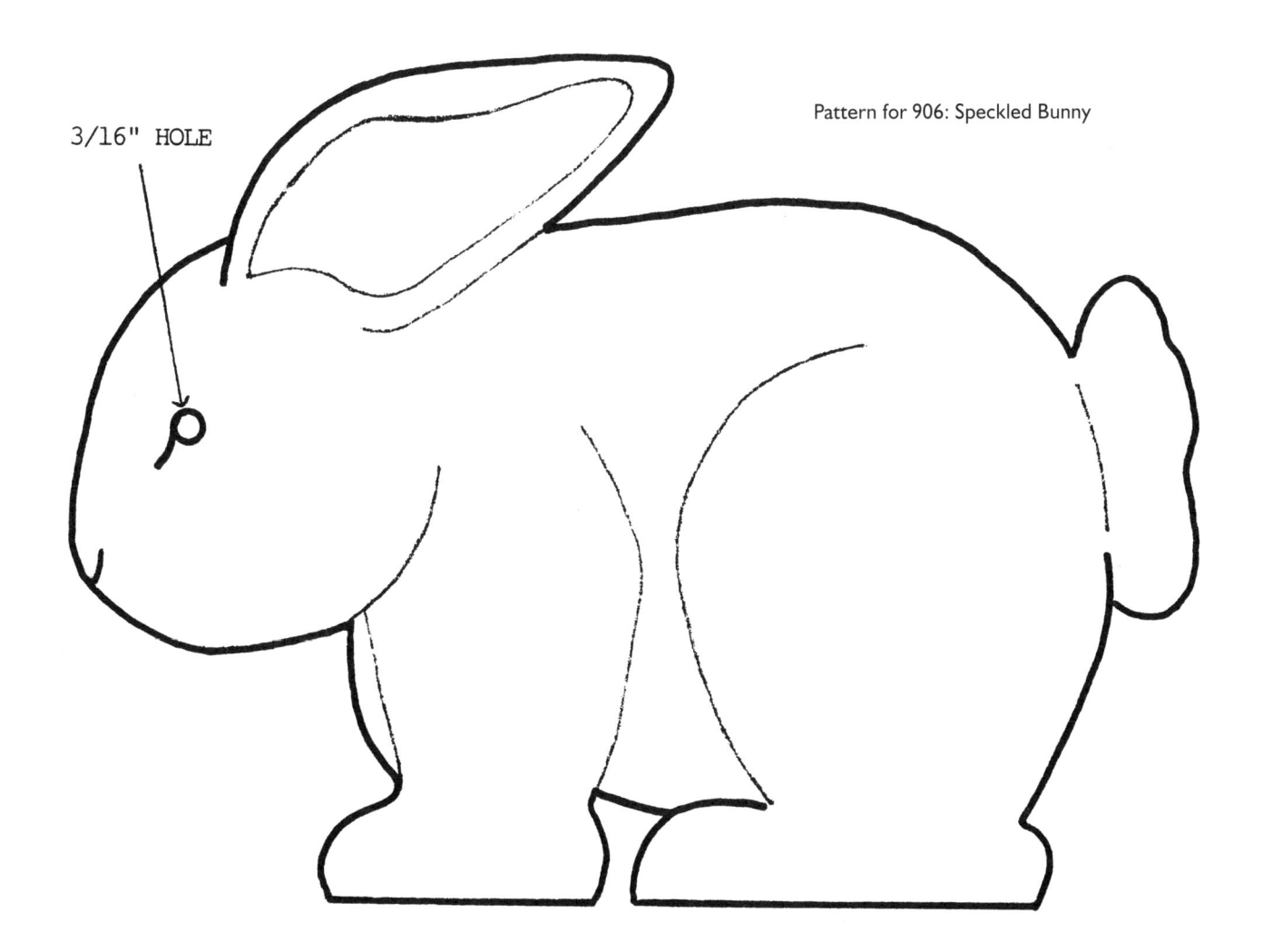

3/16" HOLE

Pattern for 906: Speckled Bunny

PATTERN 907:
FLOWER POT

SUPPLIES

5 ¼" x 4" Basswood, ¼" thick
4 ¼" x 1 ¼" Pine, ¾" thick
3 - 3 ½" pieces of 20-gauge wire
Wood glue

ACRYLIC PAINTS

Green
Light Green
Brown
Yellow
Burnt Orange
Light Orange

INSTRUCTIONS

Duplicate the pattern on a copier machine or with tracing paper. Transfer 3 of the flower pattern outlines and 3 of the leaf pattern outlines onto the basswood workpiece. Transfer the flower pot outline onto the pine workpiece. With the smallest blade recommended for the wood thickness, slowly and carefully cut out the 3 flowers. Cut in the kerf lines that form the flower petal separations on each flower. Cut out the 3 leave outlines. Cut out the flower pot. Drill the holes in the flowers and the leaves, where shown on the pattern. Using Illustration 1 (flower pot, top view) as a guide, drill holes 1 and 3 of the flower pot 3/8 of an inch in from the front edge. Drill hole 2 of the flower pot 3/8 of an inch in from the back edge. Carefully sand all surfaces of the wood pieces with 100-grid and than 150-grid sandpaper. Remove the sanding dust from the pieces with a tack cloth.

Base-coat the 3 flower pieces yellow, continuing the color around the edges and onto the backs. Base-coat the 3 leaf pieces light green, continuing the color around the edges and onto the backs. Base-coat the flower pot burnt orange, continuing the color around the edges and onto the back. Let the paint dry. Sand lightly to remove the "fuzz" raised by the paints. Remove the sanding dust with a tack cloth. Touch-up the paint if necessary.

Shade the 3 flower pieces with orange, continuing the shading around the edges and onto the backs. Shade the 3 leaf pieces with green, continuing the shading around the edges and onto the backs. Shade the flower pot with brown, continuing the shading around the edges and onto the back. Let the paint dry. Paint the brown center dots on the flowers using a paintbrush handle.

Transfer the pattern details onto the flower pot. Paint the leaves and design lines green. Let the paint dry. Dot on the light orange flower petals using a small paintbrush handle. Dot on the yellow flower petals using a small paintbrush handle. Let the paint dry. Paint the yellow center dot for the orange flower using a small paintbrush handle. Paint the yellow detail line on the orange flowers at each end of the design. Paint the orange center dot for the yellow flowers using a small paintbrush handle. Let the paint dry.

Dip one end of a 3 ½" piece of wire into glue and push it into hole 1 of the flower pot. Place a small dot of glue on the bottom of one of the leaf pieces and slide the leaves down the wire to the flower pot. Place a small dot of glue on the top end of the wire and slide one of the flowers on. Glue the second and third set of leaves and flowers on in the same manner. Make sure that the flowers are standing straight.

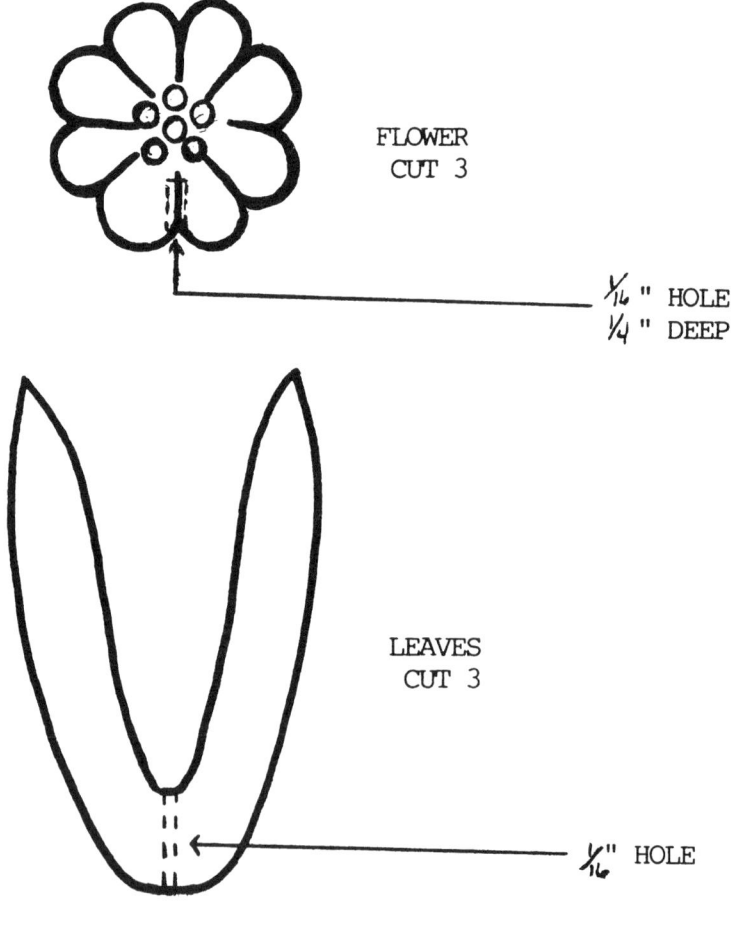

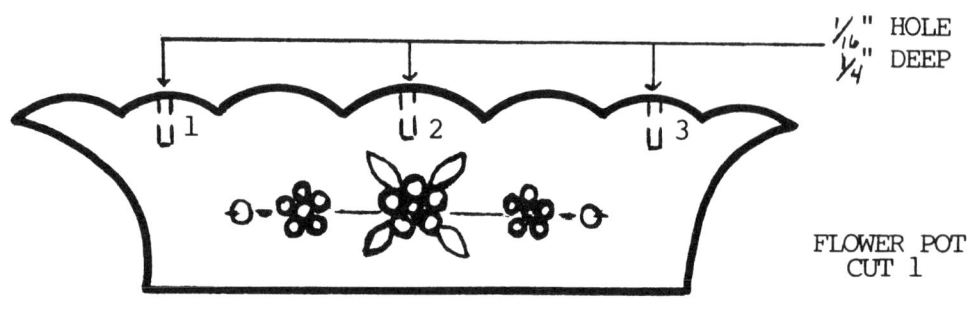

FLOWER CUT 3

1/16" HOLE
1/4" DEEP

LEAVES CUT 3

1/16" HOLE

1/16" HOLE
1/4" DEEP

FLOWER POT CUT 1

Pattern for 907: Flower Pot

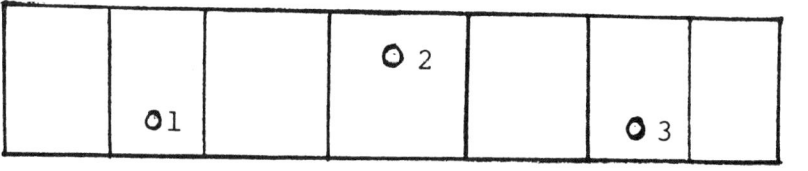

ILLUSTRATION 1
FLOWER POT
TOP VEIW

PATTERN 908:
FISH BOWL

SUPPLIES

7" x 4" Pine, ¾" thick
(2) 7" x 4" Plexiglass, 1/8" thick
Black Paint Pen (extra-fine tip)
White glue

ACRYLIC PAINTS

Black
White
Brown
Yellow
Red
Tan
Beige
Blue
Light Blue
Green
Light Green

INSTRUCTIONS

Duplicate the pattern on a copier machine or with tracing paper. Do NOT remove the protective covering from the Plexiglass pieces. Layer the wood piece and the 2 Plexiglass pieces one on top of another (wood piece on top). Secure the pieces together with masking tape so they will not separate as you are sawing. Transfer the bowl outline of Pattern "A" onto the top wood workpiece. Stack cut the workpieces with a scroll saw, using the smallest blade recommended for the combined thickness of the materials. Remove the masking tape and separate the pieces. Remove the protective covering from the Plexiglass pieces. Carefully sand the **edges** of the Plexiglass pieces with 150-grid sandpaper.

Transfer the outline of Pattern "B", for the top of the water and the sides of the bowl from the water up, onto the wood workpiece. Cut off the waste area. Sand all surfaces of the wood with 100-grid and than 150-grid sandpaper. Remove the sanding dust from the pieces with a tack cloth.

Make a reverse image pattern of Pattern "B" by placing a piece of graphite paper (graphite side up) under the pattern sheet. Trace over the pattern lines and details with a sharp pencil or a stylus. This will give you a reverse image of the pattern on the back of the pattern sheet.

Transfer the pattern details from Pattern "B" onto the front of the wood workpiece. Transfer the reverse image pattern details onto the back of the wood workpiece.

Paint the fish bowl outline white, continuing the color around the edges and paint the fish bowl outline on the back. Let the paint dry. Paint the water blue, continuing the color around the edge and paint the water on the back. Let the paint dry. Sand lightly to remove the "fuzz" raised by the paint. Remove the sanding dust with a tack cloth. Touch-up the paint if necessary.

All of the following painting instructions are for both sides of the project. Paint the water ripples light blue. Paint the sand areas tan. Let the paint dry. Paint the seaweed light green. Paint the snails beige. Paint the red areas on the fish. Let the paint dry. Paint the yellow areas on the fish. Base-coat the yellow sand areas. Highlight the seaweed with yellow. Let the paint dry. Shade the seaweed with green. Shade the sand and the snails with brown. Dot on the black eyes and tail dots with a paintbrush handle. Paint the black areas of the fish. Let the paint dry. Dot a white highlight on each eye with the tip of a round toothpick. Paint the air bubbles white. Add the details to the snails with the black paint pen.

In this instance, the rule for gluing painted surfaces is ignored. Carefully apply a thin, even spread of glue to the white fish bowl outline on the back of the project. Set a Plexiglass piece in place on top of the wood piece. Weight the pieces together until the glue dries. Turn the project over and glue the front Plexiglass piece on in the same manner.

> This pattern was reduced at 75%. Enlarge at 130%

Pattern for 908: Fish Bowl

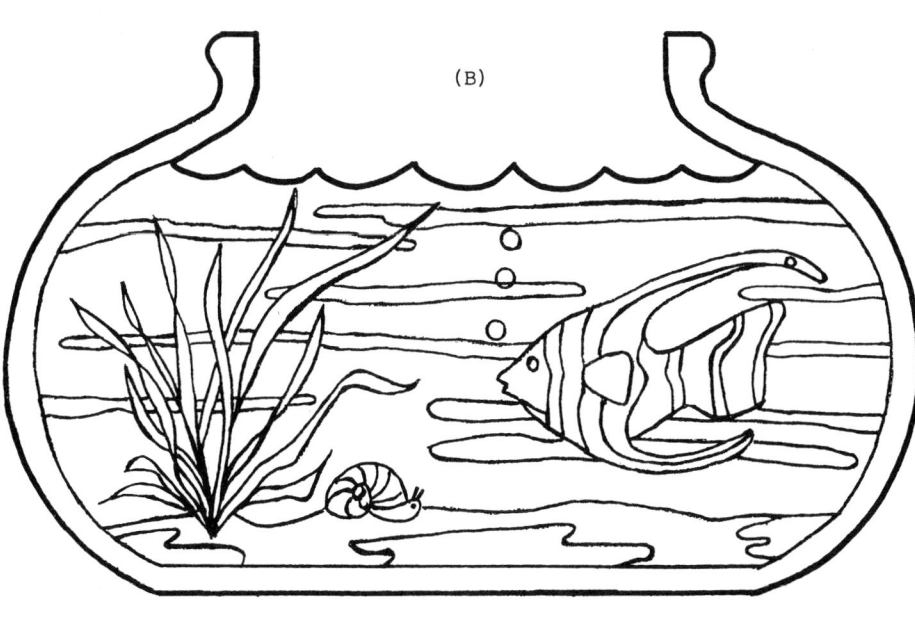

PATTERN 909:
WELCOME CAT

SUPPLIES

5 ½" x 4" Pine, 1 ½" thick
4" x 4 ½" Pine, ¾" thick
2 ½" x 7 ½" Pine, ¾" thick
Black paint pen (fine-tip)
1/8" checkerboard stencil

ACRYLIC PAINTS

White
Orange
Brown
Black
Pink
Rose
Yellow
Green

INSTRUCTIONS

Duplicate the 3 pattern pages on a copier machine or with tracing paper. Transfer the pattern outline for the head onto the 4" x 4 ½" workpiece. Transfer the outline of the tail onto the 2 ½" x 7 ½" workpiece. Transfer the body/base outline onto the 5 ½" x 4" piece of 1 ½" thick wood. Cut out the shapes with a scroll saw. Sand all surfaces with 100-grid and than 150-grid sandpaper. Remove the sanding dust with a tack cloth.

Transfer the main pattern lines onto the front and back of the workpieces. Base-coat the tip of the tail white, continuing the color around the edges and onto the back. Base-coat the paws, face and inner ears white. Let the paint dry. Paint the base areas of the body/base piece with a brown wash (3 parts brown to 1 part water), continuing the color around the edges and onto the back. Let the paint dry. Mix equal parts of orange, brown, yellow and white with a small amount of water. Use this mixture to base-coat the front legs and body, the front of the head and ears and the tail, continue the color around the edges and onto the back of the pieces. Let the paint dry. Sand lightly to remove the "fuzz" raised by the paint. Remove the sanding dust with a tack cloth. Touch-up the paint if necessary. Shade the base areas of the body/base piece with brown.

Transfer the pattern details of the face, feet and the base design onto the workpieces. Base-coat the cheek circles pink. Shade the inner ears with pink. Dot on the pink flower petals with a small paintbrush handle. Paint the eyes and the nose black. Let the paint dry. Stencil the checkerboard design on the cheek circles with rose. Shade the inner ears again with rose. Dot on the rose center for the flower with a small paintbrush handle. Paint the remaining details on the face, ears and feet with the black paint pen.

Using the front and back pattern pages as a guide, paint the brown stripes on the cat, continuing the color around the edges to connect the front and back stripes. Let the paint dry. Add definition lines to the stripes with the black paint pen. Paint the lettering (WELCOME) white. Paint the leaves green. Let the paint dry.

If you have painted the glue areas, sand the paint off where the pieces join. Glue the head and tail pieces onto the body. Clamp them in place until the glue is dry.

Pattern for 909: Welcome Cat

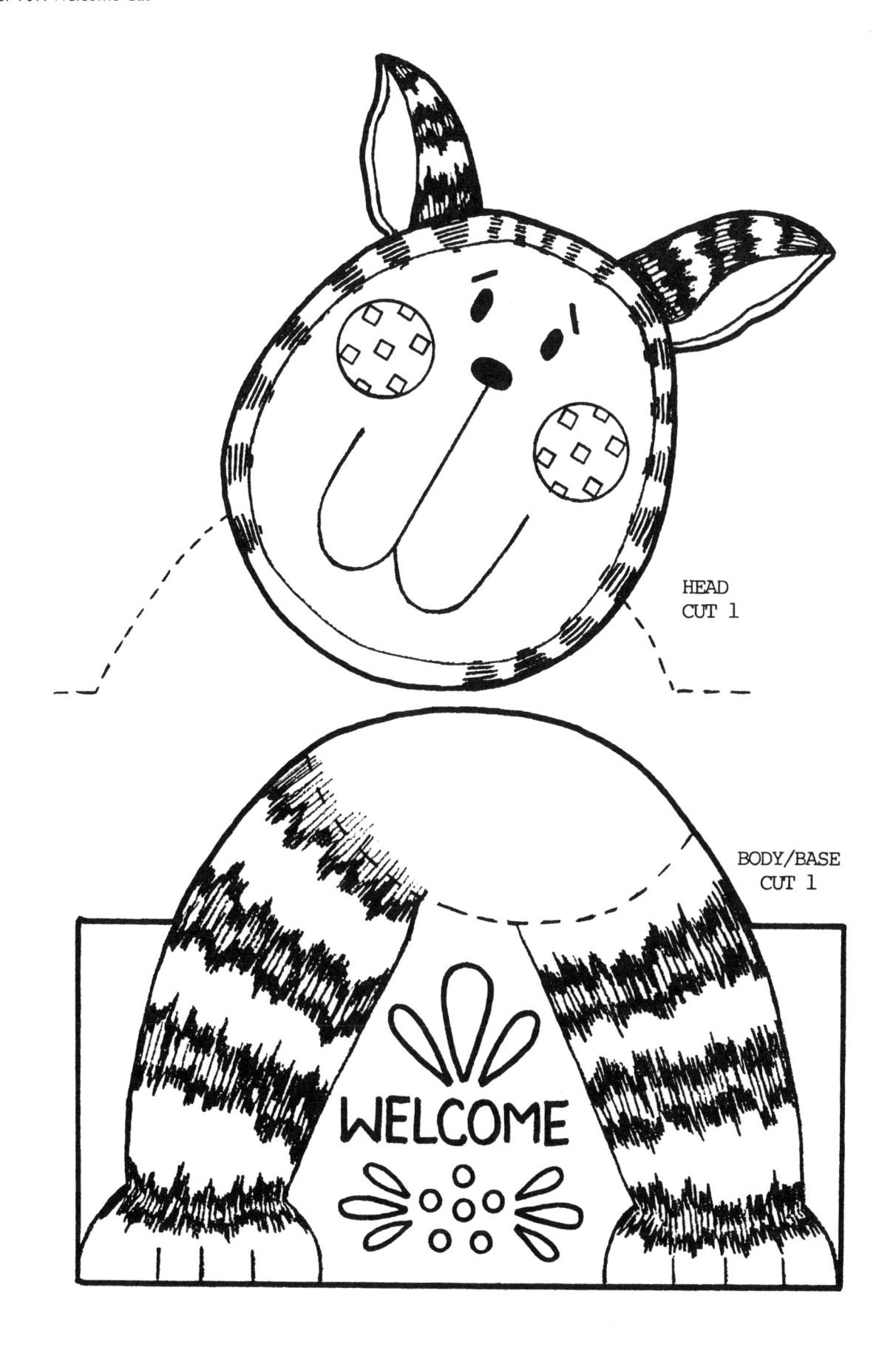

HEAD
CUT 1

BODY/BASE
CUT 1

WELCOME

91

Paint pattern for the back of 909: Welcome Cat

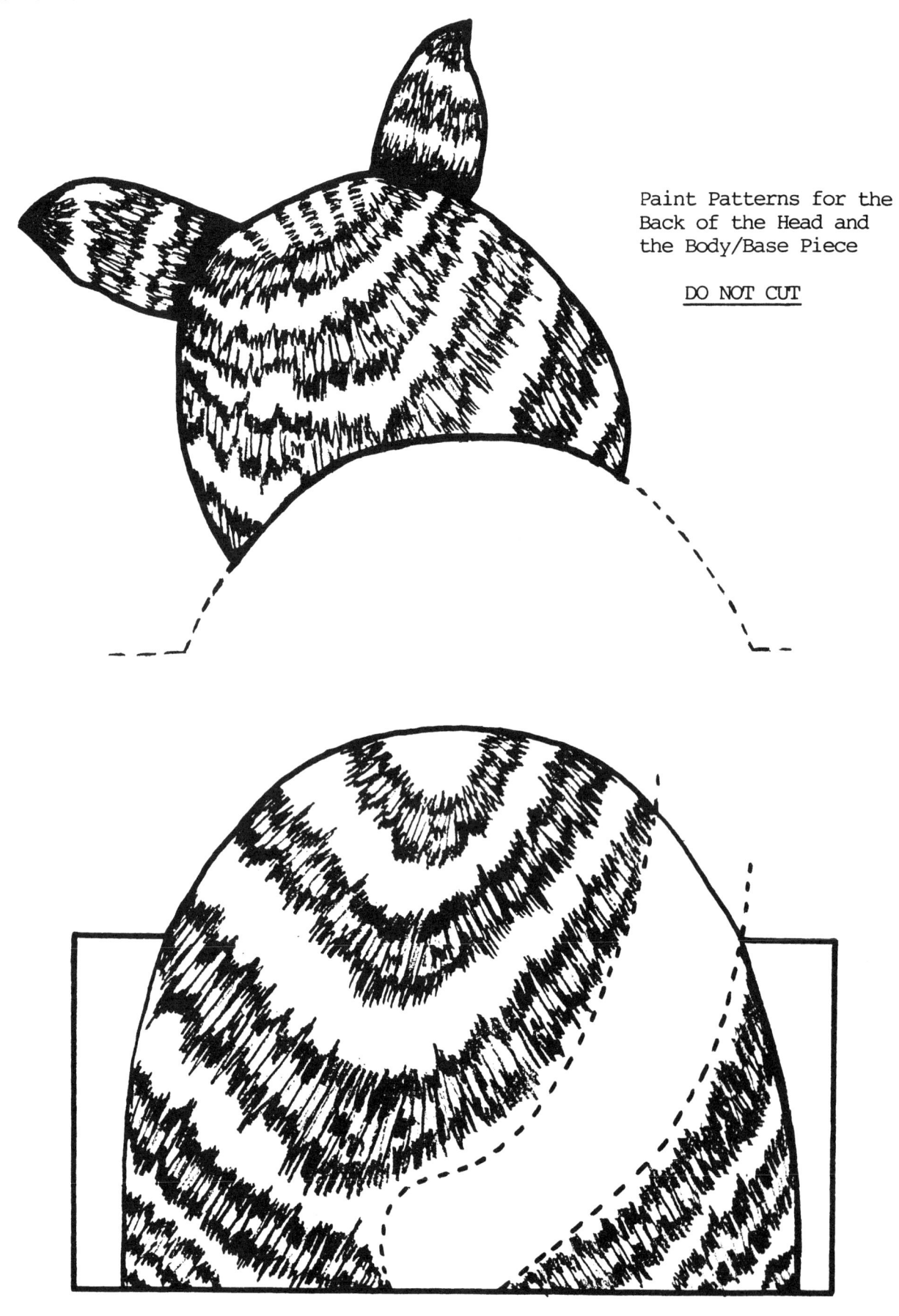

Paint Patterns for the
Back of the Head and
the Body/Base Piece

DO NOT CUT

92

Tail pattern for 909: Welcome Cat

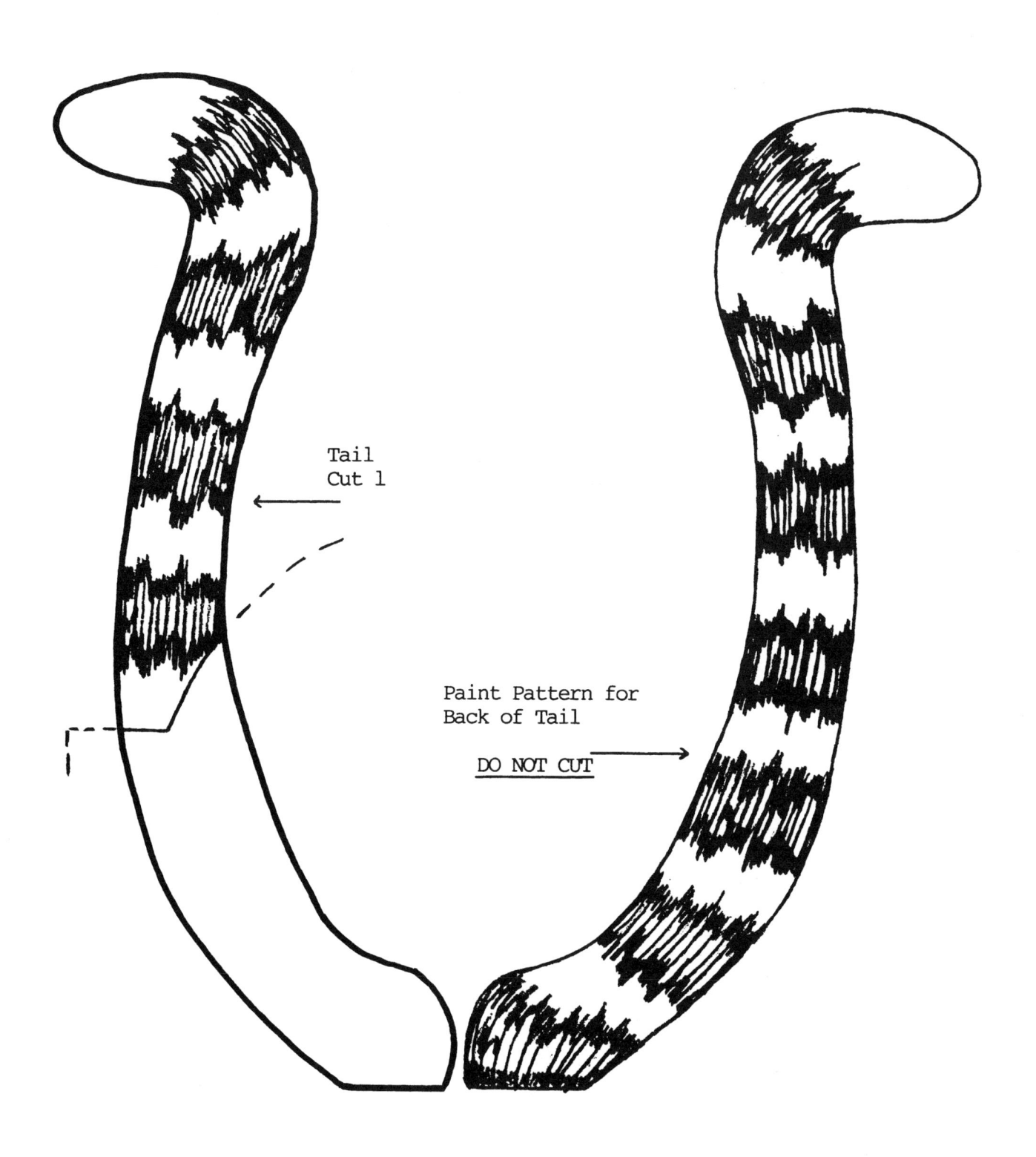

Tail
Cut 1

Paint Pattern for
Back of Tail

DO NOT CUT

PATTERN 910:
COW

SUPPLIES
9" x 6 ½" Pine, 1 ½" thick
Black paint pen (fine-tip)

ACRYLIC PAINTS
White
Black
Pale Pink
Pink

INSTRUCTIONS
Duplicate the pattern on a copier machine or with tracing paper. Transfer the pattern outline onto the workpiece. Using the smallest blade recommended for the wood thickness, cut along the cow's outline, following the arrows from the start point to the end point. This will be one continuous cut. Cut off the remaining waste areas. Sand all surfaces with 100-grid and than 150-grid sandpaper. Remove the sanding dust with a tack cloth.

Paint the edges of the cow white, continuing the color onto the back. Let the paint dry. Sand lightly to remove the "fuzz" raised by the paint. Remove the sanding dust with a tack cloth. Touch-up the paint if necessary.

Transfer the main pattern lines onto the workpiece. Paint the white areas on the front of the cow. Base-coat the nose, mouth, utters and inner ears light pink. Let the paint dry. Float pink shading onto the nose, mouth, utters and inner ears. Paint the cow's markings and hooves black. Let the paint dry.

Transfer the pattern details onto the workpiece. Paint the white for the eyes. Let the paint dry. Dot the black eye pupils on with a large paintbrush handle. Paint the nostrils black. Let the paint dry. Dot a white highlight on each eye with the tip of a round toothpick. Paint on the remaining details with the black paint pen.

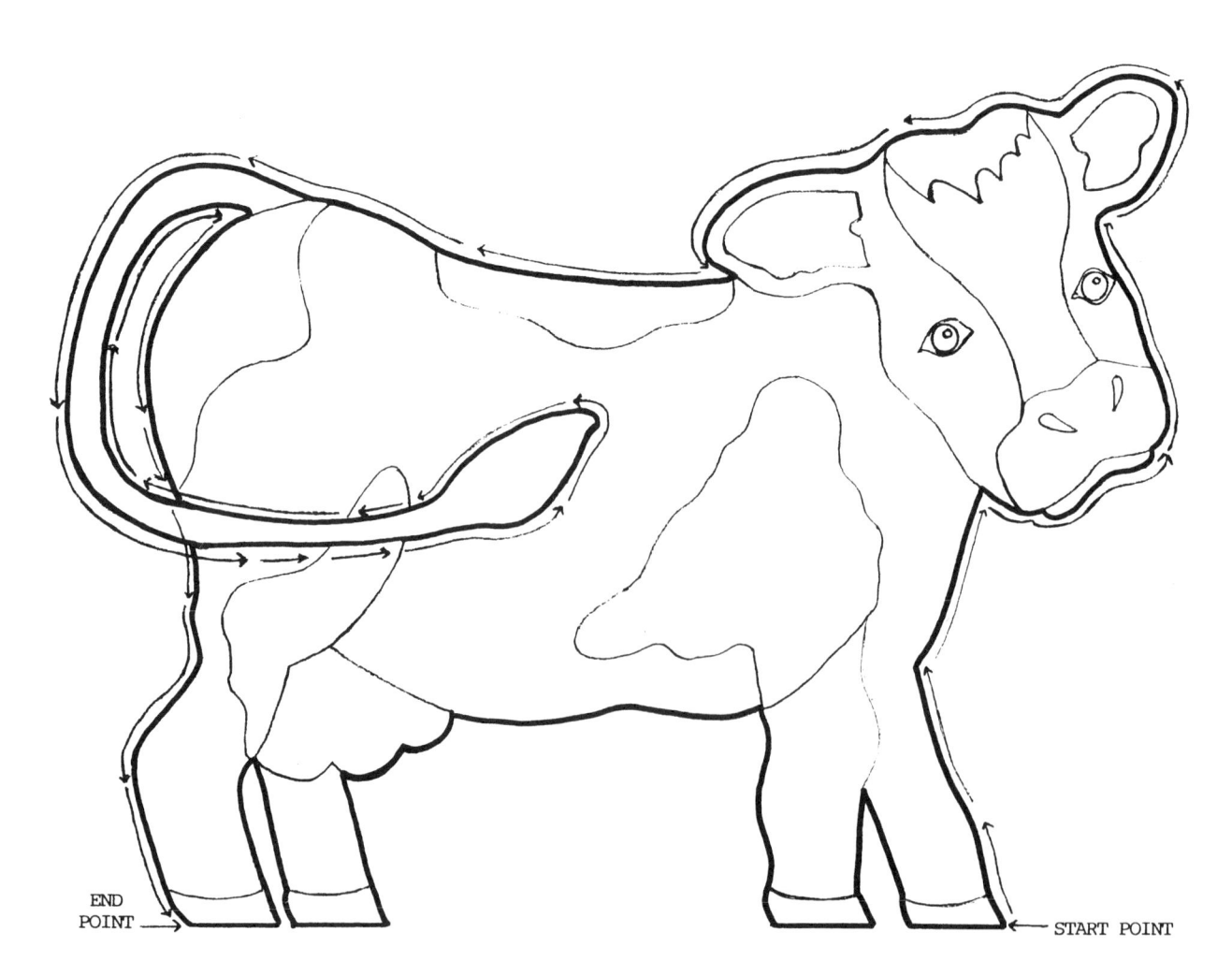

Pattern for 910: Cow

This pattern was reduced at 75%. Enlarge at 130%

Pattern 911:
PENGUIN

SUPPLIES

4 ¼" x 7" Pine, ¾" thick
Black paint pen (extra-fine tip)

ACRYLIC PAINTS

White
Black
Red
Orange
Light Orange

INSTRUCTIONS

Duplicate the pattern on a copier machine or with tracing paper. Transfer the pattern outline onto the workpiece. Cut the shape out with a scroll saw. Sand all surfaces with 100-grid and than 150-grid sandpaper. Remove the sanding dust with a tack cloth.

Transfer the main pattern lines onto the wood. Paint the black areas on the penguin's body, continuing the color around the edges of the entire workpiece and onto the back. Let the paint dry. Sand lightly to remove the "fuzz" raised by the paint. Remove the sanding dust with a tack cloth. Touch-up the paint if necessary.

Paint the white areas on the penguin's body including the white detail lines. Base-coat the hat pom-pom white. Let the paint dry. Base-coat the hat and scarf red. Base-coat the beak and feet light orange. Let the paint dry.

Transfer the pattern details onto the wood. Paint the stripes on the hat and scarf white. Dot on a black eye using a paintbrush handle. Let the paint dry. Shade the hat pom-pom with black. Mix red with a small amount of black. Use this mixture to float shading onto the hat and scarf. Float orange shading onto the beak and feet. Dot a white highlight onto the eye using the tip of a round toothpick. Let the paint dry. Paint the remaining details on the hat, scarf, beak and feet with the black paint pen.

Pattern for 911: Penguin

PATTERN 912:
LAMB

SUPPLIES

7" x 7" Pine, 1 ½" thick
Black paint pen (extra-fine tip)

ACRYLIC PAINTS

White
Black
Gray
Pink
Rose

INSTRUCTIONS

Duplicate the pattern on a copier machine or with tracing paper. Transfer the pattern outline onto the workpiece. Cut the shape out with a scroll saw. Sand all surfaces with 100-grid and than 150-grid sandpaper. Remove the sanding dust with a tack cloth.

Transfer the main pattern lines onto the workpiece. Paint the white areas on the lamb, continuing the color around the edges and onto the back. Let the paint dry. Sand lightly to remove the "fuzz" raised by the paint. Remove the sanding dust with a tack cloth. Touch-up the paint if necessary.

Base-coat the face and feet gray. Base-coat the inner ear pink. Let the paint dry. Shade the inner ear with rose. Let the paint dry.

Transfer the pattern details onto the workpiece. Dot on the white for the eyes using the eraser end of a pencil. Let the paint dry. Dot on the black eye pupils using a paintbrush handle. Paint the nose black. Let the paint dry. Paint the remaining details on the face, ears and body with the black paint pen. Paint a white highlight on the nose. Dot a white highlight on each eye using the tip of a round toothpick. Dry brush rose on for the cheeks.

Pattern for 912: Lamb

Pattern 913: WITCH

SUPPLIES

8" x 6" Pine, ¾" thick
3 ½" x 1 ¾" Basswood, ¼" thick
3 ½" x 1" Basswood, 1/8" thick
1 ¼" of 3/16" Dowel
1 ½" of 3/16" Dowel
2" Bow (Pumpkin)
Ribbon flower (purple)
Wood glue
Hot melt glue
3/8" Star stencil
Crepe craft hair (brown)
Picture frame hanger

ACRYLIC PAINTS

Purple
Yellow
Beige
Brown
Flesh
Rose
Black
Pumpkin

INSTRUCTIONS

Duplicate the pattern on a copier machine or with tracing paper. Transfer the outlines for the witch and the broom bristles onto the ¾" pine. Transfer the arm outline onto the ¼" thick basswood. Transfer the hat brim outline onto the 1/8" thick basswood. Cut the shapes out with a scroll saw. Drill the holes where shown on the pattern. Sand all surfaces with 100-grid and than 150-grid sandpaper. Remove the sanding dust with a tack cloth.

Transfer the main pattern lines onto the witch and arm pieces. Base-coat the hat and dress purple, continuing the color around the edges of the entire piece and onto the back. Base-coat the hat brim purple, continuing the color around the edges. Base-coat the sleeve purple, continuing the color around the edges of the entire piece. Base-coat the broom bristles piece yellow, continuing the color around the edges and onto the back. Let the paint dry. Sand the pieces lightly to remove the "fuzz" raised by the paints. Remove the sanding dust with a tack cloth. Touch-up the paint if necessary.

Base-coat the hand and face flesh. Base-coat the shoe black. Paint the brown lines for the broom bristles. Let the paint dry.

Transfer the remaining pattern details, as they are needed. Using a very dry, stiff bristle brush, dry brush the witch's cheek rose. Paint the eye and mouth black. Let the paint dry. Dot the beige lace holes on the shoe using a small paintbrush handle. Paint the shoelaces and the defining pattern lines on the shoe beige. Dot a beige highlight on the eye and the cheek using the tip of a round toothpick. Shade the hand with rose. Highlight the dress, shoe, face, hat, arm piece and hat brim with beige. Let the paint dry.

Cover the face, hand and shoe with masking tape. Mix beige with water to an ink consistency. Lightly splatter this mixture on the dress, hat, sleeve and hat brim with an old toothbrush or a splatter brush. Let the paint dry.

Mix pumpkin with water to an ink consistency. Lightly splatter this mixture on the dress, hat, sleeve and hat brim with an old toothbrush or a splatter brush. Remove the masking tape. Let the paint dry. Stencil the stars onto the dress with pumpkin. Paint the pumpkin stripe on the broom bristles piece.

Dip one end of the 1 ¼" long piece of dowel into wood glue and push it into the broom bristles piece. Dip the other end of the dowel into wood glue and push it into the shoe. Dip one end of the 1 ½" long piece of dowel into wood glue and push it into the hand. Wood glue the arm and hat brim in place. Hot glue the bow, ribbon flower and hair in place. Let the glue dry. Attach the picture frame hanger onto the back of the project.

This pattern was reduced at 75%. Enlarge at 130%

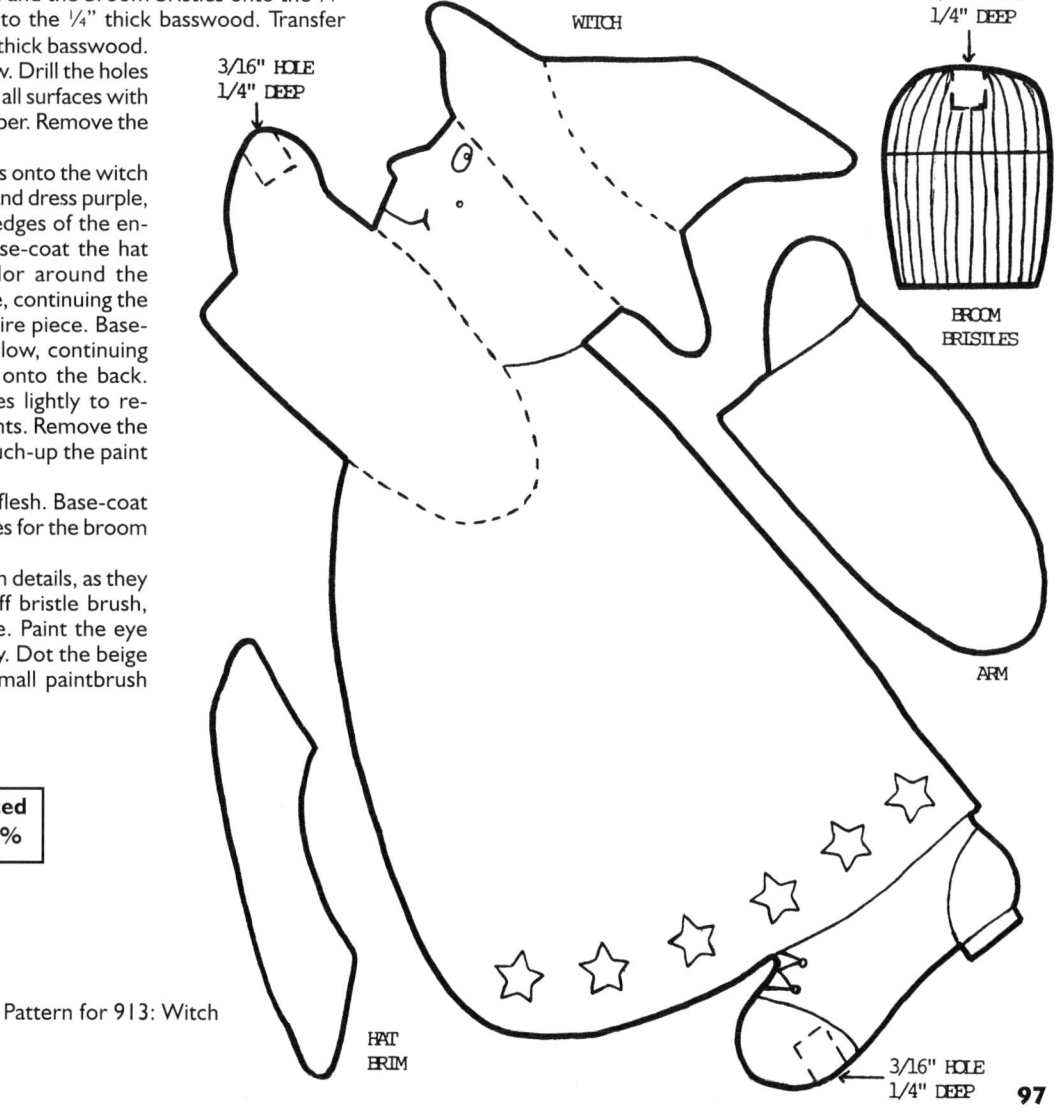

Pattern for 913: Witch

PATTERN 914:
TURTLE

SUPPLIES

10" x 6" Pine, 1 ½" thick
Black Paint Pen (extra-fine tip)
3/8" Checkerboard stencil
Wood glue

ACRYLIC PAINTS

Yellow-Green
Green
Yellow
Black
White
Light Blue

Note: DO NOT apply paint to the inside glue edges where the pieces will join. Glue will not bond permanently to painted surfaces.

INSTRUCTIONS

Duplicate the pattern on a copier machine or with tracing paper. Transfer the pattern outline, the kerf line for the mouth and all of the segmenting cut lines onto the workpiece. There is no need to transfer the eye or nose pattern details yet. Using the smallest blade recommended for the wood thickness, cut the turtle shape out with a scroll saw. Cut the kerf line for the mouth. Saw along the segmenting cut lines, cutting the turtle into 14 separate pieces. Sand the front face edges of each piece, with 80-grid sandpaper, until they are well-rounded. Sand all surfaces with 100-grid and than 150-grid sandpaper. Remove the sanding dust with a tack cloth.

Glue the 10 pieces that make up the **shell** back together. Let the glue dry. Base-coat the head, legs and tail yellow-green, continuing the color around the edges and onto the backs. Base-coat the shell green, continuing the color around the edges and onto the back. Let the paint dry. Sand the pieces lightly to remove the "fuzz" raised by the paints. Remove the sanding dust with a tack cloth. Touch-up the paint if necessary.

Stencil the checkerboard design onto the front of the shell with yellow-green. Float green shading onto the head, legs and tail. Let the paint dry. Mix green with a small amount of black. Use this mixture to shade around the outline and along each cut line of the shell. Let the paint dry.

Transfer the eye and nose patterns onto the head. Paint the eyebrow, eye pupil and the nose black. Paint the eye iris light blue. Paint the white area of the eye. Let the paint dry. Detail the eye with the black paint pen. Dot a white highlight on the eye using a small paintbrush handle.

If you have painted any of the inside glue edges, sand the paint off. Glue the head, legs and tail onto the shell. Highlight the head, legs, tail and shell with yellow. Let the glue dry thoroughly.

Pattern for 914: Turtle

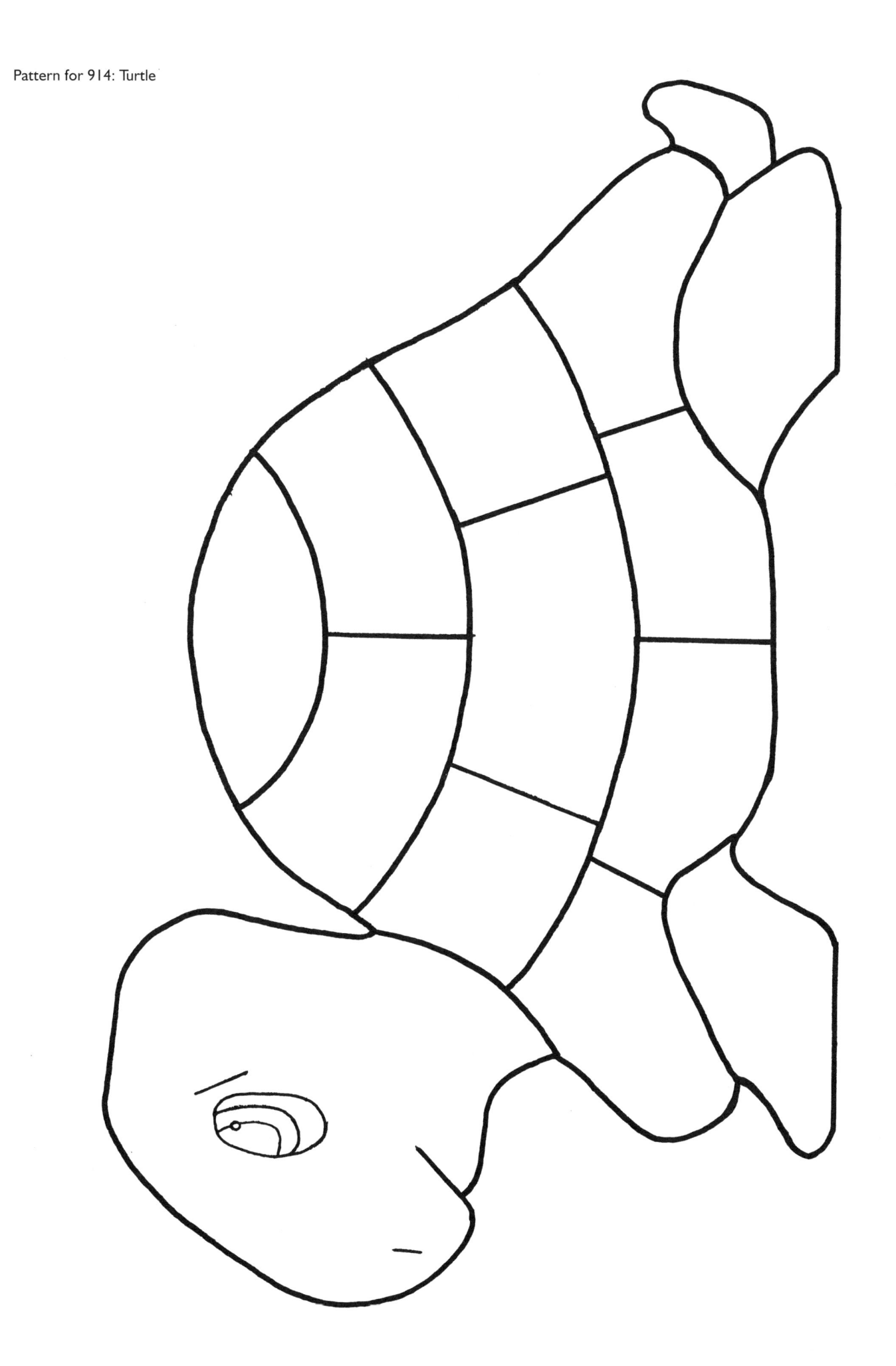

PATTERN 915: ELEPHANT

SUPPLIES

7 ¼" x 8 ½" Pine, 1 ½" thick
1 ½" x 3" Pine, ¾" thick
3" x 4" Basswood, 3/8" thick
11" x 9" piece of Fabric
2-12" Pipe cleaners
Black paint pen (extra-fine tip)
2 ½" White Bow
Wood Glue

ACRYLIC PAINTS

Gray
Black
White
Pink
Rose

INSTRUCTIONS

Duplicate the pattern on a copier machine or with tracing paper. Transfer the body pattern outline onto the 1 ½" thick workpiece. Transfer the leg pattern outlines onto the 3/8" thick workpiece. Transfer the side-view truck pattern outline onto the ¾" thick workpiece. Cut the shapes out with a scroll saw. Drill the holes, where shown on the pattern. Sand the front face edges of the leg pieces, except for the bottom straight edge, until they are well-rounded. Sand the front face edges of the trunk until they are well-rounded. Sand all surfaces with 100-grid and than 150-grid sandpaper. Remove the sanding dust with a tack cloth.

Base-coat the body gray, continuing the color around the edges and onto the back. Base-coat the legs gray, continuing the color around the edges. Base-coat the trunk gray, on all surfaces except for the back glue area. Let the paint dry. Sand the pieces lightly to remove the "fuzz" raised by the paints. Remove the sanding dust with a tack cloth. Touch-up the paint if necessary.

Transfer the main pattern design lines onto the pieces. Mix gray with a small amount of black. Use this mixture to shade around the outline of the pieces and along the main pattern design lines. Let the paint dry.

Transfer the remaining pattern details onto the body and leg pieces. Transfer the snout pattern detail onto the trunk, using the color photo as a guide. Paint the eyes and toe nails white. Using a very dry, stiff bristle brush, dry brush the elephant's cheeks rose. Paint the snout area of the trunk pink. Shade the snout area with rose. Let the paint dry.

Dot on the black eye pupils using the eraser end of a pencil. Let the paint dry. Dot a white highlight on each eye using a small paintbrush handle. Add the remaining details to the head, body, legs and trunk with the black paint pen.

Trace 4 ear patterns onto the fabric piece. Cut the ears out. Place 2 ear pieces right sides together. Sew a ¼" seam around the outer edge, leaving the opening, as shown on the pattern. Turn the ear right side out. Bend a pipe cleaner to match the curve of the ear. Insert it into the ear and tack it in place. Make the second ear in the same manner. Tuck and glue one ear into each ear hole. Adjust the ears.

If you have painted the glue areas, sand the paint off where the pieces will join. Glue the trunk and leg pieces onto the body. Glue the bow on.

¼" HOLE
½" DEEP

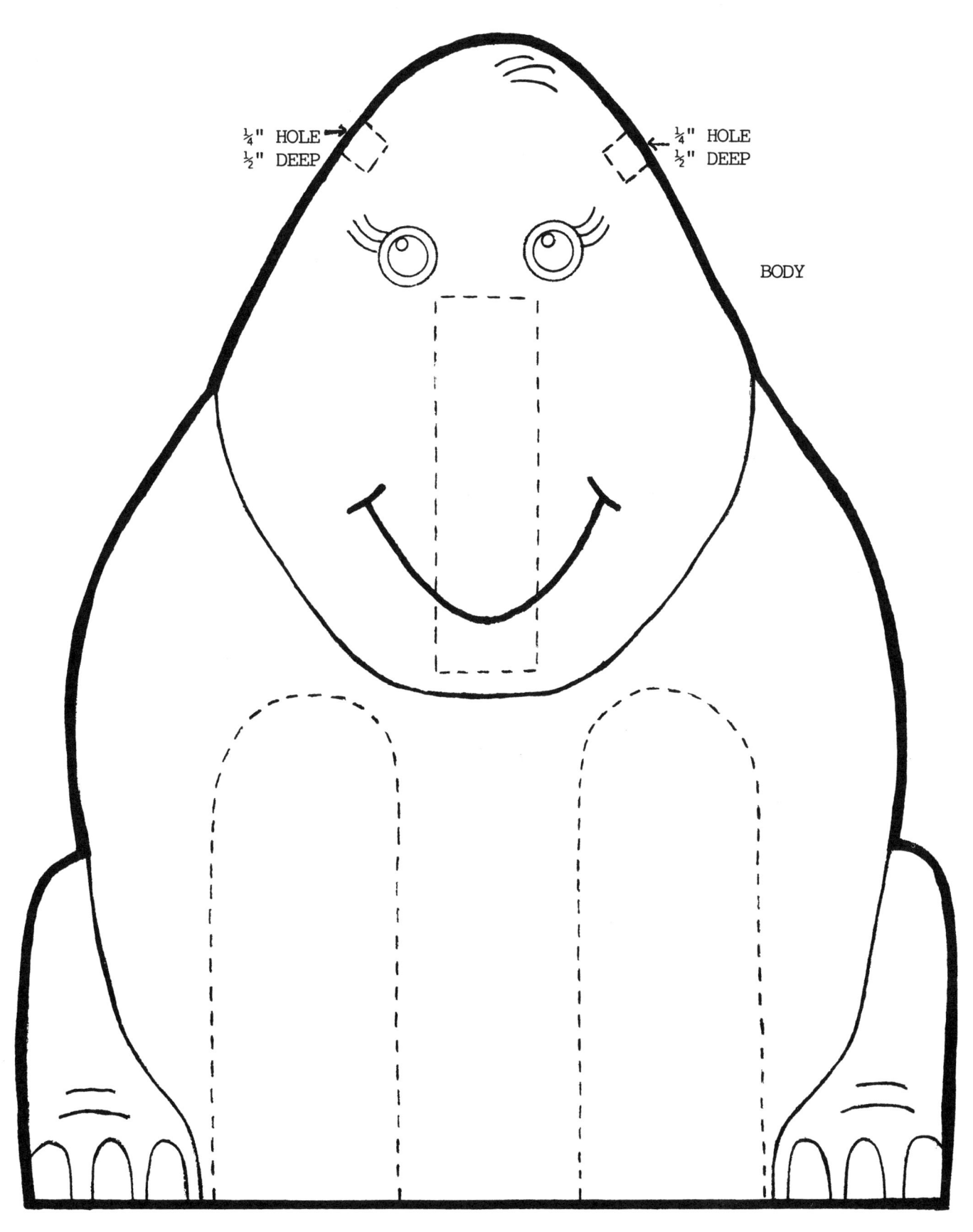

¼" HOLE
½" DEEP

BODY

Pattern for 915: Elephant (body)

Pattern for 915: Elephant (trunk, legs and ears)

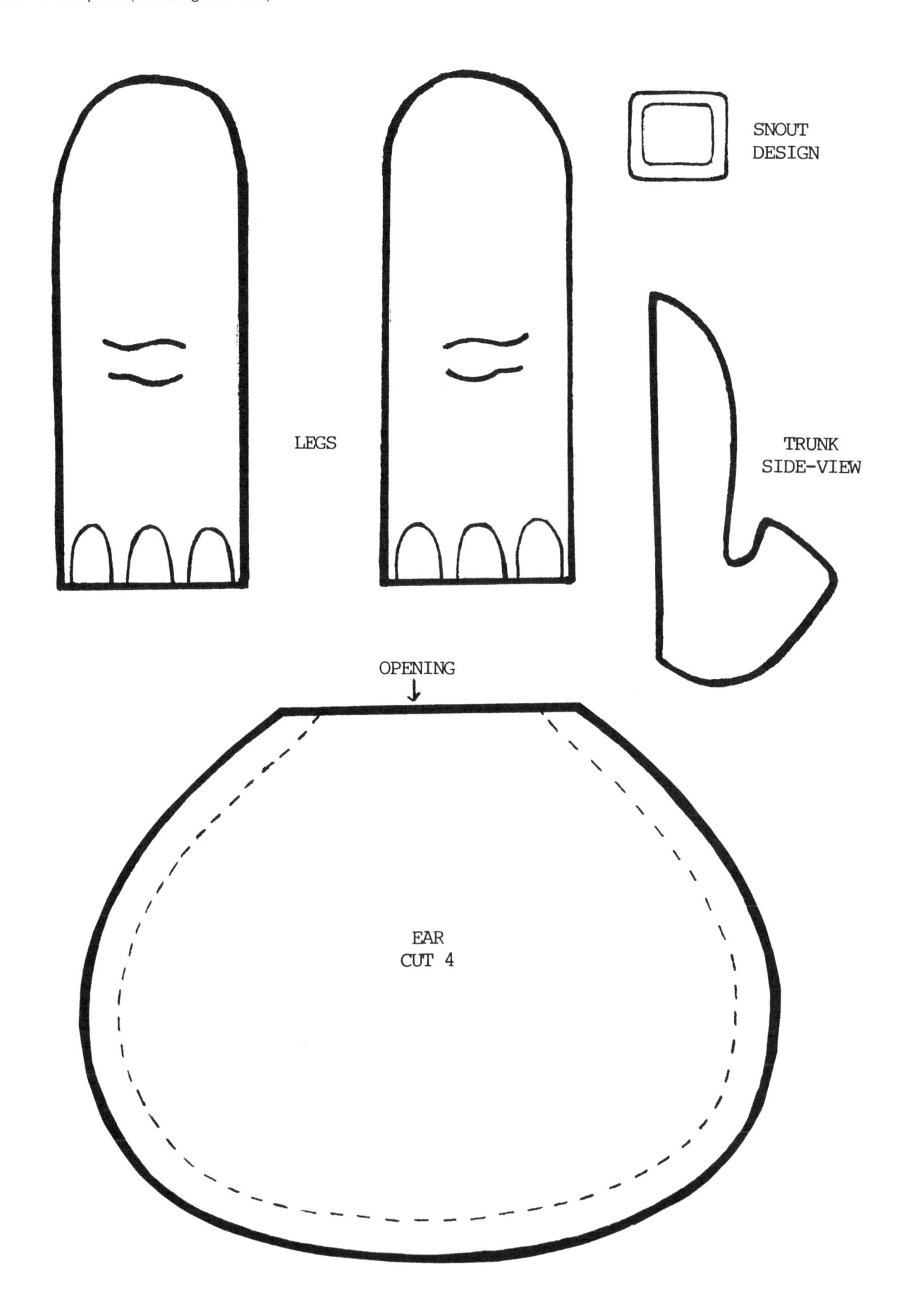

SNOUT DESIGN

LEGS

TRUNK SIDE-VIEW

OPENING

EAR
CUT 4

PATTERN 916:
SEGMENTED PUMPKINS

SUPPLIES
7" x 9" Pine, 1 ½" thick
2 ½" x 5" Basswood, 1/16" thick
Wood glue

ACRYLIC PAINTS
Pumpkin
Green
Brown

Note: DO NOT apply paint to the inside glue edges where the pieces will join. Glue will not bond permanently to painted surfaces.

INSTRUCTIONS
Duplicate the pattern page for the pumpkins and the patterns for the 3 leaves on a copier machine or with tracing paper. Transfer the outline for the pumpkins, along with all of the segmenting cut lines, onto the pine workpiece. Transfer the outlines for the 3 leaf patterns onto the basswood workpiece. Using the smallest blade recommended for the wood thickness, cut around the pattern outline of the pumpkins. Saw along the segmenting cut lines, cutting the 3 pumpkins into 12 individual pieces. Cut the leaves out. Sand all surfaces with 100-grid and than 150-grid sandpaper. Remove the sanding dust with a tack cloth.

Paint **only** the front and back surfaces on pieces 3, 6 and 7 with pumpkin. Paint the front, back and outside edges of pieces 2, 4, 8, 10, 11 and 12 with pumpkin. Paint the front, back and outside edges of piece number 1 with brown. Paint **only** the front and back of pieces 5 and 9 with brown. Paint the leaves green, continuing the color around the edges. Let the paint dry thoroughly. Sand the pieces lightly to remove the "fuzz" raised by the paints. Remove the sanding dust with a tack cloth. Touch-up the paint if necessary.

To enhance the design, sand the front face edges of the 12 segmented pieces. (For a two-sided project, sand the front and back face edges of the segmented pieces.) Sand the front face edges of the 3 leaves.

Glue the 12 segmented pieces back together in their original positions, using the pattern as a guide. Secure them tightly together with rubber bands until the glue dries. Glue the leaves on.

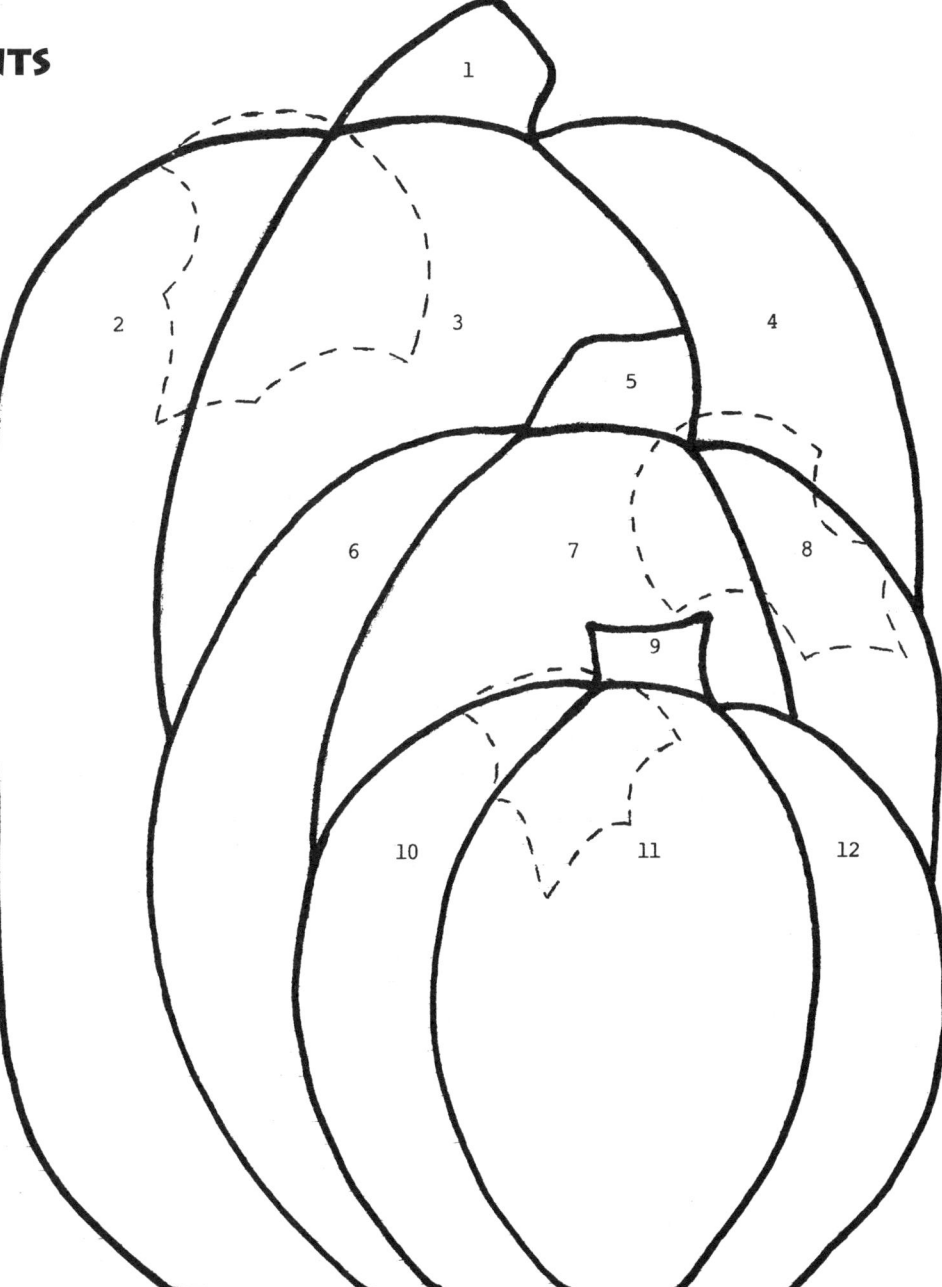

Pattern for 916: Segmented Pumpkins

These two patterns were reduced at 75%. Enlarge at 130%

Leaf pattern for 916: Segmented Pumpkins

PATTERN 917:
DINOSAUR

SUPPLIES

8" x 11" Pine, ¾" thick
3" of 5/16" Wood dowel
Varnish (semi-gloss finish)
Wood glue

Note: Use wood that has a good color and grain pattern to enhance the finished look of this project.

INSTRUCTIONS

Duplicate the pattern on a copier machine or with tracing paper. Transfer the pattern outlines for the body, 2 front legs and 2 back legs onto the workpiece. Cut the shapes out with a scroll saw. Drill the holes, where shown on the pattern. Cut the wood dowel into 4 – ¾" long pieces. Glue one piece of dowel into each of the holes drilled in the leg pieces. Let the glue dry. Sand the front face edges of the legs and all of the edges of the body until they are well-rounded. Sand all surfaces with 100-grid and than 150-grid sandpaper. Remove the sanding dust with a tack cloth.

Apply a thin, even coat of varnish to all surfaces of the body and leg pieces. Let the varnish dry. Lightly sand all surfaces. Remove the sanding dust with a tack cloth. Apply a second thin coat of varnish to all surfaces. Let the varnish dry.

If you have applied finish to the glue areas, sand the finish off where the pieces join. Glue the legs in position on the body, making sure that they are straight and even. Weight or clamp them in place, until the glue dries, to ensure a strong bond.

Pattern for 917: Dinosaur

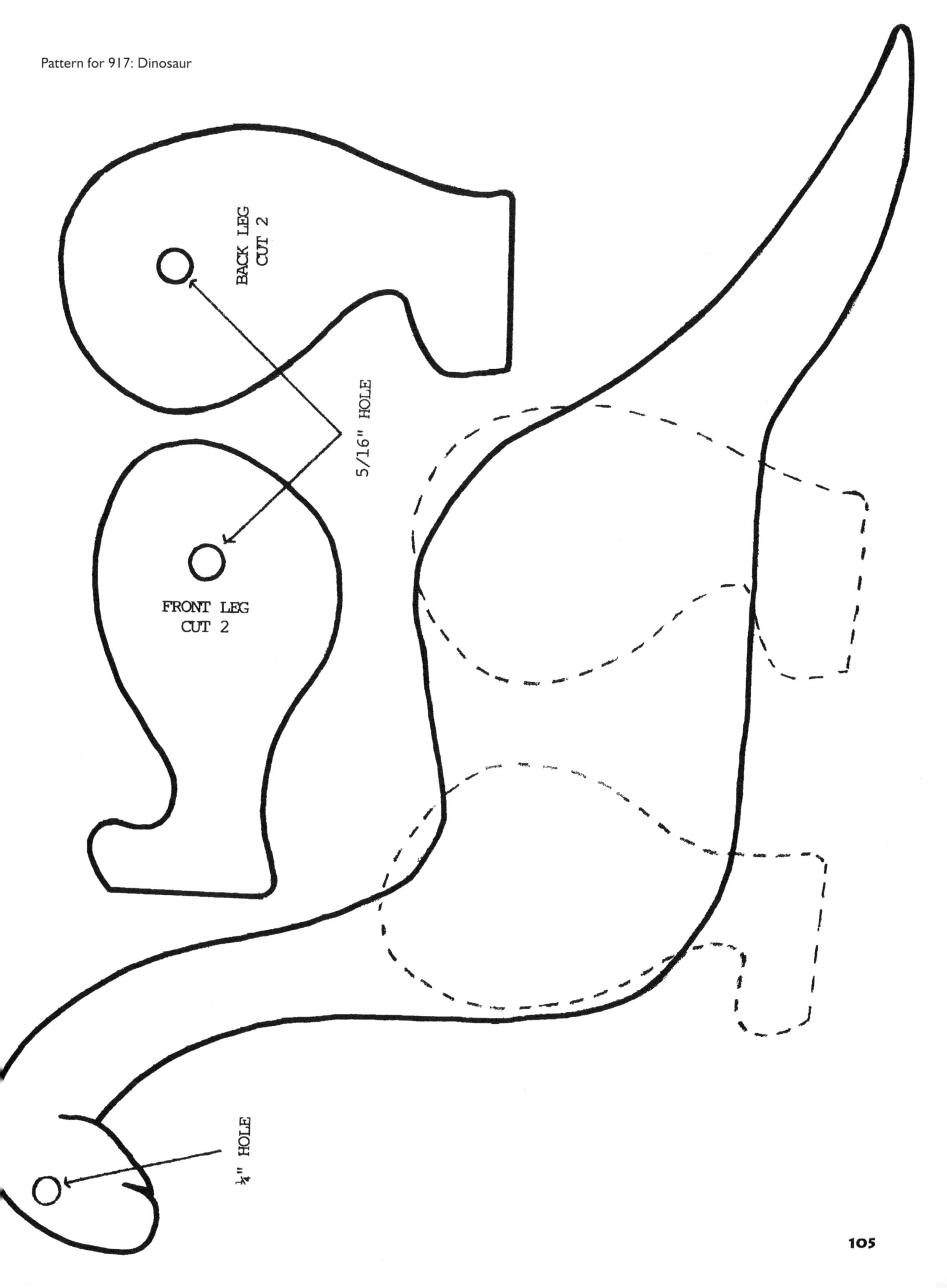

BACK LEG
CUT 2

5/16" HOLE

FRONT LEG
CUT 2

¼" HOLE

PATTERN 918:
SCARECROW

SUPPLIES

7" x 15" Pine, 1 ½" thick
5" x 6" Pine, ¾" thick
1" x 4" Basswood, 1/16" thick
10 ½" of 5/16" Wood dowel
36" of White string
3 – ¾" x 1" scraps of Fabric
Raffia
Wood Glue
White Glue

ACRYLIC PAINTS

Pumpkin
Orange
Red
Burgundy
Flesh
White
Tan
Brown
Blue
Yellow
Green
Black

INSTRUCTIONS

Duplicate the pattern sheets on a copier machine or with tracing paper. Line up and tape together the 2 halves of the scarecrow's body, trimming off the excess paper. Transfer the scarecrow's body outline onto the 1 ½" thick pine. Transfer the bird, pumpkin and base outlines onto the ¾" thick pine. Transfer the hat brim and the heart outlines onto the basswood workpiece. Cut the shapes out with a scroll saw. Cut the wood dowel into a 1 ½" piece, a 2 ¼" piece and a 6 ¾" piece. Drill the holes, where shown on the patterns. Sand all surfaces with 100-grid and than 150-grid sandpaper. Remove the sanding dust with a tack cloth.

Transfer the main pattern lines onto the scarecrow. Base-coat the following colors around the edges and onto the back of the pieces. Base-coat the hat tan. Base-coat the hat band red. Mix 2 parts flesh to 1 part white and base-coat the head sack. Base-coat the shirt green. Base-coat the pants and the bird Blue. Base-coat the hands white. Base-coat the base and the pumpkin's stem brown. Base-coat the pumpkin with pumpkin.

Paint the heart red, continuing the color around the edges. Base-coat the hat brim piece with tan, continuing the color around the edges. Let the paint dry.

Sand all of the pieces lightly to remove the "fuzz" raised by the paints. Remove the sanding dust with a tack cloth. Touch-up the paints if necessary.

Transfer the pattern design onto the shirt. Thin yellow with a few drops of water and paint the wide stripes for the plaid on the shirt. Let the paint dry. Thin red with a few drops of water and paint a narrow stripe in-between each of the wide stripes. Dot on the red buttons using the handle of a small paintbrush. Let the paint dry.

Transfer the details onto the pumpkin. Shade the pumpkin with orange. Shade the hat and the hat brim piece with brown. Shade the hatband and the heart with burgundy. Shade the head sack with flesh. Mix green with a small amount of black and use to shade the shirt. Mix blue with a small amount of black and use to shade the pants and the bird. Darken the shading on the head sack with brown. Let the paint dry.

Transfer the face design details onto the scarecrow. Transfer the design details onto the bird. Paint the scarecrow's eyes white. Paint his nose red. Using a very dry, stiff bristle brush, dry brush the cheeks and chin with red. Paint the bird's beak pumpkin. Paint the pumpkin's leaf green. Let the paint dry.

Shade the bird's beak with orange. Dot black eyes on the bird using a small paintbrush handle. Dot black eye pupils on the scarecrow using a slightly larger paintbrush handle. Paint the scarecrow's mouth black. Add the line details to the bird, shirt and pants with black. Detail the pumpkin with brown. Darken the line details on the head sack with brown. Let the paint dry.

Highlight the bird, the hat and the hat brim piece with white. Dot a white highlight on the scarecrow's and the bird's eyes using the tip of a round toothpick. Highlight the scarecrow's nose with white. Outline the scarecrow's eyes and nose with black. Highlight the bird's beak with yellow. Let the paint dry.

Wood glue short lengths of raffia around the scarecrow's face for hair, starting each piece in the area where the hat brim piece will be positioned. Wood glue the hat brim piece in place. Glue a few pieces of raffia to the outside edge of each hand, right under the shirtsleeve cuff. Wood glue the heart on the shirt.

Spread a thin layer of white glue on the back of the fabric pieces and position them on the pants. Cut the string into 3 equal pieces. Tie one of the pieces into a bow and glue it in place under the scarecrow's chin. Wrap a piece of string around the top of each shirtsleeve cuff and tie it in to a bow. Dot a drop of white glue on the knot of each bow.

Wood glue the 1 ½" length of dowel into the hole drilled in the bent arm. Wood glue the 2 ¼" length of dowel into the hole drilled in the arm that hangs straight down. Let the glue dry.

Glue one end of the 6 ¾" length of dowel into the hole drilled in the base. Put a small amount of wood glue on the bottom edge of each pant leg and on the top of the dowel. Place the scarecrow on the base with the dowel wedged straight up between his legs. Adjust the dowel so that the bottom edge of the pants rest on the base and top of the dowel is glued to the bottom edge of the shirt.

Wood glue the pumpkin onto the base. Wood glue a few pieces of raffia to the base. Wood glue the bird onto the scarecrow's shoulder.

Pattern for 918: Scarecrow (top half)

HAT BRIM

5/16" HOLE
1/4" DEEP

HEART

HEART
5/16" HOLE
1/4" DEEP

107

Pattern for 918: Scarecrow (bottom half)

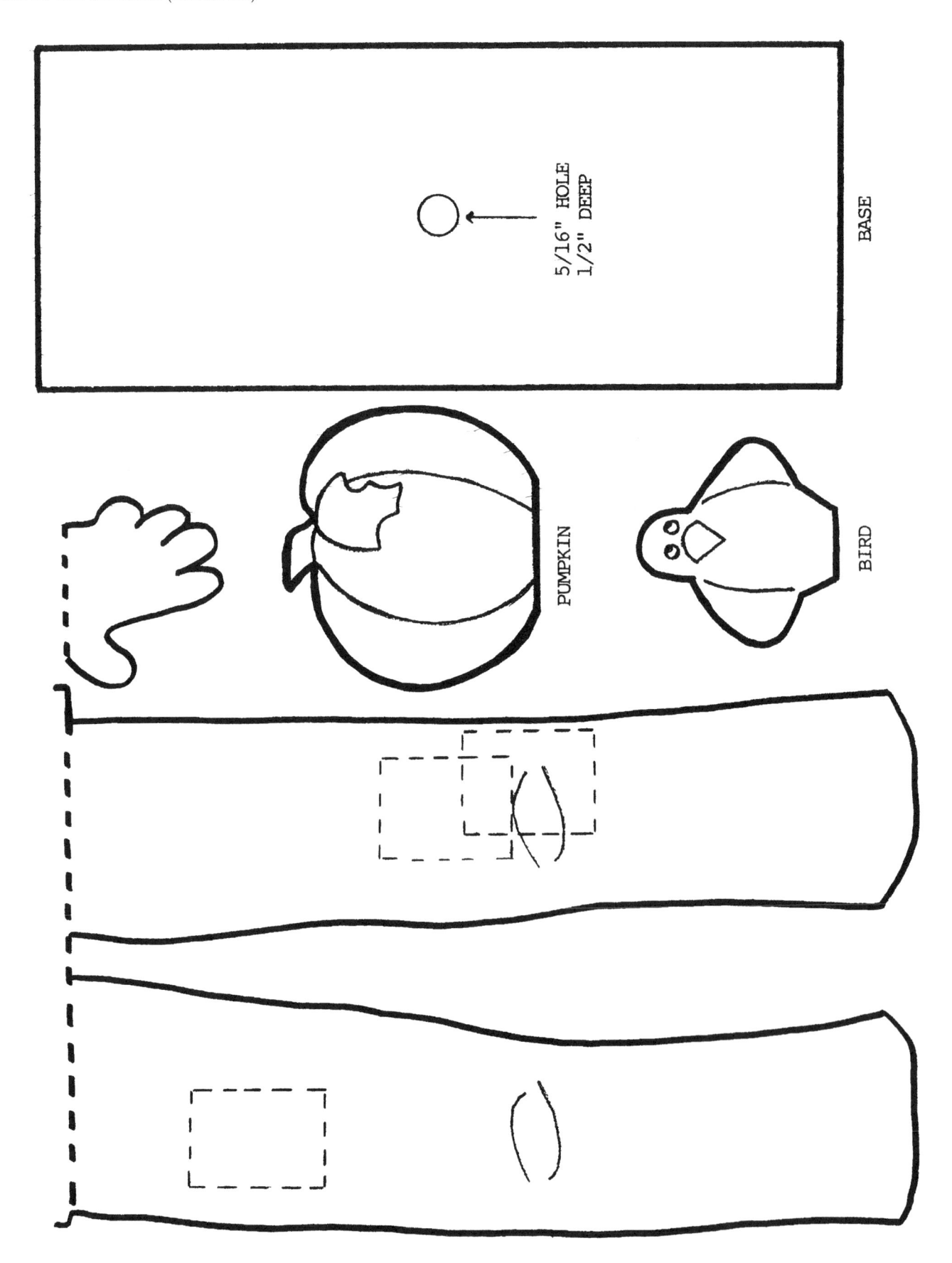

BASE

5/16" HOLE
1/2" DEEP

PUMPKIN

BIRD

108

PATTERN 919:
BIRD IN NEST WREATH

SUPPLIES

3 ½" x 3 ½" Basswood, ¼" thick
4" x 5" Basswood, 1/8" thick
6" Grapevine Wreath
Spanish moss
Hot melt glue
Wood glue
5" of 20-gauge wire

ACRYLIC PAINTS

Light Blue
Blue
Light Orange
Orange
Light Green
Green
Yellow
Black

INSTRUCTIONS

Duplicate the pattern on a copier machine or with tracing paper. Transfer the bird's body pattern onto the ¼" thick wood. Transfer the tail, beak and 8 leaf patterns onto the 1/8" thick wood. Carefully cut out the shapes with a scroll saw. Sand all surfaces with 100-grid and than 150-grid sandpaper. Remove the sanding dust with a tack cloth.

Base-coat the leaves light green, continuing the color around the edges. Base-coat the beak light orange, continuing the color around the edges. Base-coat the bird's body and tail pieces light blue, continuing the color around the edges. Let the paint dry. Sand lightly to remove the "fuzz" raised by the paints. Remove the sanding dust with a tack cloth. Touch-up the paint if necessary.

Float green shading onto the leaves. Float orange shading onto the beak. Float blue shading onto the bird's body and tail pieces. Highlight the beak and the leaves with yellow. Let the paint dry. Paint the detail lines on the leaves green. Paint the detail lines on the tail blue. Dot on the black eyes with a small paintbrush handle. Let the paint dry.

If you have applied paint to the glue areas of the bird pieces, sand the finish off where the pieces will join. Glue the beak and the tail in place on the bird's body with wood glue. Let the glue dry.

Hot glue the Spanish moss onto the front of the wreath to form a nest. Hot glue the bottom of the bird onto the inside of the wreath. Hot glue the leaves onto the wreath. Thread the wire through a few of the vines on the back of the wreath and twist the ends together to form a hanger.

This pattern was reduced at 75%. Enlarge at 130%

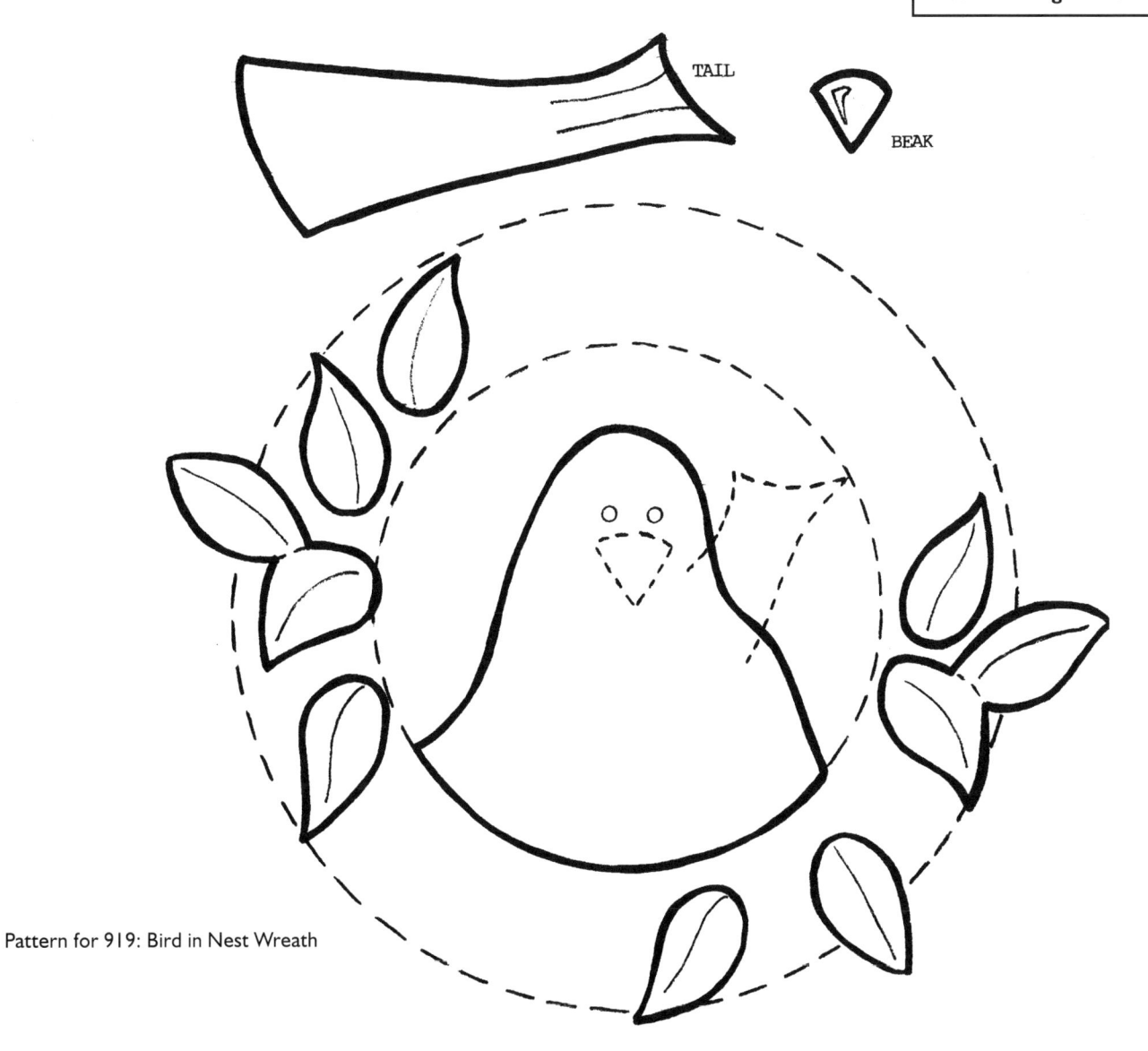

Pattern for 919: Bird in Nest Wreath

PATTERN 920:
ANGEL WITH MOSS HAIR

SUPPLIES

6" x 9 ½" Pine, 1 ½" thick
4" x 3" Basswood, ¼" thick
3" x 8 ½" Basswood, 1/8" thick
3 - 8" pieces of 20-gauge wire
3 - 5/8" White buttons
Brown paint pen (extra-fine tip)
3" x 22" piece of Fabric
Spanish moss
Wood glue
Hot melt glue
14" of ¾" wide Lace

ACRYLIC PAINTS

Beige
Brown
Burgundy
White
Rose
Flesh

INSTRUCTIONS

Duplicate the pattern sheets on a copier machine or with tracing paper. Transfer the angel's body pattern onto the 1 ½" thick pine. Transfer the wing pattern onto the 1/8" thick wood. Transfer the arm piece pattern and 3 flower patterns onto the ¼" thick wood. Cut the shapes out with a scroll saw. Cut the petal design kerf lines on the flowers. Drill the holes, where shown on the pattern. Sand all surfaces, including the inner edges of the kerf cuts, with 100-grid and than 150-grid sandpaper. Remove the sanding dust with a tack cloth.

On the body piece, base-coat the head, neck and hand flesh, continuing the color around the edges and onto the back. Base-coat the hand area of the arm piece flesh, continuing the color around the edges. Base-coat the flowers burgundy, continuing the color around the edges. Base-coat the dress and apron beige, continuing the color around the edges and onto the back. Base-coat the sleeve area of the arm piece beige, continuing the color around the edges. Base-coat the wing piece beige, continuing the color around the edges and onto the back. Let the paint dry. Sand the pieces lightly to remove the "fuzz" raised by the paints. Remove the sanding dust with a tack cloth. Touch-up the paint if necessary.

Transfer the lines and the design details onto both sides of the wing piece. Paint the lines and the design details using the brown paint pen.

Transfer the design details onto the body and the arm pieces. Using a very dry, stiff bristle brush, dry brush the cheeks with rose. Paint the mouth black. Dot on the black eyes using a small brush handle. Mix brown with water to form a wash. Use the mixture to paint the stripes for the plaid on the dress and on the sleeve area of the arm piece. Let the paint dry.

Float brown shading on the dress and apron and on the sleeve area of the arm piece. Dot a white highlight on each eye using the tip of a round toothpick. Dot on the white collar using a small paintbrush handle. Highlight the flowers with white. Let the paint dry.

If you have painted the glue areas, sand the paint off where the pieces will join. With the wood glue, glue the wing and the arm pieces in place. Let the glue dry. Hot glue a button in the center of each flower. Hot glue the Spanish moss to the angel's head for hair. Hot glue the lace around the bottom edge of the apron, starting and ending in the back. Wrap the fabric piece around the angel's head, tie it into a bow and hot glue it in place.

Curl each length of wire around a thin piece of dowel. Dip one end of each wire in wood glue and push it into one of the flowers. Glue the other end of each wire into one of the holes drilled in the hand.

Pattern for 920: Angel with Moss Hair (body)

BODY

111

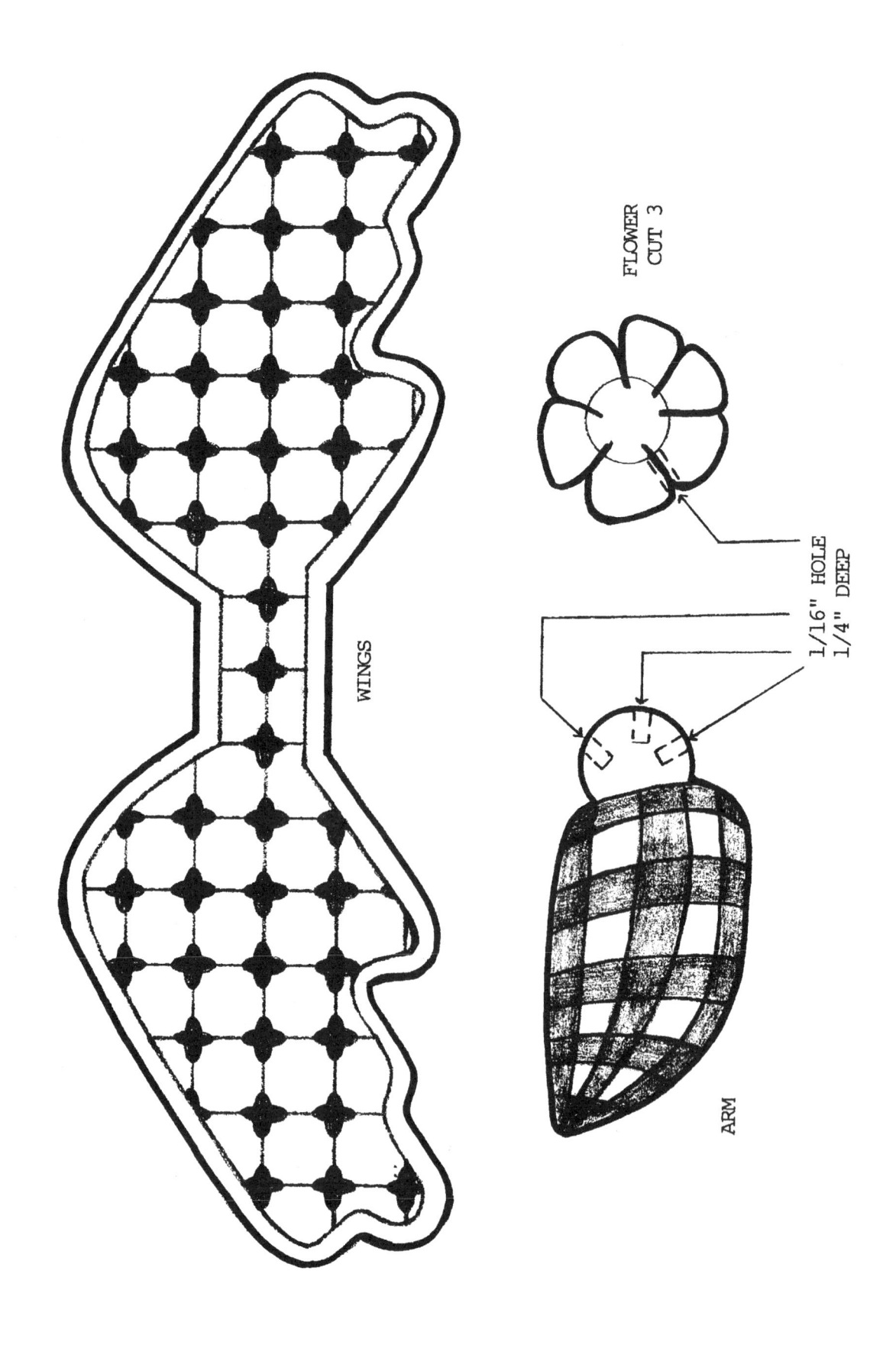

Pattern for 920: Angel with Moss Hair (wings, arm and flower)

FLOWER
CUT 3

1/16" HOLE
1/4" DEEP

WINGS

ARM

GALLERY

Pattern 825A: Bunny Puzzle, Pattern 825B: Bunny Puzzle (fabric ears), and Pattern 825C: Bunny Holding Heart

Pattern 826A: Dog Puzzle and Pattern 826B: Dog Puzzle (fabric ears)

Pattern 827: Inchworm Puzzle

Pattern 860: Apple Puzzle

Pattern 861: Pear Puzzle

Pattern 862: Grape Puzzle

Pattern 829: Santa Puzzle, Pattern 830A: Santa Key Chain or Magnet, Pattern 830B: Santa Tree Ornament, and Pattern 830C: Santa Shelf Decoration

Pattern 831: Heart Santa

Pattern 871: Santa with Hat

Pattern 832: Santa Heart Face

115

Pattern 835: Christmas Angel

Pattern 870: Angel with Flower

Pattern 828: Tree Puzzle

Pattern 833: Inner/Outer Tree

Pattern 834A: Standing Tree and Pattern 834B: Standing Tree

Pattern 874: Holiday Tree

Pattern 836: Christmas Wreath

117

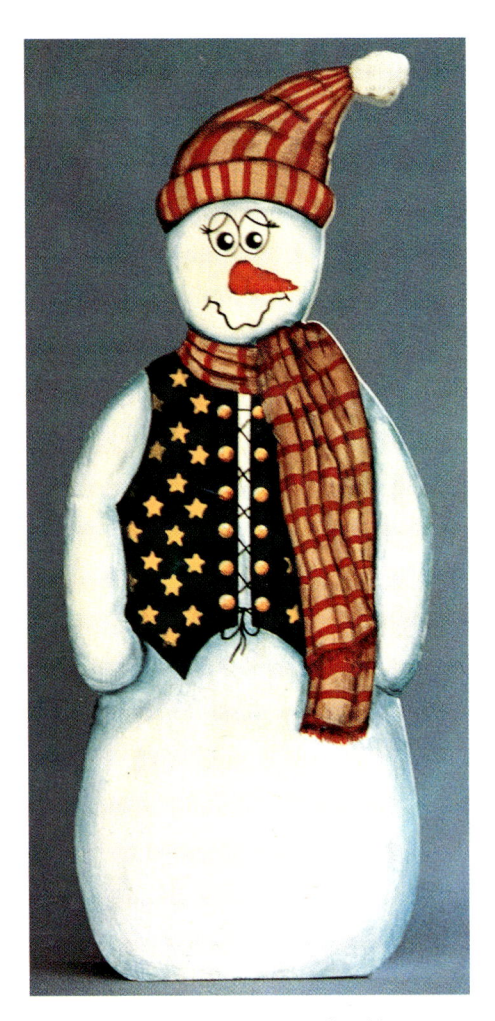

Pattern 872: Snowman with Scarf

Pattern 837: Snowman with Star Vest

Pattern 905: Boo-Ghost

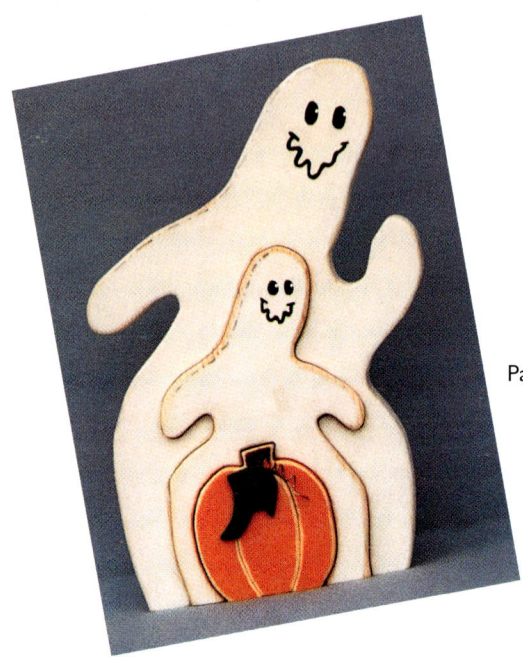

Pattern 904: Ghosts and Pumpkin

Pattern 902: Three Pumpkins

Pattern 903A: Tall Pumpkin and Pattern 903B: Tall Pumpkin

Pattern 901: Inner/Outer Pumpkin

Pattern 916: Segmented Pumpkins

Pattern 913: Witch

119

Pattern 875: Holiday Turkey

Pattern 918: Scarecrow

Pattern 898: Butterfly Wreath

Pattern 899: Butterfly Wall or Lawn Ornament (3-D)

Pattern 900: Butterfly Wall or Lawn Ornament (flat)

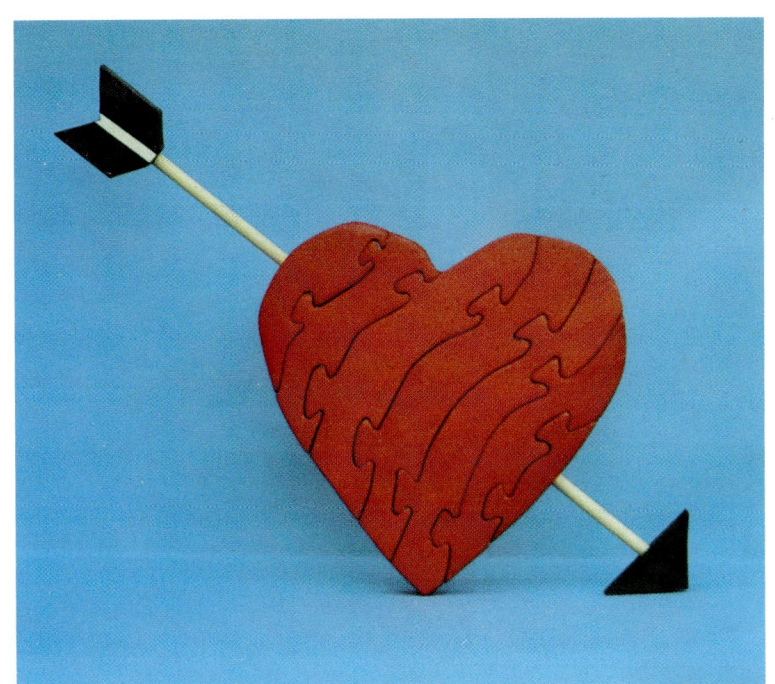

Pattern 840: Heart Puzzle

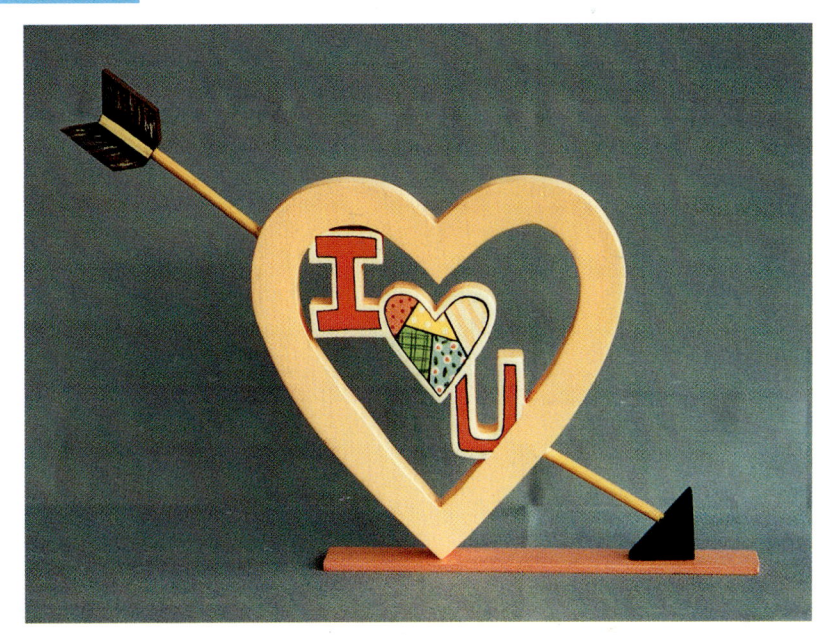

Pattern 841: I-Love-You Heart

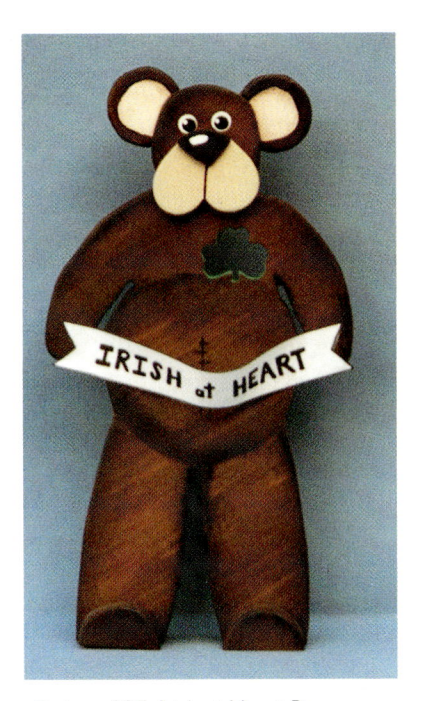

Pattern 887: Irish at Heart Bear

Pattern 886: Irish Shamrock Heart

Pattern 845: Bunny Wreath

Pattern 846: Six-Egg Basket

Pattern 876: Holiday Eagle

Pattern 844: Spring Is In The Air

Pattern 907: Flower Pot

Pattern 919: Bird in Nest Wreath

Pattern 920: Angel with Moss Hair

Pattern 891: Double Bow and Pattern 890: Single Bow

Pattern 877: Three Bears

Pattern 878: Goldie

Pattern 888: Sitting Bear

Pattern 869: Bunny

Pattern 867: Cat

Pattern 868: Dog

Pattern 880: Boy Bunny with Sucker

Pattern 881: Girl Bunny with Balloon

125

Pattern 917: Dinosaur

Pattern 850B: Toy Bunny (fabric ears) and Pattern 850A: Toy Bunny

Pattern 851B: Toy Dog and Pattern 851A: Toy Dog (fabric ears)

Pattern 908: Fish Bowl

Pattern 873: Reindeer

Pattern 911: Penguin

Pattern 906: Speckled Bunny

Pattern 912: Lamb

127

Pattern 910: Cow

Pattern 915: Elephant

Pattern 909: Welcome Cat

Pattern 914: Turtle

Made in the USA
Columbia, SC
02 June 2018

Acknowledgements:

Thank you Nick, Nicholas, Adria, Marin, and Saltydog...I love you all infinity times infinity. Nick, I am so thankful for our time together in China. It's where it all happened! How many amazing places did we explore together?! The family and life that we have built together is in for so many exciting changes this year and I am so excited for all that is to come! Marin, welcome to our world sweet baby girl!
And once again, thank you Lei for your patience and expertise in helping create this book! You are awesome!
--KN

Copyright © 2018 by Kimberly Naylor
Illustrated by Lei Yang
Edited by Meredith Tennant
All rights reserved.

Travel Bug Press 2018
ISBN: 978-0-9979493-2-2

modern: recent fashion or style; ahead of its time

natural resource: materials that are found in nature and can be used by people in different ways

orbits: to go all the way around something

Pinyin: the system used to sound out Chinese characters into words using the alphabet

plant: a factory where electricity is made

population: the number of people in a certain area

ports: the cities, towns, or other places where ships load or unload

Portugal: a country in Europe; see map 1

Portuguese: people or things from Portugal

rush hour: the time of day when a lot of people are using the roads, trains, buses, and subways; usually, before and after normal work hours

secluded: hidden away from view

shipping: putting things on ships to be sent to other places

skyline(s): the outline of buildings or mountains (often at a distance) against the background of the sky

sorrow: sadness

strokes: the lines that are drawn to form a character or characters

territory: an area or region of land

tomb: an underground area or space where the dead are buried

UK (United Kingdom): a country in Europe made up of England, Wales, Scotland, and Northern Ireland. The capital is London. See map 1

GLOSSARY:

abroad: in or to a different country or countries

accomplishment: something done well with achievement and skill

ancient: really old

architecture: the art and science of designing buildings

autonomy (autonomous): freedom and independence; able to make your own rules

bustling: very busy

cavalry: soldiers who fought on horseback

character(s): pictures that have a meaning; each character is a word or idea

chariots: a carriage pulled by horses and steered by a person

clan: a group of people of the same family or class

contribution: something that is given to help a person, a cause, or a movement

cultures: the customs, arts and sciences, food, behavior, and achievements of a particular group of people

dense (densest): very close together, crowded

destination: the place that you are going to

dialects: a form of language that is particular to a certain area or group of people

dynasty: a family of rulers

facade: the front of a building

fusion: a way of bringing together two different things

governed: ruled or was in charge of

irrigated: watered

majestic: grand, wonderful

Map 2.

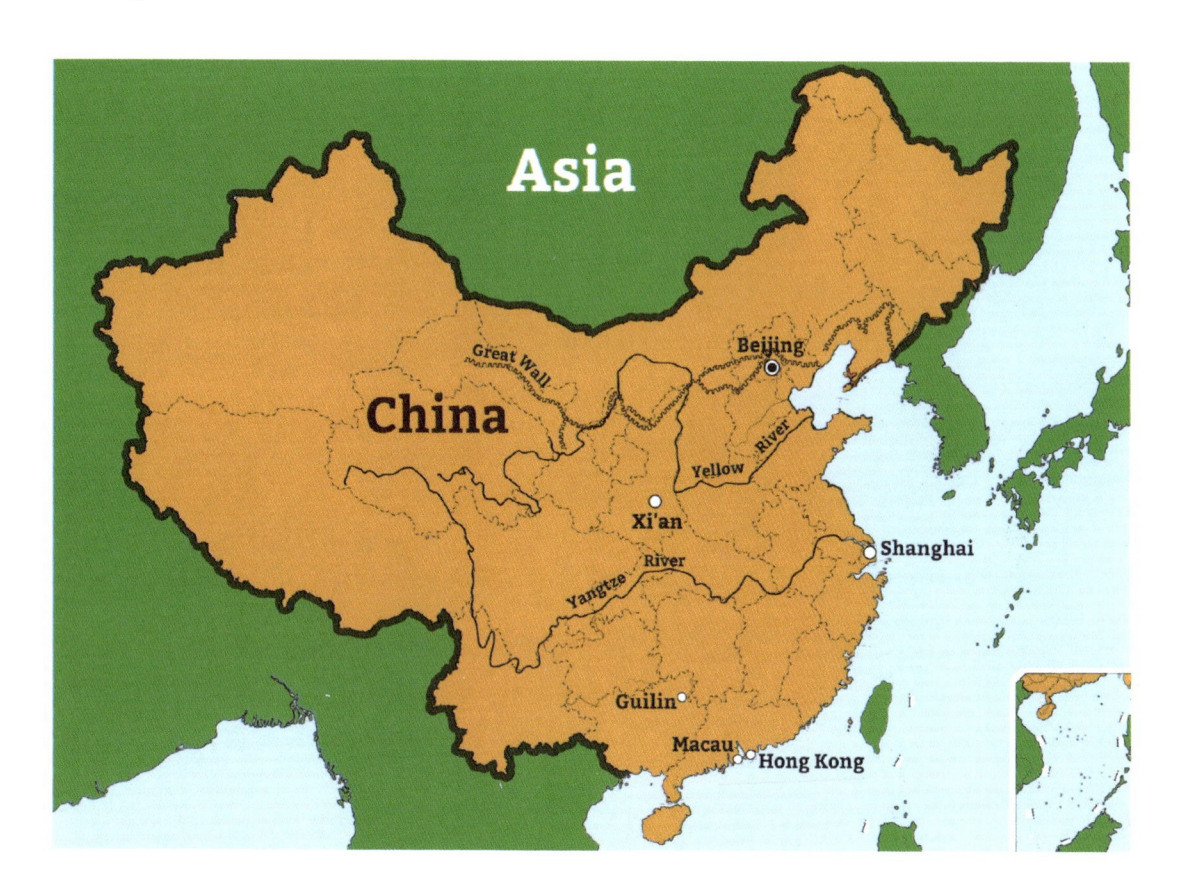

Map 1.

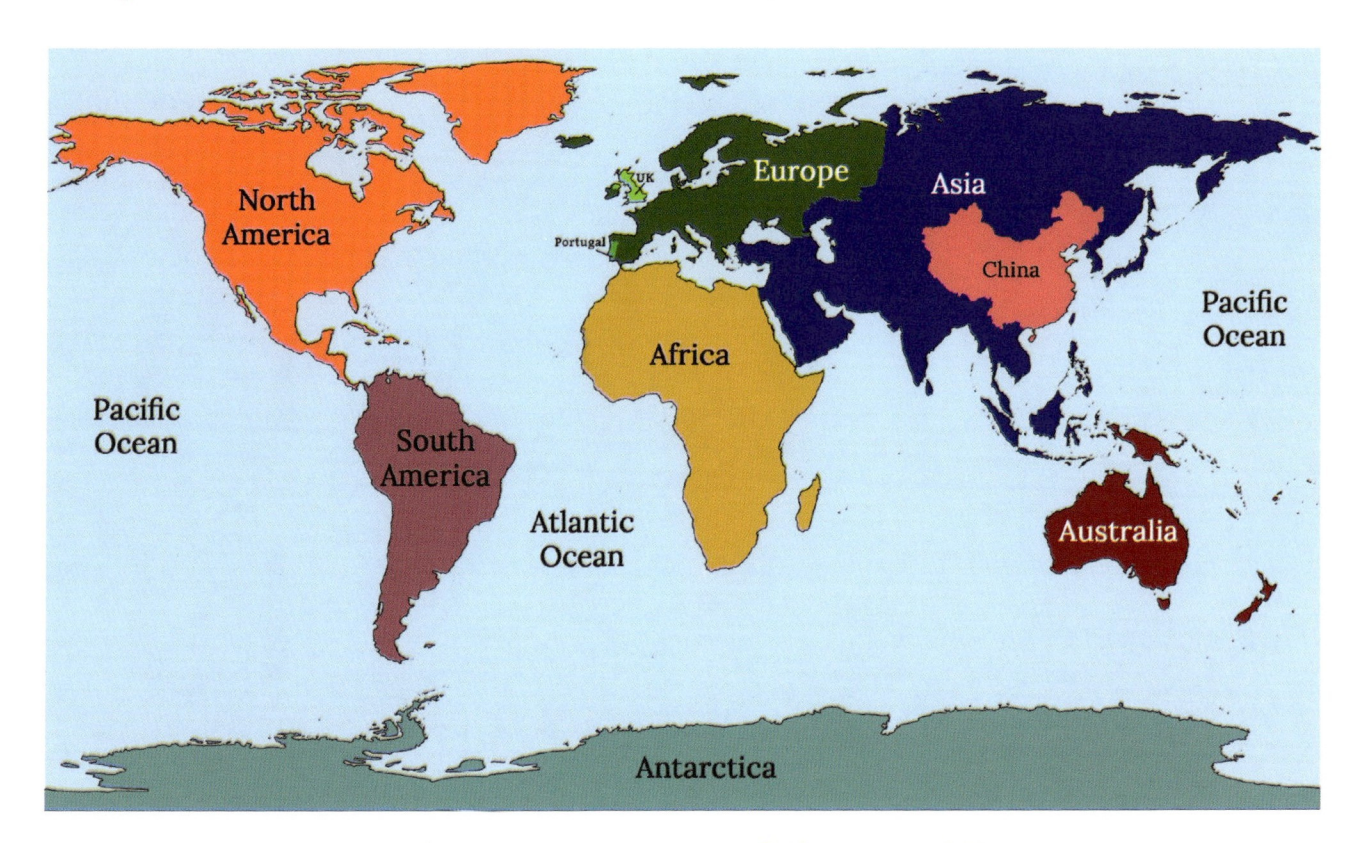

The continents of the world

The places can look different,
the people not like you,
but we all want the same in life:
Peace, Love, and Happiness-to name a few.

So when you go off traveling
to an amazing destination,
respect the people, culture, and land
and have an awesome vacation!

Zai Jian, we must leave you.
We learned so much with you here!
China is a beautiful country
and a place that we hold dear.

But there's something to remember
and please don't forget:
The more you learn of our world,
the smaller it can get.

Next door is the pretty Yu Garden
It's something of which we are quite fond.
We can bring our snacks and walk around
then go feed the fish in the Koi pond.

The City of God Temple also makes our to-do list. If you like to eat snacks, this place is not to be missed.

Let's ride bikes along the river which will give us quite the view of one of the world's best skylines. It's one of Shanghai's top things to do.

But don't get me wrong,
it's not all work and no play.
There are fun places to see.
We'll show you some, if we may.

It is known for its business,
its shipping and ports
for the moving of containers
filled with things of all sorts.

Before we leave you,
before we say goodbye,
there is one more stop to visit
a <u>modern</u> city called Shanghai.

A city so <u>bustling</u>
and filled with skyscrapers,
lots of busy people--
the movers and shakers.

上 海
shàng hǎi
(Shong-hi)

Go see the Big Buddha known for its large size. He sits up on a mountain ruling over the skies.

Is it just me or does he look like he's giving high fives?

Hong Kong has <u>secluded</u> beaches where you can find a lot of space. Hike the mountains and kayak the bay. It's a naturally beautiful place.

It also has many man-made wonders.
But just where should we go?
How about Ocean Park and Disneyland?
Ride the rides and see the shows.

Victoria Harbor is spectacular.
Let's go see it this afternoon.
We can take the Star Ferry
to view both Hong Kong and Kowloon.

We are in for a real treat next
up on Victoria's Peak.
The tram will take us to the top
to give us the view we seek.

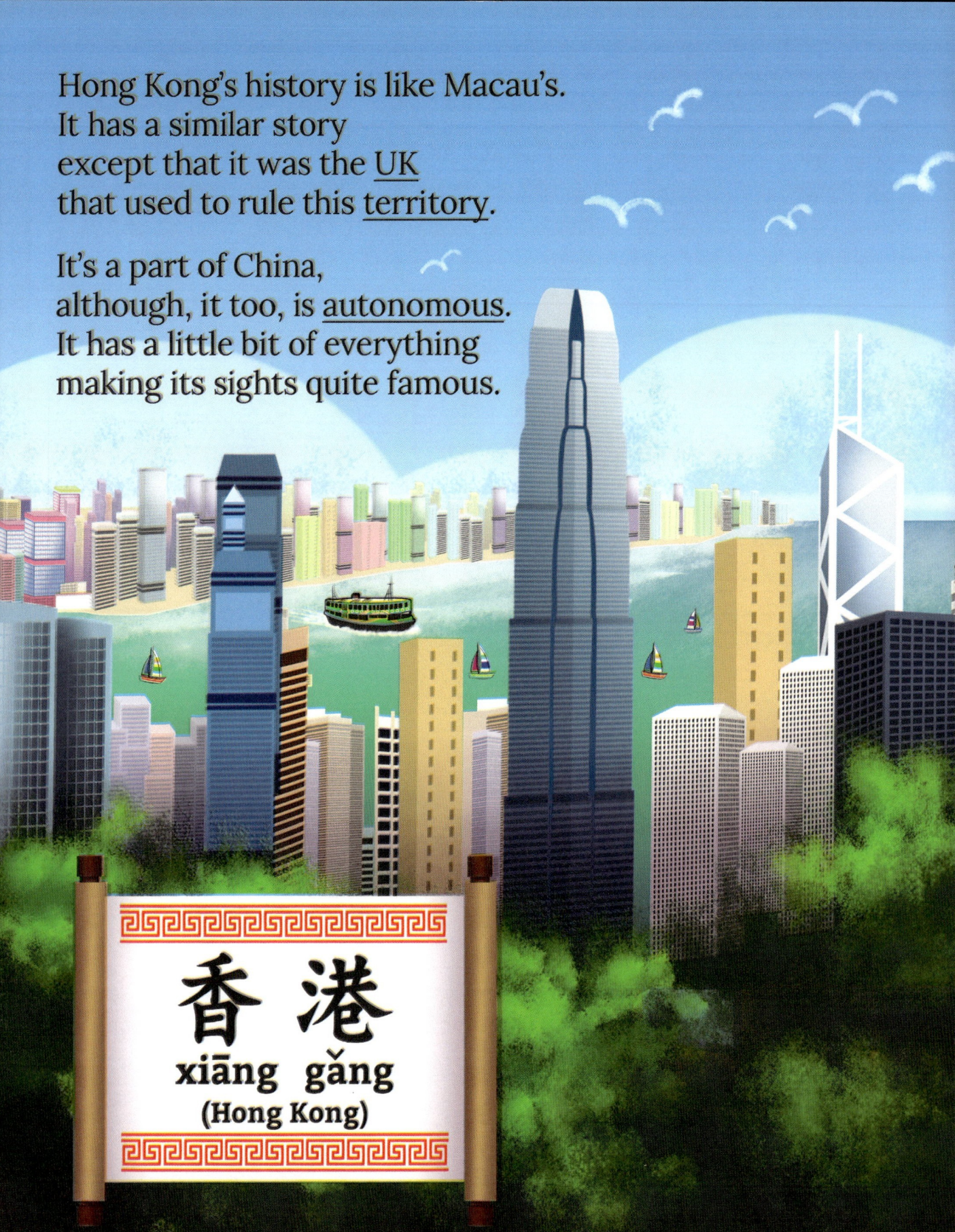

Hong Kong's history is like Macau's.
It has a similar story
except that it was the UK
that used to rule this territory.

It's a part of China,
although, it too, is autonomous.
It has a little bit of everything
making its sights quite famous.

香 港
xiāng gǎng
(Hong Kong)

Macau can rule itself.
That's called <u>autonomy</u>.
It has its own laws
and its very own money.

Climb the steps to St. Paul's.
The <u>facade</u> is all you'll see.
A fire destroyed the rest of the church
that was here originally.

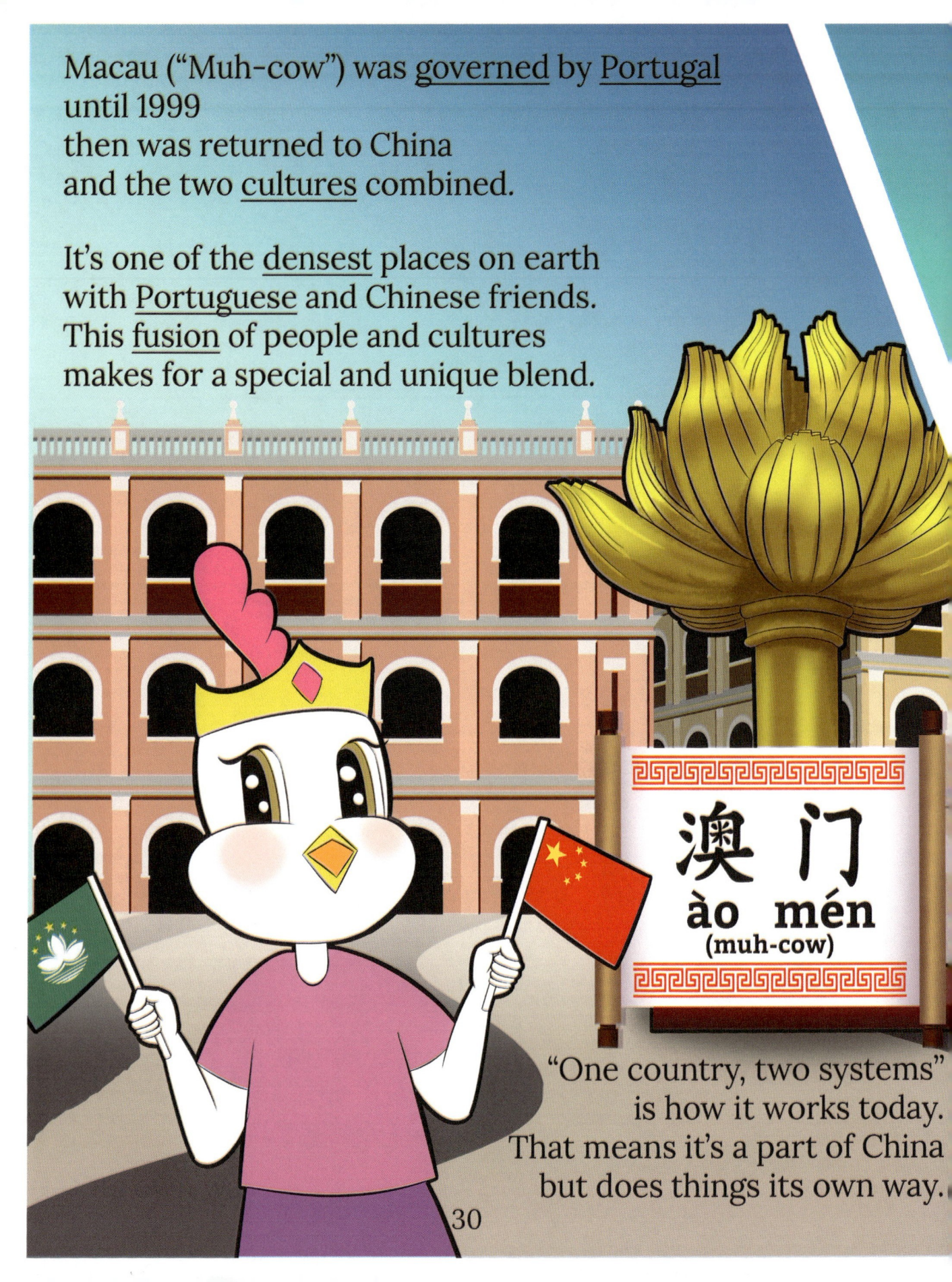

Macau ("Muh-cow") was governed by Portugal
until 1999
then was returned to China
and the two cultures combined.

It's one of the densest places on earth
with Portuguese and Chinese friends.
This fusion of people and cultures
makes for a special and unique blend.

澳 门
ào mén
(muh-cow)

"One country, two systems"
is how it works today.
That means it's a part of China
but does things its own way.

But from the top you can see
the fishermen on their boats.
They use birds called cormorants
to catch fish in their throats.

These birds are specially trained
to hunt fish and go fetch.
Rings are placed around their necks
so they don't swallow the catch.

Guilin is our next stop.
Can you say "gwee-leen?"
The Li River and mountains
make up this <u>majestic</u> scene.

You can even climb some.
One is called Moon Rock.
You must sweat to get there-
it's surely an uphill walk.

桂 林
guì lín
(gwee-leen)

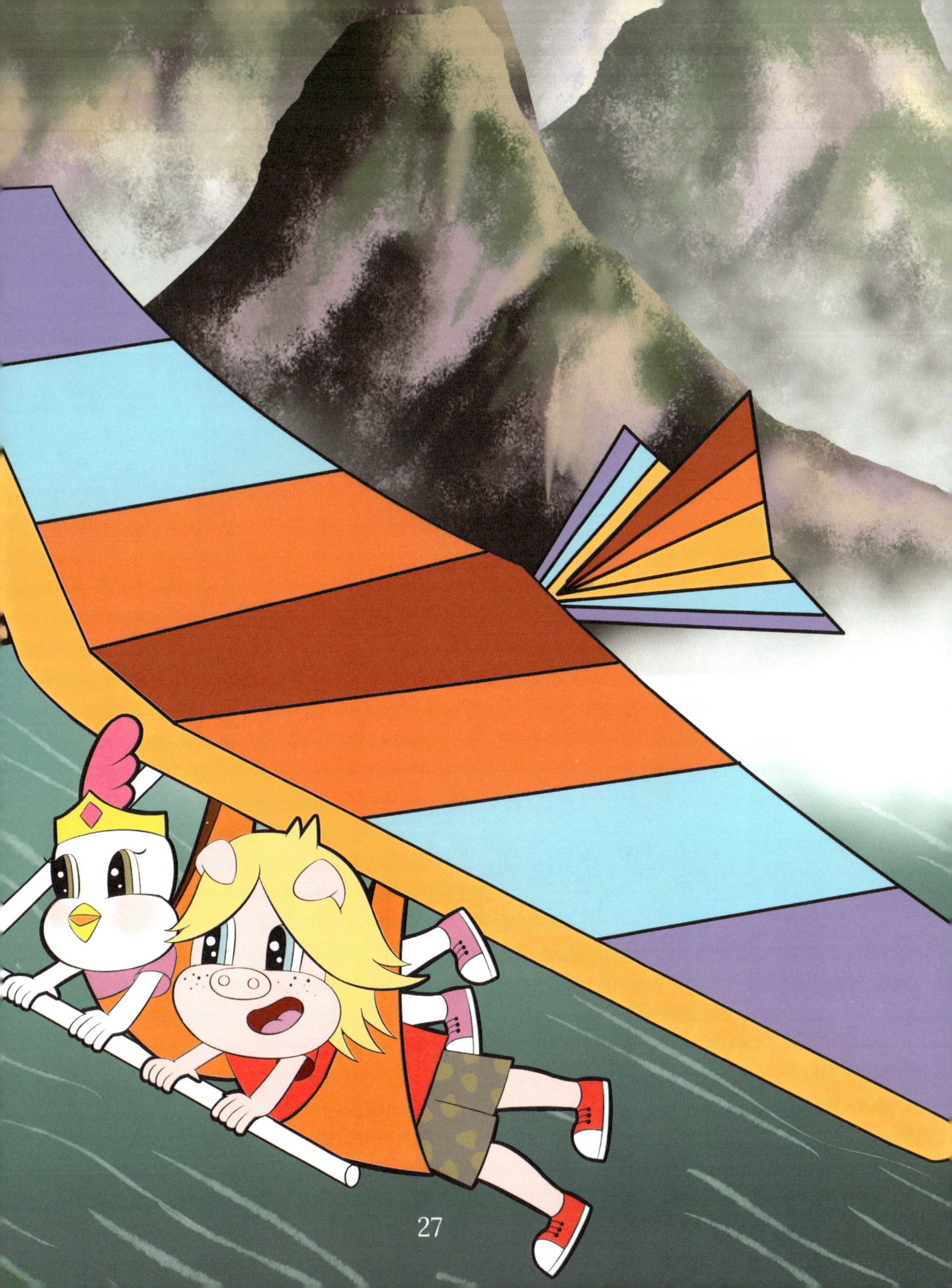

Along the Yangtze River,
sits the Three Gorges Dam.
Using water, a <u>natural resource</u>,
it creates electricity, Ham.

This <u>plant</u> is number one.
The world's largest power station—
moving water real fast
to power the great nation.

When the 1st emperor died,
he wanted a tomb of great size
for peace in the afterlife
and protection from all these guys.

Eight thousand men in all
and lots of horses, too.
Cavalry and chariots-
quite an impressive crew!

Where to next, big brother?
Now let's head to Xi'an!
Oh! I've heard of that place--
rows of statues go on and on!

The Terracotta Army
is its official name.
Thousands of clay soldiers
and no two are the same.

西 安
xī ān
(shee-on)

Its name means Yellow River but is also called The Great <u>Sorrow</u> because of the damage and deaths it caused a long, long time ago.

Sadly, throughout its history, it has flooded and changed its course making the people who lived there leave and move away by force.

Flowing around parts of the Great Wall is Huang He, a river so grand. It's where the ancient Chinese fished, farmed, and irrigated their land.

It stretches 4000 miles
across the earth's face.
Apparently, the astronauts
have tried to take pictures of it from space.

It is quite the accomplishment,
an amazing contribution, for sure.
Imagine all the people and hard work it took
to build this piece of architecture.

The ancient Chinese were creative and smart
making lots of inventions and great works.
They invented the kite, silk, and the compass;
and, of course, paper printing and fireworks!

There is a wall in China.
It twists and turns and snakes.
Its purpose was to protect
the land inside its gates.

The <u>ancient</u> rulers knew
this couldn't be just any wall.
They had to make it Great
so built it 3 stories tall.

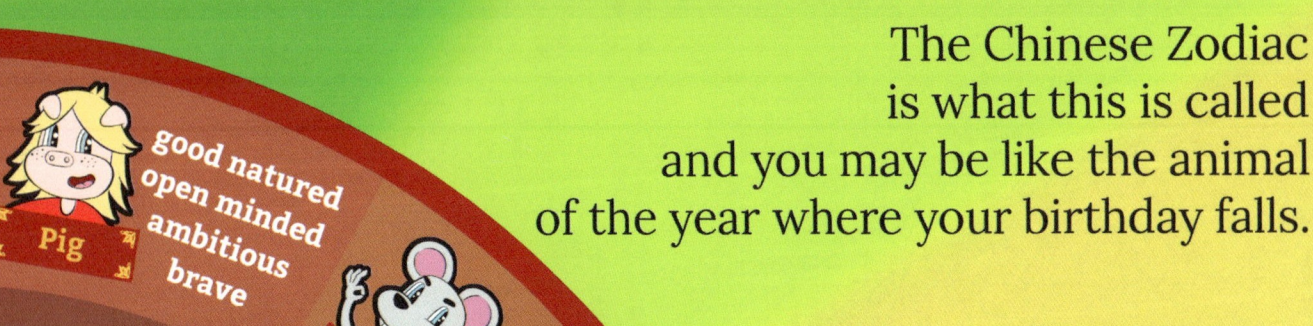

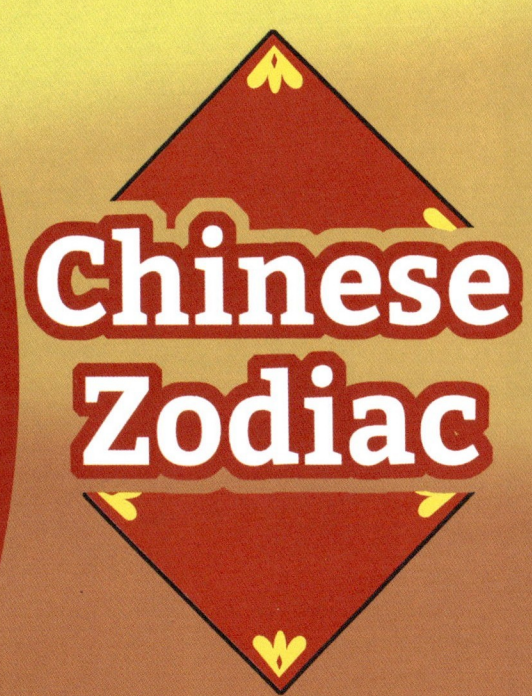

The Chinese Zodiac is what this is called and you may be like the animal of the year where your birthday falls.

Chinese Zodiac

Pig — good natured, open minded, ambitious, brave
1971, 1983, 1995, 2007, 2019, 2031, 2043

Rat — quick-witted, lovely, smart, kind
1972, 1984, 1996, 2008, 2020, 2032, 2044

Ox — hardworking, patient, honest, strong
1973, 1985, 1997, 2009, 2021, 2033, 2045

Tiger — self-confident, competitive, charming, brave
1974, 1986, 1998, 2010, 2022, 2034, 2046

Rabbit — responsible, alert, gentle, kind
1975, 1987, 1999, 2011, 2023, 2035, 2047

Dragon — hardworking, easygoing, natural, smart
1976, 1988, 2000, 2012, 2024, 2036, 2048

Are you an honest ox?
Or a rabbit who is kind?
What year were you born?
Look at the wheel and see what you find.

The planet Jupiter orbits around the sun.
It takes a whole twelve years
for its trip to be done.

生 shēng

肖 xiāo

This special wheel
is based on these twelve years.
There is one animal
for each year here.

Dog — hardworking, sincere, helpful, brave
1982, 1994, 2006, 2018, 2030, 2042, 2054

Chicken — tenderhearted, trustworthy, responsible, generous
1981, 1993, 2005, 2017, 2029, 2041, 2053

Monkey — adventurous, confident, fearless, smart
1980, 1992, 2004, 2016, 2028, 2040, 2052

Goat — creative, gentle, kind, shy
1979, 1991, 2003, 2015, 2027, 2039, 2051

Horse — strong sense of humor, born performer, energetic, animated
1978, 1990, 2002, 2014, 2026, 2038, 2050

Snake — born leader, clever, wise, calm
1977, 1989, 2001, 2013, 2025, 2037, 2049

18

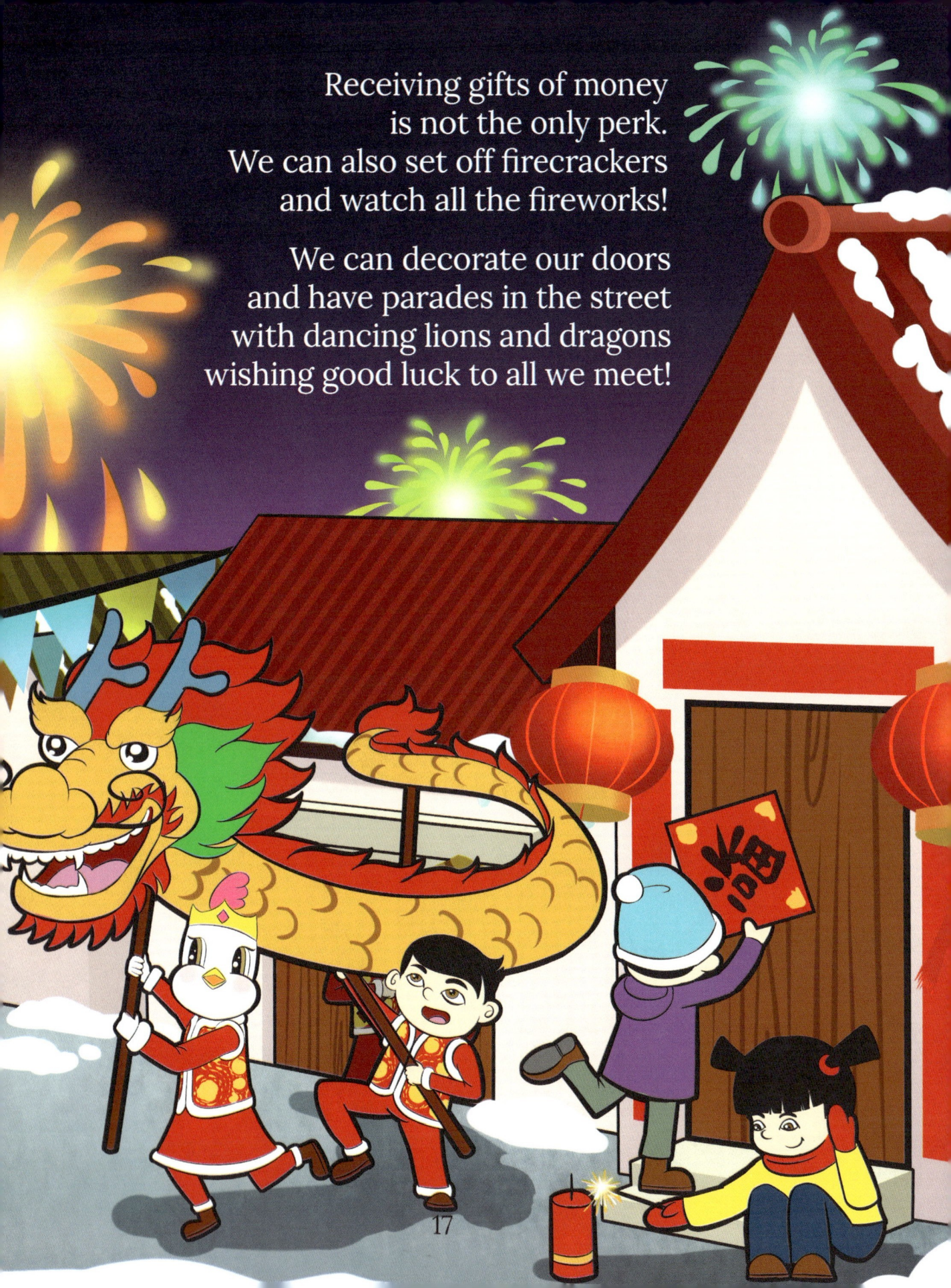

Receiving gifts of money is not the only perk. We can also set off firecrackers and watch all the fireworks!

We can decorate our doors and have parades in the street with dancing lions and dragons wishing good luck to all we meet!

Happy New Year
新 年 快 乐
xīn nián kuài lè
(shin-nyen kwhy-luh)

Every year the Chinese celebrate Chinese New Year where people get together with their families from far and near.

Now it's time for a party! "Happy New Year" to you! Here is a red envelope and it's filled with money too!

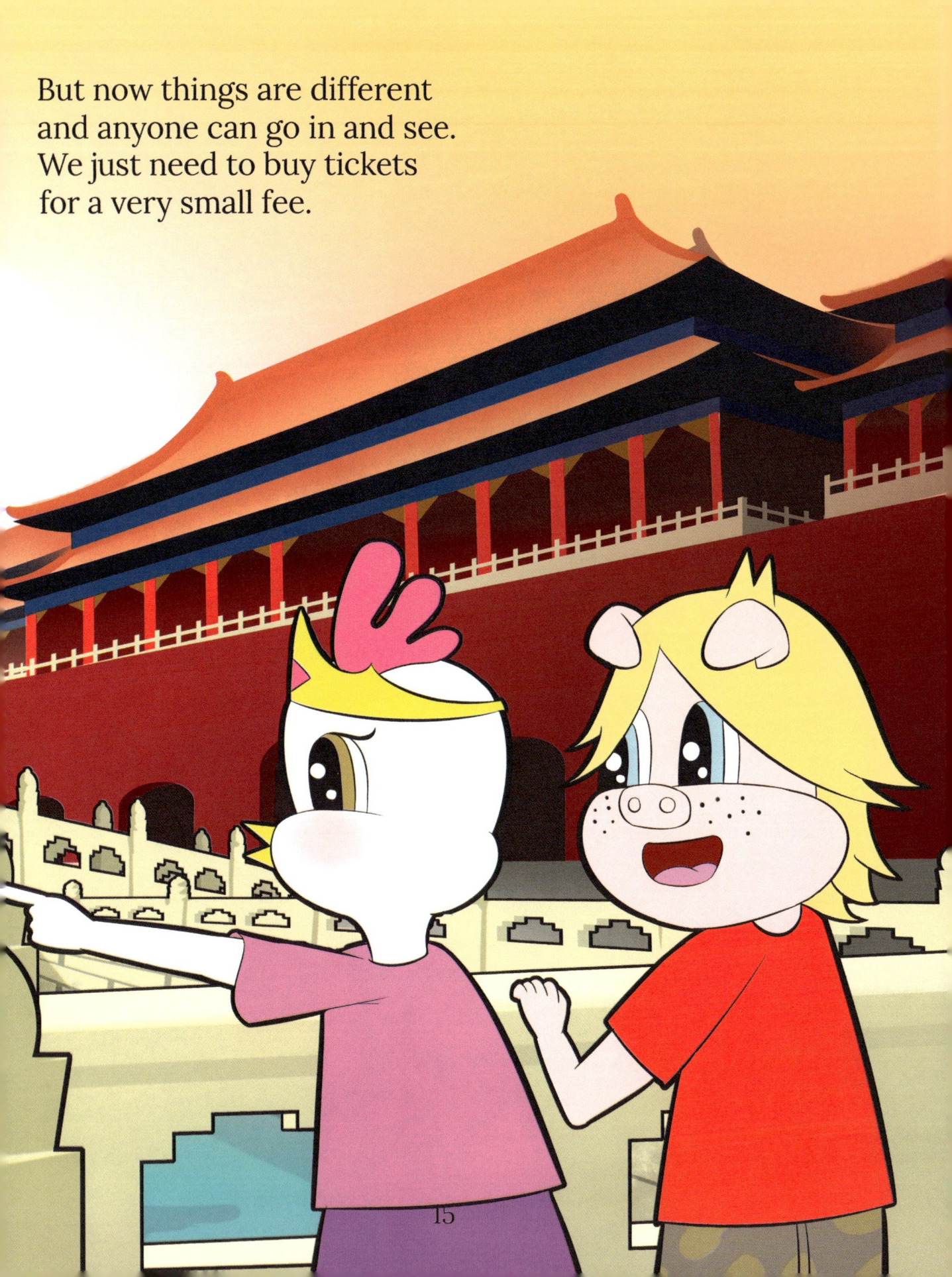

But now things are different
and anyone can go in and see.
We just need to buy tickets
for a very small fee.

Beijing is an ancient place
whose meaning is "north city."
There are many interesting sights here
like the Forbidden City.

Who built this palace?
And how long did it take?
The Ming dynasty did it.
It took 14 years, for goodness sake!

For 500 years
during the Ming dynasty rise,
only the king and clan lived here-
not for regular guys.

If you find yourself here, consider yourself in luck and definitely try this tasty dish– a Beijing specialty: "Peking Duck."

First we're off to Beijing! (Bay-jeeng)
It's the capital of this place.
It's the third largest city in the world
taking up quite a lot of space.

北京
Beijing

Can you say this: "kuai zi?" (kwy-zuh)
The Chinese word for chopsticks.
At first they are hard to use.
Is someone playing tricks?

筷 子
kuài   zi
(kwy-zuh)

But if you keep trying,
you will surely learn soon
that you can eat what you want
without a fork, knife, or spoon.

Center to Chinese daily life
are the markets that line the street.
You can get almost any food there—
we think that's pretty neat.

Almost every meal includes
a dish with some white rice.
You can eat it with chopsticks
usually for no extra price.

The cities are <u>bustling</u>.
The crowds are thick and <u>dense</u>
with more than 1.3 billion
kids, ladies, and gents.

地铁 Subway

Cars, trains, buses, and bikes
are how most get around.
Don't get caught in <u>rush hour</u>
trying to cover a lot of ground.

China is number one in terms of population. This means they have more people than any other nation.

The word for China
was created long ago.
It's meaning is ancient.
Can you say: "zhong guo?" (jong gwo)

中　国
zhōng　guó
(jong gwo)

Zhong guo means "middle land" because they thought China sat centerstage in the universe- it's as easy as that.

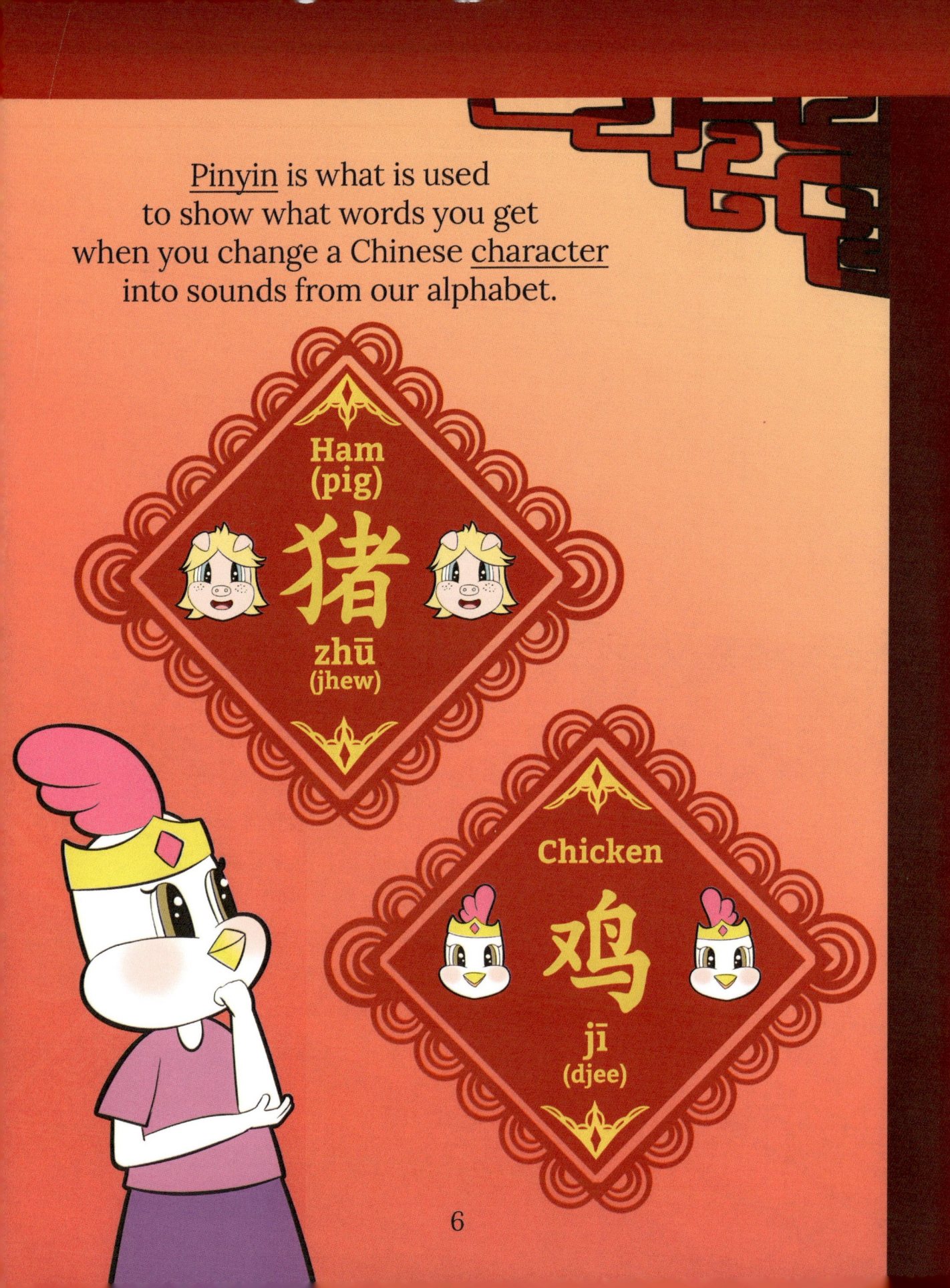

Pinyin is what is used to show what words you get when you change a Chinese character into sounds from our alphabet.

Ham (pig)

猪

zhū
(jhew)

Chicken

鸡

jī
(djee)

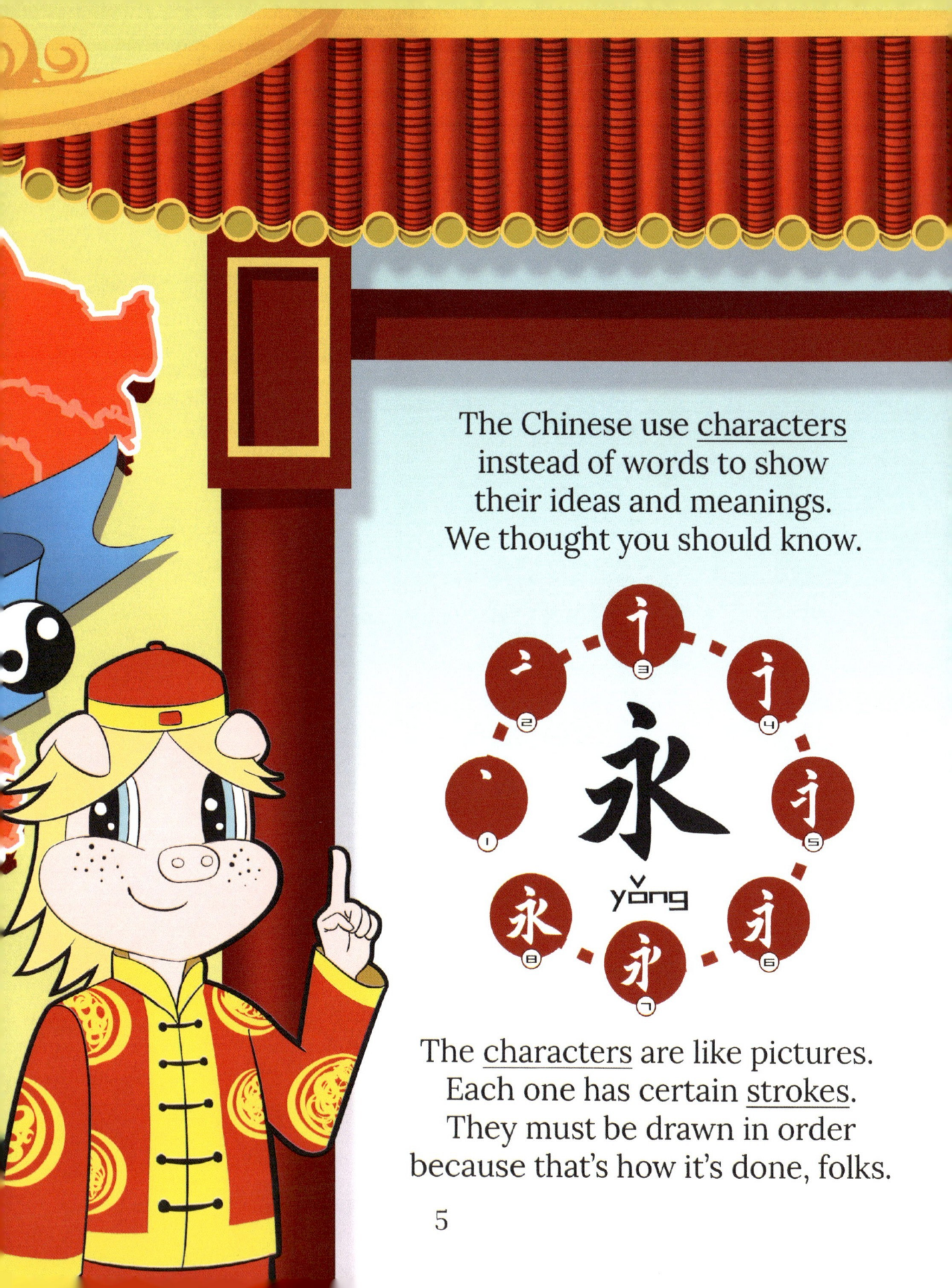

The Chinese use characters
instead of words to show
their ideas and meanings.
We thought you should know.

yǒng

The characters are like pictures.
Each one has certain strokes.
They must be drawn in order
because that's how it's done, folks.

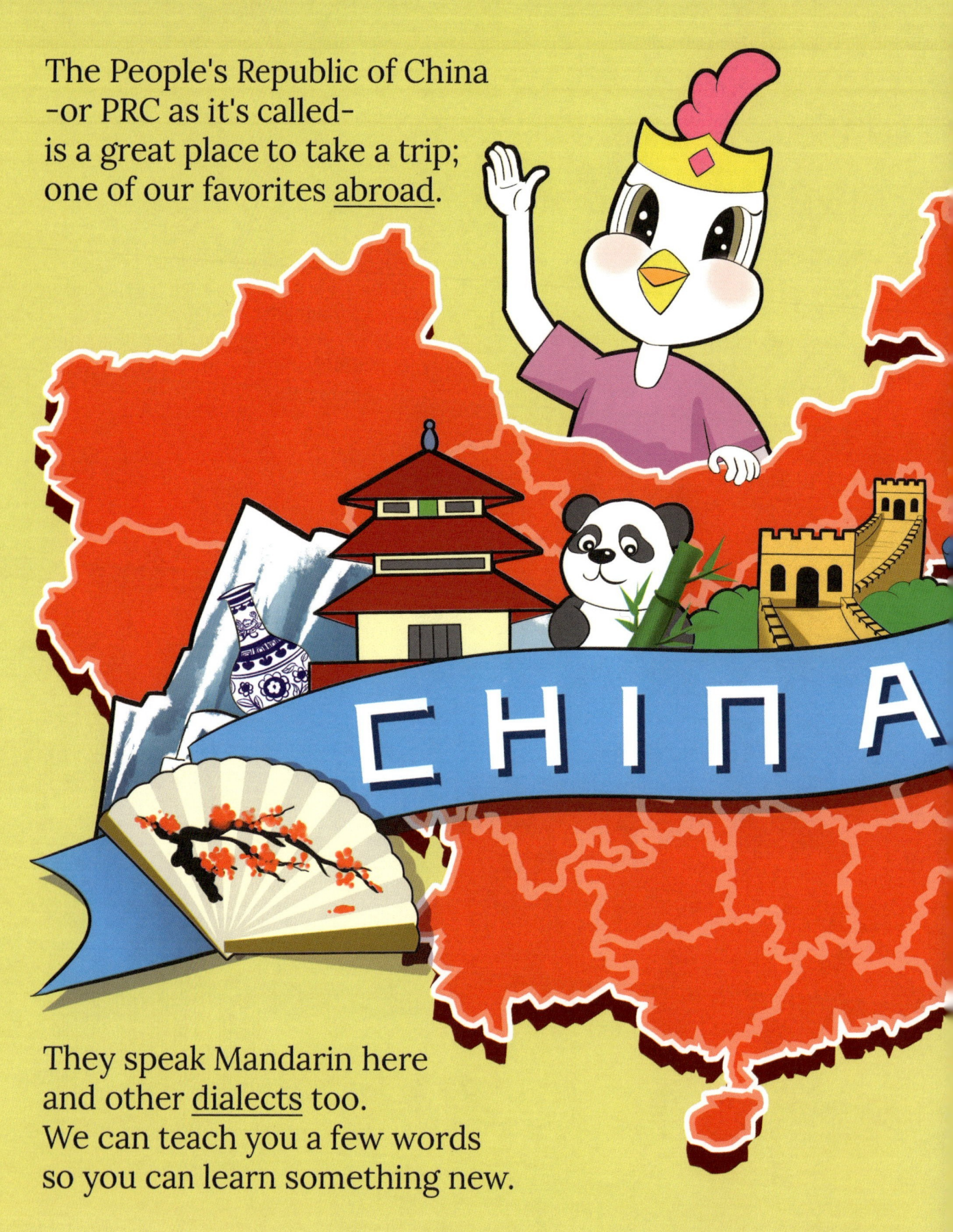

The People's Republic of China
-or PRC as it's called-
is a great place to take a trip;
one of our favorites abroad.

They speak Mandarin here
and other dialects too.
We can teach you a few words
so you can learn something new.

Hh Ii Jj Kk Ll Mm Nn Oo Pp Qq Rr Ss Tt Uu Vv Ww Xx Yy Zz

FACTS ABOUT CHINA:
1. Largest <u>population</u> in the world
2. Captial city: Beijing
3. Official Language: Mandarin
4. Money: Yuan or Renminbi
5. Home of the giant panda

Panda

2008 Summer Olympics

Beijing
Xi'an
Shanghai
Guilin
Hongkong
Macau

Let's learn something new about our <u>destination</u>. We think it will help us have a great vacation!

CHINA

China's Flag

Renminbi

Ni hao! My name is Chicken and this guy is Ham. Today we go to China to discover a new land.

Ham and Cheggs Do China

By Kimberly Naylor

Illustrated by Lei Yang